REDISCOVERING SELF-HELP
Its Role in Social Care

SOCIAL SERVICE DELIVERY SYSTEMS
An International Annual
Founding Series Editors:
DANIEL THURSZ
JOSEPH L. VIGILANTE

MEETING HUMAN NEEDS
1: An Overview of Nine Countries
edited by DANIEL THURSZ and JOSEPH L. VIGILANTE
Volume 1   1975   ISBN 0-8039-0314-6 hardcover   ISBN 0-8039-0589-0 softcover

2: Additional Perspectives
From Thirteen Countries
edited by DANIEL THURSZ and JOSEPH L. VIGILANTE
Volume 2   1976   ISBN 0-8039-0590-4 hardcover   ISBN 0-8039-0591-2 softcover

REACHING PEOPLE
The Structure of Neighborhood Services
edited by DANIEL THURSZ and JOSEPH L. VIGILANTE
Volume 3   1978   ISBN 0-8039-0817-2 hardcover   ISBN 0-8039-0818-0 softcover

REACHING THE AGED
Social Services in Forty-Four Countries
edited by MORTON I. TEICHER, DANIEL THURSZ, and JOSEPH L. VIGILANTE
Volume 4   1979   ISBN 0-8039-1365-6 hardcover   ISBN 0-8039-1366-4 softcover

LINKING HEALTH CARE AND SOCIAL SERVICES
International Perspectives
edited by MERL C. HOKENSTAD, Jr., and ROGER A. RITVO
Volume 5   1982   ISBN 0-8039-1819-4 hardcover   ISBN 0-8039-1820-8 softcover

SOCIAL SERVICE DELIVERY SYSTEMS
An International Annual
Volume 6

REDISCOVERING SELF-HELP

Its Role in Social Care

Editors

DIANE L. PANCOAST
PAUL PARKER
and
CHARLES FROLAND

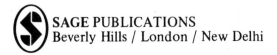

SAGE PUBLICATIONS
Beverly Hills / London / New Delhi

For information address:

SAGE Publications, Inc.
275 South Beverly Drive
Beverly Hills, California 90212

SAGE Publications India Pvt. Ltd.
C-236 Defence Colony
New Delhi 110 024, India

SAGE Publications Ltd
28 Banner Street
London EC1Y 8QE, England

Printed in the United States of America

Library of Congress Cataloging in Publication Data

Main entry under title:

Rediscovering self-help.

(Social service delivery systems ; v. 6)
Includes bibliographical references.
1. Self-help groups—Addresses, essays, lectures.
2. Social service—Addresses, essays, lectures.
3. Medical care—Addresses, essays, lectures. 4. Self-
care, Health—Addresses, essays, lectures. I. Pancoast,
Diane L. II. Parker, Paul, 1950-   III. Froland,
Charles. IV. Series.
HV547.S44 1983   361.7   83-3126
ISBN 0-8039-1990-5
ISBN 0-8039-1993-X (pbk.)

FIRST PRINTING

CONTENTS

PREFACE

There is an element of presumption in the writing of any book. This book may be more presumptuous than most. It deals with an area—self-help—that has only recently been recognized as a significant force in human services. It is still a vague and ill-defined field of study, making international comparisons especially difficult. Even a cursory scan of the biographies of the contributors reveals diversity in professional training, experience, and current affiliation and indicates just how scattered this development currently is. Furthermore, despite some broad similarities in purpose and function, the formally organized welfare services differ vastly from one country to another, and there was no room in this book for detailed discussion of the formal sector.

What led us onward was our excitement at finding colleagues in other countries who were involved in experiments with self-help, asking the same sorts of questions and making the same sorts of speculations that we were. We hope that this book will begin similar voyages for its readers.

As a point of embarkation we provide some definitions and set out some key issues in an introductory chapter. Separate sections deal with informal helping and self-help groups, enabling the reader to focus on the area of greatest interest. A final section contains chapters that deal more broadly with self-help in a policy context. We could not resist the temptation to have the final word, so our last chapter expresses what we have learned from the contributions of our colleagues.

Early on, we made the decision to include only chapters from "Western" industrialized countries because we felt that similarities in their historical development and political and economic systems would provide the best chance of making meaningful comparisons. Within this group, we must confess that representation is based as much on availability ("networking") as on an intent to cover all developments. Omission of a particular region or country should not be taken as a lack of interest in self-help there.

We think that the development of this field in the United States could profit from the more theoretical and political approach the Europeans bring to it. Perhaps the American emphasis on a more eclectic, pragmatic pattern of development holds something useful for them as well. Still, we have assumed that the greatest readership for this book will be among professionals and students in the United States, and we apologize for any inconvenience this may cause to other readers. In spite of the fact that one of the editors is British, at least *some* of our ethnocentricity was intended.

If we needed any reminder of the difficulties of international communication, it was provided by observing the valiant struggles of the authors for whom English is not their native tongue. Indeed, that some of the language and terminology may puzzle or jar the American reader is indicative of some of the important distinctions between the ways self-help and professional services are conceptualized in the United States and in other countries. For example, there is no way adequately to translate *solidarité*, a word that is used by both our French and Quebec authors, without a long treatise on its historical use and the cultural implications of its combined meanings of mutual aid, traditional ties, and militant striving by oppressed groups for a better life.

We want to thank all of the authors for the enthusiasm and energy with which they met our invitation to contribute and the responsibility with which they met our deadlines. We also want to acknowledge the support we received from the Regional Research Institute for Human Services at Portland State University and its director, Dr. Arthur Emlen. Dr. Nancy J. Chapman of the Institute deserves our special thanks for being understanding about the logistical pressures we were under and willing to let us juggle our other responsibilities. Finally, as with any book, there is the person whose secretarial skills and patient good humor *really* make it possible. Thank you, Judy May.

Portland, Oregon   Diane L. Pancoast
                                                      Paul Parker
                                                      Charles Froland

INTRODUCTION

CHARLES FROLAND,
DIANE L. PANCOAST,
and PAUL PARKER

This book is about relationships—specifically, the ways human service professionals can relate their work to self-help initiatives. Because of the need to encompass such a variety of different political and cultural contexts, the perspective finally adopted on this issue has been cast in broad terms of reference. Professional services in social and health care systems mean quite different things when viewed against a backdrop of different national legislation designed to meet divergent social welfare objectives. Self-help action is expressed in a variety of different forms as cultural traditions and local needs combine in ways that defy tidy definition. Thus, the focus has been directed to a more general question of how formal and informal ways of giving and receiving help can find common ground. We have spoken elsewhere of these as two worlds of care: the world of informal, private caring relationships arising out of family, community, and other social ties and the world of professional, governmentally financed services (Froland, Pancoast, Chapman, & Kimboko, 1981). While the two spheres generally function independently of one another, there is an area of overlap. This is the area that this book attempts to explore in a cross-cultural framework.

At present it is probably fair to say that the area of overlap is not large. However, the results of efforts under way in many Western countries suggest that the potential for activity in this area to have both positive and negative effects on the larger worlds of formal services, self-help, and mutual aid is great. We intend neither to predict whether this potential will be realized nor to suggest that it should be realized. Rather, our intention is to illustrate what has occurred and to point out its relevance to policy and practice in social and health care from the varied perspectives of authors in a number of different countries.

A strong, though paradoxical, justification for an international collection can be found in the *intra*national diversity of approaches to self-help and its relationship to professional services. As this book will show, there is no single pattern or set of responses within countries, and the repeated message is that those who would be involved should make their assessments and decisions accord with the particular case in point, while making use of any material perceived to be appropriate. In a field where there are few rules, if any, to dictate policy or practice, a wide-ranging collection of ideas, contexts, and examples can serve as a valuable stimulus to imaginative practitioners and policymakers. Ideas drawn from another country are as likely to be useful as those from one's own. As long as we remember that the differences in the ways people in the various countries represented here help each other, both formally and informally, are at least as important as the similarities, we can profit from an attempt to draw out some common themes.

In this introduction we take the opportunity of setting out a few points of reference that have guided our thinking in organizing the book, in the hope that they will help the reader develop useful contrasts and comparisons in the chapters that follow. First, we explain why we have chosen to title the book, *Rediscovering Self-Help.* While we cannot present a full-scale historical analysis of the phenomenon, we feel that current efforts must be understood in the context of self-help initiatives in the past and of social and economic changes that have occurred in Western societies. We want to develop the thesis that the renewed interest in self-help constitutes a sort of "quiet rediscovery," a subtle shift that has important implications for systems of social and health services. Then we make the point that, while we have lumped together a wide variety of types of informal helping to make a convenient contrast with governmentally provided, formally organized services, there are important distinctions between self-help and informal caregiving that must be kept in mind in order to do justice to the complexities of these arrangements. Finally, we draw attention to the key issues in policy and practice that thread throughout the individual chapters and have served to organize our review.

EARLY MANIFESTATIONS OF SELF-HELP

Self-help is by no means a new phenomenon. Indeed, setting aside semantics and definitional nuances for the moment, the activity of self-help is as old as human society. But the philosophical construction placed on the term has undergone many revisions. "Self-help" has seen much growth and evoked much attention in Western countries in the last decade. However, the concept had already been presented in two sharply contasting forms the better part of a century ago. Rather than attempting a historical review of self-help, we offer a brief comparison of interpretations from the nineteenth century, which serve to demonstrate some of the issues that have made their way to the present.

Samuel Smiles was twenty-five when Queen Victoria ascended the throne in 1837. He died in 1904. He was therefore chronologically a most Victorian man. His magnum opus, *Self-Help, with Illustrations of Character, Conduct and Perseverance,* is the apotheosis of Victorian middle-class values. To Smiles, help from without was "often enfeebling in its effects" (p. 21), "government is negative and restrictive" (p. 22), and the best institutions "leave [man] free to develop himself and improve his individual condition" (p. 22). His book is a catalogue of men who, by character, resourcefulness, and "self-help," managed to rise out of their common origins to achieve prosperity, status, and Victorian virtue. *Self-Help* is a capitalist's bible, with just enough reference to "the great principle of doing to others as you would be done by" (p. 37) to suggest an awareness of the relationship between religion and the rise of capitalism.

In contrast, Prince Peter Kropotkin (1842-1921) emerged from a radically different political and social background with a work on self-help that he entitled *Mutual Aid* (1902). An anarchist and an atheist, he condemned the role of religion and churches, which preached "charity, which bears a character of inspiration from above, and, accordingly, implies a certain superiority of the giver upon the receiver" (p. 283). Kropotkin argued that mutual aid is a natural human force, in which the social and economic needs of a community are symbiotically strengthened. He identified a great range of settings in which mutual aid had flourished and continued to exist even in turn-of-the-century Europe—for instance, in harvesting procedures in Switzerland, Italy, and France, and in the formation of workers' unions and associations. However, he also suggested that certain environments are less conducive to mutual aid than others: "In the cities . . . the absence of common interest nurtures indifference" (p. 277). While, like Smiles, Kropotkin did not look to the state and government for salvation, his reasons were very different; he rejected the imposition of formal discipline and hierarchy which government bureaucracy requires. Finally, he divided mutual aid into two types: standing institutions of mutual support and acts of mutual aid that have their origin in personal or social sympathies.

Already it is possible to see certain issues emerging: the delicate and often paradoxical relationship between individualism and cooperation; self-help as an alternative to, or a unit within, the established system of government; self-help as a means of addressing specific problems or as a holistic philosophy. At this point, the most important issue raised is the implied existence of two basic models of self-help. One, predominantly offered by Smiles and supported in part by Kropotkin, is a clinical model: self-help is a means of individuals and small groups dealing with their own problems, struggling to survive in a world for which they are not ideally designed. The other, which is essentially a structural model, presents self-help as a natural and healthy way for communities to organize themselves both for internal social satisfaction and, where necessary, against loss of control and self-awareness. This second model was Kropotkin's main thesis.

Self-help and mutual aid in the twentieth century have continued to develop expressions that were responsive to the demands of the times. Thus, in America, for instance, the earlier part of the century saw the growth of the unions and ethnic self-help associations. From the 1930s to the 1950s, groups such as Alcoholics Anonymous, Recidivists Anonymous, and Gamblers Anonymous epitomized the philosophy that "a problem shared is a problem eased," and some of those organizations established national structures and identities that still exist. However, from the 1950s to the 1970s, a new force emerged, the increased politicization of self-help, which is associated with the civil rights movement, the women's movement, consumer groups, and the like. Recently there has been an unprecedented proliferation of service-oriented self-help groups and activities, offering specialized support to a wide range of people.

This brief comment on growth and change in the field of self-help is intended simply to indicate that not only is self-help not a new discovery, it is a mechanism that is evidently adaptable to historical circumstances. Other contributors have given similar historical perspectives for their own countries. It is clear that there has been no single, universal trend across time, but the present international context of self-help does exhibit striking similarities across national boundaries.

While it is essential to keep in mind the important differences in history, culture, and politics among the countries represented in this book, it is also useful to remember that they have many things in common. These common elements form the context within which the new forms of self-help are becoming an important force, and they distinguish these countries from many others where the issues would surely be framed differently. Some important common elements are:

(1) *Economic.* All of the countries represented in this volume have mature, industrialized economies that have experienced a declining growth in gross national product, relatively high inflation, and rising unemployment in recent years. While each country certainly has its own unique economic difficulties, conditions shared worldwide have encouraged debate about many similar types of economic policies for responding to limited prospects for growth.

(2) *Political.* All of these countries have had stable democratic governments for many years. Democratic values of free association, participation, and pluralism are supported by these societies. Economic issues have tended to dominate political debate in the past decade, with many countries turning to conservative parties after a period of more leftist administrations, although France has recently elected a socialist government.

(3) *Social and Democratic.* These countries are characterized by a large middle class which dominates the social ethos. Most of these countries are basically urban societies with sparsely scattered rural populations. Demographically, the elderly are becoming a larger proportion of the populations and will continue to increase proportionally until the end of the century. Due to better health care, more people with chronic health problems are living longer. Another significant change is the increasing proportion of women who are working outside the home, particularly those with small children.

Many of these countries have experienced an increase in pluralism, amounting in some cases to separatism. Although this has created some destructive divisions along religious or racial lines within these countries, it has also led to an emphasis on self-sufficiency and pride within various formerly oppressed groups and a greater appreciation of diversity and the rights of minorities in the larger society.

(4) *Social Welfare.* Within the past century, each of these nations has developed a social welfare system that provides a "safety net" for its citizens and some basic economic support for all citizens who can no longer work. Other supports, such as health care and housing, are also provided, although the coverage varies more widely from country to

country. Overall, there is a general feeling of entitlement to certain governmental services and an expectation of equitable distribution.

(5) *Professional Social Work.* Every country represented in this book has at least one profession identified with the delivery of social welfare services. These professions have all the usual trappings: training schools, diplomas, certification, and professional associations. The period of the 1960s and 1970s was a time of turmoil and questioning of basic ideology and methodology in these professions. More recently, cutbacks in services have threatened the jobs of many, adding insecurity to the general confusion in professional identity and leading to demoralization in what are called in the United States the helping professions.

PHILOSOPHICAL SHIFTS

The societal conditions and changes discussed above have predictably been accompanied by new trends at the individual, institutional, and community levels, which in turn have motivated a renewed interest in self-help. At the individual level, there seems to have been a general reorientation to self-help values in the past two decades, although it has been expressed differently according to various cultural influences. We are not suggesting that a broad-scale intrapsychic transformation has occurred within the general public. The change is at a more modest, even tentative, level, and indications of it must be pulled together from a variety of scattered sources. The rising popularity of self-help books in the United States and, to a lesser extent, in Europe is one indication. The questioning of traditional roles and lifestyles and the creation of supportive contexts in which to explore new roles in like-minded company are less widespread, but culturally significant nonetheless.

There are obviously many ways in which the urge to take control of one's personal circumstances can be satisfied by self-help action, although perhaps only a few will come to official attention as full-fledged self-help groups. Most occur informally within one's personal circle. It is likely that enduring patterns of self-help and mutual aid are being called into play to meet different patterns of need. For example, the fundamental shift in the role of women in Western countries away from their "kin-keeping" functions is making necessary a revision in the distribution of the tasks of caring for dependent family members as women seek greater independence or enter the workplace. In many instances this redistribution will require the refashioning of self-help to respond to the altered requirements for care.

If one accepts the premise that there is a strong, individual propensity to look to informal means of self-help to solve problems and that this is rooted in traditional democratic values, the case for individual rediscovery does not rest solely on this ground. Closely allied with self-help values, there has also been a shift toward reprivatization of individual need. The emphasis on self-help may be a constructive attempt to repersonalize services by assuming greater control of both means and ends. Certainly, reprivatization can be seen in the greater political support given to proponents of smaller government, but it is less clear whether this stems from a reaction to past institutional excesses, a necessary invention in the face of scarcity, a convenient rubric for conservatives, or a new philosophy. In this regard, the individual rediscovery of self-help is more of a quiet realization than a popular movement. Just as important, it derives not from an infatuation with yesterday's social forms, but rather from attempts to manage today's social forces.

Social welfare institutions have also undergone significant changes in the last several decades that have increased their interest in self-help action. Economic and political changes both within nations and between them have created an institutional need to share and in some cases to devolve responsibility for meeting social need. The last decade has witnessed economic shocks that have repeatedly shaken the public confidence engendered by the postwar boom. Shortages of national resources, declining growth, inflation, and a host of other economic ills have proven intractable to fiscal and monetary policy, at least in the short run. One result has been to question whether the government necessarily should serve as the agent of first resort, particularly with respect to social and health care. With cutbacks, professional providers have also become increasingly disillusioned and demoralized. Increasing attention has been directed to the possible role voluntary organizations can play in filling the gaps left by governmental retrenchment.

This retrenchment comes at a time when there has already been a push to expand the role of the community in the provision of services. Surprisingly nonpartisan, the general call is to push for greater citizen representation in policy, to place services closer to those served, to increase voluntarism in publicly funded care, and, indeed, to give specific recognition to the importance of informal means for meeting needs. To say that these interests constitute a movement is perhaps to wield a broad brush with little concern for what surface it covers. No doubt there are internal inconsistencies that prevent the adoption of a unified platform. However, there can also be no doubt that within the helping professions of social work, nursing, psychology, psychiatry, and even other branches of medicine, there are strong constituencies who argue for equal participation of clients and their families, friends, and neighbors in caregiving activities. These arguments are not necessarily based on expediency, economy, or faddism; more often they arise from a concept of services that departs from the traditional view of helping, in which the haves dispense to the have nots. In this view, assistance is only really useful when it is mutually activated by all parties to care.

While certainly not leaders in the rediscovery of self-help values, professionals and the governments that give them sanction have found ample, although conflicting, reasons to undertake the search. An ambivalence lies at the heart of the institutional reluctance to embrace self-help initiatives with greater commitment. It is created by a conflict between the need to find a substitute that can be used on an occasional, controlled basis and the need to find a full partner who can share the burden of responsibility with an increasingly overwhelmed formal sector. It remains to be seen how governments and professionals will resolve this dilemma. Indeed, the decision may be taken from their hands by the pressure of events.

Communities represent the third arena in which self-help values can be expressed. It is sometimes argued that industrialized, Western countries have experienced a shift away from slower, organic, and quiltlike evolution toward whole-cloth planning of housing estates, condominiums, and suburbs without traditions, which have left a spatial regularity that often encompasses a social vacuum. Where local communities once may have offered the natural building blocks for social integration, they now often represent unfortunate accidents of geography that give rise to parochial interests and social alienation. No longer can one expect to share more than a parking strip with one's neighbors.

This view of the disintegrated community has been popular in the sociological literature, but it is neither a representative description of the present nor an accurate contrast with the past. While one can find wastelands among communities today, such conditions were not absent among communities of days gone by. One has to be careful not to confuse form with substance, for even among ostensibly impoverished and transient neighborhoods, one can find richly interwoven social bonds to assist residents with a wide variety of needs. So the question becomes not whether there are still communities that are capable of self-help. Nor is it a question of whether communities may now have greater reason to engage in self-help than before, because of assaults by governmental interventions, population mobility, or economic development. Rather, it seems safe to begin with the assumption that self-help values have persisted and to ask what has changed in the way these values are manifest that now leads us to think they are being rediscovered. Several changes can be identified.

First, community self-help initiatives appear to have become more political, intent on obtaining greater resources from outside the community and determined to exert greater self-determination in the use of these resources. Whether directed toward governmental programs or private enterprise, the intent is to have greater local participation in decisions that affect the economic and social conditions of the community.

Second, self-help initiatives at the local level reflect a greater emphasis on communities of interest rather than communities of propinquity. Greater geographic mobility, more specialization in the definition of needs and issues, and perhaps even the increased speed of information sharing brought on by the electronic revolution in media all have contributed to the shift to a greater proportion of ties based on common interests. While neighborhoods are still the base for some social bonds, the relevant ties for many who must deal with the social diversity of the urban scene are developing increasingly from among disparate contacts. Out of these, a collective identity based on mutual interests can be forged.

Third, the changes in institutional initiatives that we discussed above have produced a response, in turn, of new community self-help values and objectives, with governmental programs taking place closer to communities. Local power blocs and specialized interest groups may have accelerated in proportion to the greater complexity of governmental programs and other public resources being directed to the local level. In these respects, self-help action still serves a mediating function but with regard to a more diverse set of institutional incursions into private life.

Thus, the rediscovery of self-help taking place in communities may indeed be one of form rather than an alteration of social or political values. Where once more general forms, such as fraternal organizations or clubs, may have sufficed, now more diverse and specialized organizations may have become necessary. The observation of greater numbers of self-help organizations may therefore say less about the overall level of self-help activity than it does about the process by which self-help actions attempt to become a more effective force in modern communities.

WHY LINK SELF-HELP
AND INFORMAL CARE?

This book contains material covering professionals' relationships to two types of help-giving resources: informal caring networks and self-help organizations, which we are conveniently lumping together as "self-help." What, if any, is the link between the two, other than that professionals and academics who are interested in one are often interested in the other? Self-help groups are characteristically self-aware, as well as self-determining; they have objectives, strategies, philosophies, and an organizational structure that is consciously formed. "Informal caring networks" is really no more than a term used to describe the structure within which people give and receive goodwill and good deeds in their own personal social groups. While there undoubtedly are motivations and patterns to be traced within informal caring networks, there are not the same senses of self-awareness and self-determination that are the hallmarks of self-help groups. A member of a self-help group, if asked the reason for his or her participation, is usually well prepared to answer. A person who is known to be a source of help in a social network, if asked a similar question, may simply not comprehend the context of the question! This is because the content of the helping exchange is a secondary product of the principal activity, which, put succinctly, is living as a social being. In contrast, the order of priorities is reversed in the self-help group, where the goals of the group are the grounds for meeting, and any other social satisfactions are spin-offs.

Similarly, self-determination is considered to be not only a basic tenet of self-help philosophy, but also a major preoccupation of groups in action. Some of their self-awareness is focused on the objective of maintaining control over their own organization, without succumbing to institutional manipulation or colonization. Informal helping systems, on the other hand, have in the past been so free to exercise self-determination that it has not presented itself as an issue; only recently has there been sufficient institutional curiosity in the resource potential of such systems to constitute any threat to their natural equilibrium.

In comparing self-help groups and informal helping networks, there is also a contrast in longevity of "membership." Anyone wanting to join a self-help group will choose it in response to a self-determined interest, and frequently that person's membership lasts only as long as his interest or need is stimulated. In practice, active membership is often brief or spasmodic. Helping interaction within social networks, on the other hand, is an endemic condition. It is not something that people take up and then give up; it is with them, to greater or lesser degree, from birth to death. The link between self-help and informal helping networks is not a link of similarity based on definition of need or of membership, self-awareness, or longevity. It might be argued that both represent an alternative to professional services and a resource that may be of use to the formal sector. But that would also be true of traditional volunteer organizations, which are not included in this book. One link that is sometimes forged between informal help and self-help, although it is by no means a necessary condition for the existence of either, is suggested by the need of self-help groups for an organizational framework. Bruce Stokes (1981, p. 130) describes it thus: "The most appropriate structure for self-help activities are local social networks—the web of friends and acquaintances that surrounds each person. The most intimate social networks are made up of people who encounter each other on a daily basis. Informal networks often coalesce into formal ones." Self-help groups are often emerging out of informal helping networks or helping to create them. Our earlier empirical research showed that agencies which understood this relationship between self-help and informal helping and developed a combination of supportive approaches were able to deploy their own resources most effectively (Froland et al., 1981).

Thus, we have chosen to use the term "self-help" in order to describe a broad variety of helping activities that may represent a continuum of arrangements for engaging in mutual aid. This continuum can be seen to counterpoint the structure of formal aid provided by governmental services. In some instances, the relationship between informal and formal provisions of care has been seen as a dichotomy—doing for oneself versus being done for. However, this may be more a reflection of the maturation of the welfare state in developed countries rather than a rejection of its basic provisions.

Basic benefits (such as food, money, housing, and health care) have come to be accepted, with national variations, almost as social rights. Institutional care and other services for the mentally ill, mentally retarded, and physically handicapped are also regarded as an entitlement, although the generally poor quality of many of these services makes them undesirable to many. The social control functions of the welfare system in adult penology, juvenile delinquency, and child abuse and neglect are also widely accepted. In a sense, the area that is left for various forms of informal care is residual—the more spontaneous, day-to-day exchanges of assistance that make ordinary life possible—no less important than the formal services but more resistant to bureaucratization. In another sense, the area in which informal care is still paramount is remedial—compensating for shortcomings and deleterious effects of the formal sector.

ISSUES IN POLICY AND PRACTICE

Our review of the changes occurring in many Western countries does not point toward a rediscovery of self-help action with unified or widespread impact. Rather, the evidence suggests the presence of varied motivations behind the renewed interest with at times conflicting values coming into play. These conflicts may become particularly notable within the context of attempts to find a mutually beneficial way in which professional services and self-help initiatives can interact. Unresolved issues are reflected in inconsistent policies and confused practices.

At this point it will be useful to outline in broad terms the scope of these issues in order to provide a framework for the chapters that follow. Our outline may give greater or lesser attention to what is relevant in each country, but it is intended to stimulate thinking about the larger implications of relating formal and informal sources of help.

Taken together, the issues prompt questions about the ability of informal and formal sources of care to respond to social need, how these services may interact in mutually beneficial ways, and what a system of services would potentially become if the integration of formal and informal care were encouraged more broadly. In presenting each issue area, we first provide a general description and then present a list of illustrative questions. Throughout, we use the terms "self-help" and "informal helping" interchangeably because we expect that each issue can apply to either source of help.

PHILOSOPHICAL BASIS

Strategies for bringing formal services and self-help activities or informal helping together will involve the expression of certain philosophical beliefs, principles, or assumptions. We think it will be important to make these philosophical points clear in order to understand what values are being emphasized and what tradeoffs are being made among competing values. Illustrative questions that may be asked include:

- How is the burden of care distributed?
- What assumptions about people's needs and abilities in relation to helping are being made?

- Will the general welfare of some groups and not others be increased? What does this imply about various groups' access to resources?
- Does family responsibility for meeting need receive greater or less emphasis?

ROLE OF SELF-HELP AND INFORMAL HELPING

The role of self-help and informal helping activities vis-à-vis the formal sector may be explicitly decided by professionals or others within the formal system of services. In other cases, when self-help or informal activities have appeared spontaneously, implicit definitions will have been made. Questions include:

- How important to formal services is the incorporation of self-help or informal helping seen to be? Is it a means to an end or is it an end in itself?
- Is informal helping seen as a substitute for formal services or a supplement?
- What assumptions about the capacity of self-help are being made?
- How might the role definition change according to different problems, populations, needs, and other aspects of the focus of interaction?

INCENTIVES FOR DEVELOPING A PARTNERSHIP

For there to be a sustained effort to combine formal and informal sources of help in mutually beneficial ways, there must be certain incentives provided to each side. When we think of incentives, we must examine the motives and exchange relationships that may either promote or work against the development of an equal partnership. Questions include:

- What incentives do formal service providers need to enter a partnership? Do they need special training? Are certain criteria for selecting staff important?
- Will there need to be changes in the mission or accountability of the formal agency to accommodate informal helpers? Are certain philosophical beliefs necessary to develop a partnership?
- What are positive and negative implications of providing incentives? What are appropriate incentives? Is there a danger of overdoing it?

POLITICAL CONSIDERATIONS

The prospects for developing a partnership between formal and informal sources of help can involve important political considerations. Depending on the current political climate, the presence or absence of certain political interest groups, and other aspects of the political structure of a country, the nature of the relationship may change drastically. Questions include:

- Which political constituencies are for or against the development of a relationship? How will this influence the prospects for a relationship?

- Where might the idea of developing broader cooperation between formal services and informal help fit with the statutory framework underlying the system of service?

- To what extent will advocacy for self-help, informal help, volunteerism, and the like be traded off against other social rights in the political arena (such as the right to equal access to services)?

- Will there be an ideological conflict with existing power groups (such as labor unions, professional societies, and civil rights groups)?

- To what extent might the development of a greater emphasis on self-help promote either greater factionalism or pluralism at the local level?

INSTITUTIONAL CONSIDERATIONS

The idea of a broader-scale relationship between formal and informal sources of help raises an issue of whether or not it may be institutionalized. Questions include:

- What level of government should be concerned about promoting greater cooperation? How should policy be developed?

- Can cooperation by systematized? Would this be an appropriate direction to pursue or are spontaneous or experimental modes better for the present?

- To what extent may the idea be seen as providing a solution to meeting needs in rural areas or other underserved areas?

- To what extent is the danger of cooptation or colonization real? How can it be prevented?

- Would more systematic attention to the relationship between informal care and formal services actually result in cost savings?

The list of issues is long. That they can be formulated at all is indicative of the progress that has been made in recent years. The chapters that follow do not pretend to give final answers. They do take us a long way by the application of analytical precision and practical experimentation. The development of the relationship between institutional services and self-help will continue to be a dialectic, fueled by recent political, social, and economic forces which have given it a new urgency.

REFERENCES

Froland, C., Pancoast, D., Chapman, N., & Kimboko, P. *Helping networks and human services.* Beverly Hills, CA: Sage, 1981.

Kropotkin, P. *Mutual aid.* Boston: Porter Sargent, 1902.

Smiles, S. *Self-help, with illustrations of character, conduct and perseverance.* St. Louis: Crawford & Co., n.d.

Stokes, B. *Helping ourselves: Local solutions to global problems.* New York: Norton, 1981.

I

INITIATIVES IN
INFORMAL CARE

1

PATTERNS OF PARTNERSHIP
Three Models of Care for the Elderly

GORDON GRANT and CLARE WENGER
United Kingdom

Recent years have seen an expansion of well-grounded evaluative social care research in the United Kingdom (Goldberg & Connelly, 1981). Amidst this development the needs and support of the elderly have always been prominent (M. Abrams, 1980; Hunt, 1978; Power, 1978; Wenger, 1982). The role and tasks of social work in this country have been subject to a recent review as a result of which a community-based model of social work has been recommended (National Institute for Social Work, 1982). There are, however, indications that social work practice is subject to a wide variety of powerful organizational and environmental pressures (Glastonbury, Cooper, & Hawkins, 1980; Parry, Rustin, & Satyamurti, 1979; Black, Bowl, Burns, Critcher, Grant, & Stockford, in press), so greater emphasis on interweaving of formal and informal care systems will require even more careful scrutiny of organizational arrangements and relationships to the community. This chapter is an attempt to crystallize some of the problems and possibilities this will create for social care of the elderly in the community.

We begin by outlining the structure of statutory services in the United Kingdom before describing three innovatory programs that have attempted to bring about greater fusion of formal and informal care. Issues in advancing a partnership are then discussed in some detail before we finally assess the real prospects for change.

27

THE ORGANIZATION OF STATUTORY
SOCIAL SERVICES: IMPLICATIONS FOR
DEVELOPMENT OF INFORMAL CARE

Within Great Britain a major commitment has been made to the development of a universal, integrated personal social services system. Legislation during the 1960s and 1970s has attempted to remove the vestiges of "poor law" stigma attached to receipt of "welfare" services. At the cornerstone are the local-authority social services (in England and Wales) and social work (in Scotland) departments. Descriptive accounts of these forms of organization are reported elsewhere (Westland, 1978; Gandy, 1976). The Seebohm and Kilbrandon reports, which provided the foundation for a restructuring of personal social services organization, saw these departments as only one of a network of services rather than self-contained units. It was envisaged that coordination with other services, mobilization of community resources, encouragement and development of community identity, and mutual aid would be necessary to bring departments into contact with the entire community. Indeed, this was largely reiterated by the Barclay Committee (National Institute for Social Work, 1982). The expectation was that a community orientation would help to reduce perpetuation of rigid distinctions between givers and takers of services, besides creating the conditions for partnership between those working in formal and informal care systems.

Despite the tradition of organized voluntary activity in this country, the existence of many voluntary agencies is contingent on grant aid or subsidy from the local authority or indeed from central government. Thus we can see how the level of voluntary organized action may reflect not only general economic well-being but the flavor of political control at local government level.

The organizational reforms of the early 1970s have been followed by a period of administrative stability and consolidation, if at a time of economic decline. This has allowed considerable attention to be focused on the structure and effectiveness of area social services teams, the "local" outlets of statutory social services, and on their relations with the community at large. Elucidation of the complexities of fusing statutory with other sources of care therefore requires some understanding of the varied, and conflicting, pressures and expectations placed on teams, a subject to which we return later. The problems of interweaving formal and informal care can perhaps be best explored initially by discussion of concrete examples of community-oriented approaches to social care.

THREE CONTRASTING COMMUNITY-ORIENTED
CARE SCHEMES FOR THE ELDERLY

We have to acknowledge that our choice of care schemes is arbitrary and therefore not representative of the growing range of alternatives. Nevertheless, those we have chosen have attracted much publicity and are in the forefront of more radical and thought-provoking initiatives. Although each has a different aim, all raise some common issues and present interesting possibilities for further action. The Gofal scheme and patch-based social services are examples of experiments initiated by local authorities, whereas neighborhood care is an illustration drawn from the many types of voluntary organized action.

The Gofal scheme is but one example of an attempt by social services departments to mobilize or generate extra help in the community to meet the needs of the frail elderly eligible for residential care. Principles on which the project is based have been described by Challis and Davies (1980), who have been evaluating the original parent project. Based on the premise that many of the frail elderly would prefer to remain in their own homes if adequate support were available, the scheme is designed to build more flexible, individually tailored packages of care for clients in conjunction with the services currently available. At the same time it is hoped to use resources more efficiently through postponement or reduction of the need for residential care. Gofal-type schemes embody a number of innovatory operating principles:

(a) provision of a decentralized budget to experienced social workers who take responsibility for coordination and development of care for elderly people;

(b) establishment of an upper limit on expenditure for all departmental services per client to raise consciousness of the cost-effectiveness imperative and to ensure that limited resources do not become too narrowly focused on too few clients;

(c) use of knowledge of unit costs of departmental services to allow opportunity cost principles to enter social workers' decision-making frameworks;

(d) design, by project social workers, of helping agreements between the agency and paid helpers in individually tailored contracts;

(e) involvement of elderly clients and, where necessary, family carers in all the decision-making processes connected to the foregoing.

When clients are referred to the project worker, an assessment visit is made and the elderly person is given the option of receiving Gofal care as an alternative to a residential place. Almost all opt for the experimental scheme and then participate in discussions about the design of a suitable package of home-based care. This usually involves a mixture of intensive domiciliary, personal, and socio-emotional care that can be organized during unsocial hours such as weekends, evenings, and nights as well as during the daytime. Already established home help or district nurse visits continue. Where possible, helpers are recruited through the personal network of the client, through the Job Centre or, as the project progresses, from the worker's pool of helpers. The project worker subsequently makes a contractual arrangement with a helper for such care to be provided.

Neighborhood Care (or Good Neighbor) schemes in the United Kingdom exist in the thousands; recent research into their organization suggests that they are so varied in their aims, origins, and functions that common elements are difficult to discern (Abrams, Abrams, Humphrey, & Snaith, 1981). However, as examples of voluntary organized effort directed at the care and support of elderly and handicapped persons in the community, neighborhood care schemes usually:

(a) embody a need to accept and support a measure of formal organization as the unavoidable means of promoting informal neighborly relationships;

(b) restrict immediate caring objectives to activities that are feasible within the available framework of "local" resources and contacts;

(c) endeavor to recruit unpaid helpers, street wardens, and secretarial staff from the immediate vicinity to reduce distinctions between givers and receivers of care;

(d) embody helping functions within the context of "organizing" care, visiting, and surveillance for needy persons, while also extending neighborly relationships;

(e) situate their activities somewhere between statutory bodies and the community, their relationship to the former being characterized by a certain amount of ambiguity and contingency rather than by extremes of support and neglect.

More frequent types of help include friendly visiting, shopping for the housebound, and transport, especially for outpatients and visitors to hospitals. However, constant or regular surveillance of those at risk is very much the cornerstone of these schemes, with the result that they have come to play an important gatekeeping role in providing a needed means of access to resource-distributing bodies, such as housing departments or primary health teams, as well as with the "outside world" in general.

In endeavoring to synthesize common features of *patch-based community-oriented models of organization,* Hadley and McGrath (1980) characterize these models as embodying:

(a) locally based teams, focusing on small areas or patches;
(b) the capacity to obtain detailed information about the patch;
(c) accessibility and acceptability of the patch to users;
(d) close liaison with other local agencies and groups;
(e) integration of all field and domiciliary workers within patch teams;
(f) participative forms of management in patch and area teams;
(g) the exercise of a substantial degree of autonomy by the team vis-à-vis the local authority.

One of the central aims of patch working is to heighten the commitment by social services departments to preventive social work and to interventions that extend beyond the more traditional reactive model of service delivery. Since much of the focus of patch teams has fallen on the elderly in the community, we feel we can justify including some discussion of these experiments in this chapter. The underlying philosophy of this approach is that a small team which covers and is based within a small area, is more visible, more accessible, and more likely to build in local knowledge and understanding not only of existing informal care networks but also of unmet needs.

Staffing and Role Relationships

In the Gofal scheme the project social workers are an integral part of a specialist social services team for elderly and handicapped persons. They receive referrals in the main from other field social workers and so deal with those elderly persons who are already social services clients and who have become eligible for residential care. In this way it has been possible to maintain a low profile and keep practice experimental until such times as more established working methods and better informed eligibility criteria can be operated with confidence. This has meant that project workers are providing a specialist role within a specialist team.

Whereas the process of "accepting" clients was initially based on negotiations with other team members, operating criteria are now crystallized and case transfers take place extremely smoothly. As the scheme has become better known, referrals have also been channeled directly to the project workers, especially from medical social workers attached to hospital, and general practitioners. The scheme has passed beyond the experimental stage and is now under line management control. At the fieldwork level it is regarded as an established part of the department's community services and has been expanded to other area teams.

What ties project workers to helpers they recruit is a working contract that the workers are responsible for designing. Contracts have symbolic as well as practical meanings for helpers. Besides making explicit what tasks need to be undertaken in the care of an old person, they are a measure of the value the statutory agency places on work helpers undertake, and they provide some reinforcement of the need for reliability. The contracts are backed by a commitment from project social workers to provide helpers with professional support and advice at all times. Helpers are encouraged to take a wide view of client need by being cued into alternative forms of domiciliary care that may also have been mobilized, thereby encouraging them to provide an overarching surveillance role. This creates the capacity for integrated or multidisiplinary team approaches. Though in one sense "binding," the contracts themselves are viewed as negotiable. Helpers see them as setting the limits and boundaries to their care of the elderly, but they are encouraged to renegotiate or review them as circumstances change.

Operationally, Gofal thus rests on teamwork among social worker, helper, client, and any significant other carers. It is an attempt to blend professional and lay resources. Of the first seventy-four helpers recruited into the scheme, most were unskilled women, and only one or two had relevant professional experiences. However, most, being young or middle-aged mothers or persons used to caring for dependent relatives, had a vast fund of personal experience of caring on which they could draw. Broadly speaking, the scheme has attracted helpers from socioeconomic groups comparable to those who work as home helps, and it clearly provides an additional and valued source of local part-time work for predominantly working-class women in a low-wage area.

The neighborhood care schemes described by P. Abrams and colleagues are backed by a variety of bodies including local authorities, churches, and a multiplicity of voluntary organizations. Only a minority had paid organizers or a paid secretariat, and the researchers found that it was impossible to identify these schemes as a distinct type of caring project on the basis of any single organizational principle. Their administrative diversity is seen by Abrams and colleagues as a reflection of tension between dispersal and centralization caused by the fact that schemes were committed simultaneously to providing care *and* to promoting neighborliness, the former requiring coordination and control and the latter devolution of responsibilities of the "street warden" pattern.

Relationships between organizers and their helpers in good neighbor schemes appear to be fluid. Friendly visiting of the elderly and routine surveillance are typically unstructured, informal, and comprehensive in their demands. To quote the research team, "the essence of the job is just being there, being trusted and being in touch." If it is difficult to tell an inquirer just what one is doing, it is clearly going to be difficult to define what the role relationship between helper and organizer should be. There is only rarely an element of payment as reward for work done in these schemes, and there is no formal working contract. If altruism and the desire to be a helping hand are primary reasons for becoming involved in good neighbor schemes, it is easy to understand why a fluidity in role relationships is necessary. While enabling helpers not to feel tied down, it also means they can just as easily opt out. As we shall see later, this leads to problems in maintaining a stable and committed helper work force.

It is a premise of patch "philosophy" that unqualified workers and ancillary staff have the potential to offer practical and supportive care of a high standard and that greater prominence should be given to these workers and volunteers to broaden their roles. Teams are integrated and adopt a form of management based on participative democracy. In summarizing the findings of several patch-based case studies, Hadley and McGrath (1980) suggest that this helps to break down barriers to the community by facilitating more direct access to services. This, along with a geographical patch focus, is reported to make it more difficult for workers to hide behind jargon or bureaucratic procedures when dealing with clients, which in turn forces workers to be more honest about the limits of their own work and of the department's resources.

Patch workers have had to be careful not to take over too many caring tasks from the family, for families thus become overdependent. Nevertheless, a start has been made by some teams to arrange care contracts with informal carers. Questions about how best to engage care networks are still, however, very much under discussion. Patchworkers or their nearest equivalent, neighborhood visitors, in some areas appear to have had a good deal of success in negotiating relationships with local community leaders and key others to arrange ways of monitoring and supporting the elderly. Most of the help required by the elderly is of a practical, common-sense, and visiting nature, for which specialized skills may not be necessary. Furthermore, it seems in some instances that by the demonstration of their ability, unqualified patchworkers have neutralized any felt status differences between themselves and qualified personnel.

The available data suggest that patch teams have also endeavored to break down barriers between field and domiciliary workers. In many of the teams, home help organizers and wardens of sheltered housing complexes are almost as much a part of the team as patchworkers and their team leaders. One detects a desire to embrace teamworking approaches to practice and a readiness to tackle issues on a proactive rather than just a reactive basis. For the moment, patch teams appear to be able to live with their hybrid composition of individuals, qualified and unqualified, professional, auxiliary, and volunteers alike. As a result of increased integration of workers in some patch teams, qualified staff are freed for more specialized duties and unqualified workers express their appreciation of having qualified workers around to whom they can turn for advice and consultation. Cases appear to be freely discussed between workers, and a "team" approach to problems has become more evident, with the development of a more collaborative style. We look with interest to see whether the desire for heterogeneous team composition and multidisciplinary teamwork can be sustained given, on the one hand, bureaucratic requirements for control and conformity and, on the other, the need for flexibility, responsiveness, and informality in coexistence with the community.

Intrateam relationships seem least complicated in the Gofal scheme if only because project workers and other social workers are still operating within a reactive system. However, the ability and freedom to disburse payments and work out contracts with helpers has been a binding force among clients, helpers, and project workers. Where more than one helper works with the same client, informal cooperation and flexibility have developed. There is greatest fluidity and flexibility in relationships between members of good neighbor schemes, but linked to this is a predisposition for helpers to leave, particularly if there seems to be too little for them to do. This creates problems with manpower stability and the accumulation of expertise. In patch teams, status rivalry between members has been minimized, and there is a strong suggestion that the broadened roles of auxiliary and volunteer personnel are gradually making it possible for bridges to be built with the community.

Intervention Strategies

Within the Gofal scheme, the integration of formal and informal care becomes almost automatic once it has been decided to assess the client's eligibility for the experimental service. However, the client is not always seen as a reliable source of insight, for reasons that include fear of coercion to leave home, dementia, or loss of memory, each of which may lead to under- or overstatement of need. This is avoided by extending the exploration of need beyond the client to informal carers, but only with the client's permission. Breaches of confidentiality are thereby minimized.

Not only does this lead to more reliable and comprehensive judgments about client need; it also allows the professional social worker to begin to assess the strengths and weaknesses of available care from family, friends, and neighbors.

The social networking conducted here can be most taxing for project personnel, since it involves a multidimensional juggling act to keep care options open prior to formation of a satisfactory long-term package of support.

Poorly conceived packaging of support may lead to stresses among participants at later stages, which, in small rural communities or urban neighborhoods, could have serious consequences for future involvement. These are not our views but those of the principal project organizer, who is closer to the action (Williams, 1981), and we have every reason to respect the validity of the perspective he offers.

Of the first 74 helpers recruited by project personnel, 17 were identified through the client or members of the client's social network; the remainder were attracted mainly through local job centers or by advertising. Whatever the recruitment source, matching of helpers to clients is carried out on the basis of geographic proximity rather than any attempt at psychological screening or matching, on the assumption that citizens are supportive of one another most of the time. This appears to have worked; turnover of helpers is low. It also reinforces the findings of an earlier major study of volunteer care of the elderly (Power, 1978). More significant, the proximity factor has been instrumental in minimizing travel by helpers to clients. Were domiciliary services of formal agencies to be operated on a similar premise, it seems likely that this would start a minor revolution in the reduction of operating costs, especially in rural areas, where travel time and expense are major considerations.

Another salient feature in the strategy of intervention in the Gofal scheme is the rule of the rota, where several helpers are mobilized to assist particularly high-need clients. Rotas are organized so that no helper is committed every evening or all weekend, which minimizes disruption to family life and thus keeps motivation buoyant. A further consideration is that of maximizing interchangeability between helpers, so that substitutable cover can be provided as well as complementary interweaving. Helpers are also encouraged to display initiative in reorganizing the schedule of support among themselves in consultation with clients, knowing that project social workers are always available as supporting agents. This reduces demands on social workers and frees them to undertake other tasks. Although this has become an underlying principle, careful professional judgment has to be exercised to avoid "dumping" problems on helpers. Thus, once all the initial exploration and assessment work is over, the social work role embodies brokerage, community development, and network-monitoring dimensions. All of these spring out of seeing clients as part of care networks and viewing persons in or around those networks as potential caregivers.

Although these precepts could be regarded as implicit in the neighborhood care schemes described by P. Abrams and colleagues, their work suggests that the shortage and "inappropriateness" of helpers are the two most frequently cited problems. By far the most frequently mentioned prescription for greater success was more helpers. Despite being highly localized, the small geographic base from which these schemes operated was not sufficient by itself to generate helpers. However, as Abrams and his colleagues comment, recruitment problems may tell us more about the expectations of organizers who are paid or work with the statutory authorities than they do about the actual availability of helpers. Another problem has been that both schemes and volunteers are often more numerous in those areas where needs are least, and less available where greatest.

The main difference between helpers in the Gofal scheme and those in neighborhood care projects is that the former are paid, while the latter, with only one or two exceptions, are not. Though we know from the emerging research findings about Gofal that motivations for helping were complex and highly individualistic, they were definitely *not* typified purely by altruism or sheer monetary gain. Some sense of personal commitment was usually combined with a variety of pragmatic considerations. Within the neighborhood care schemes, however, there is a strong suggestion that lack of payment opportunities militated against regular, consistent, and long-term commitments from helpers. Presumably this meant that clients with high dependency, chronic needs were among the most difficult to support. One of the needs most frequently expressed by clients was for transport, and with increasing costs few volunteers can continue to help with no financial reimbursement. The intimation is that the costs of being a good neighbor may be high and the rewards modest, and that difficulties arise from not being able to remedy this imbalance.

The patch systems described by Hadley and McGrath (1980) are predicated not only on the need for geographic decentralization of teams to bring them closer to the community but also on the accompanying desire for greater control over the executive decision-making processes—in short, more delegated authority for teams. Available data do not, except in outline, inform us of how helpers and volunteers are recruited, but it is a claim of patch protagonists that the outposting stratagems employed facilitate earlier identification of need and thus assist preventive work.

A report by Currie and Parrott (1981), which describes in detail the operation of a patch team in Nottinghamshire, does in fact indicate that a decentralized base significantly increases referrals, particularly those coming directly from clients rather than third parties or other agencies, and that it is possible to deflect or deal with many inquiries or contacts informally, without having them routed through the formal welfare system. It is claimed that this is made possible only by bringing patch teams and their ancillaries into closer contact with the community. One of the fears Currie and Parrott's work seems to have allayed is that the patch team would be overworked: Though increased referrals accrue from this method of working, the patch team was not swamped and indeed found the new situation one with which they could cope. Only longer-term monitoring will tell whether cumulative knowledge of local patches results in effective preventive work and an ability to build lasting support networks for those in need in the community.

So far our knowledge of the costs and success of these alternative approaches, let alone their cost-effectiveness, is extremely limited. A first analysis of the parent scheme on which Gofal was based has, however, shown that enhancement of community support provided to the frail elderly results in significantly better outcomes on quality-of-life measures as well as being cheaper than conventional statutory support (Challis & Davies, 1980). Evaluation research of a similar kind seems to be in order for patch and neighborhood care approaches, but this also needs to be complemented by careful analysis identifying what skills and decision-making paradigms are required of the key workers.

Siting

The Gofal project is based on Anglesey, an island off the North Wales coast in a rural Welsh-speaking area. It is but one of several comparable initiatives springing from the momentum of the original pilot project in Kent in the southeast of England (Challis & Davies, 1980). We are now able to see these schemes operating in seaside resorts, retirement settlements, stockbroker belts, and economically depressed areas, both rural and urban. Replication work is being monitored by a small body of researchers scattered around the country who are endeavoring to pool their experiences and collaborate in analyzing and disseminating findings. The schemes do not owe their origins to the whims of passing political fancy, for they are to be found in localities representative of a wide range of political complexions. This in itself may be a useful indicator of future developmental potential.

Abrams and coworkers present more substantial evidence of the crossing of geographic and political boundaries in their review of over 1000 good neighbor schemes. The regional distribution was not even, and it became clear that regions with the lowest levels of need enjoyed the best provision of social care from good neighbor schemes. The converse was reported not to be the case. The researchers concluded that the incidence of schemes has more to do with the availability of helpers and organizers, particularly where there is a large supply of people (mainly women) who not only do not do full-time work but can also afford to meet the costs involved in being a good neighbor. In short, such schemes appear to flourish best where need and a certain level of prosperity exist side by side.

The distributional pattern of patch-based schemes is still emerging. The most publicized initiatives (Cooper, 1980; Bayley, Parker, Seyd, & Tennant, 1981; Currie & Parrott, 1981) appear to be based around small towns or villages with mining connections. This may be related to their visibility as communities with relatively well-defined boundaries, which would be conducive to a patch focus, but it is clearly not a precondition, since patch schemes are known to be operating in scattered rural areas as well as in central London (Hadley & McGrath, 1980). Moreover, there has been recent publicity about newly emerging patch-based initiatives in places as far flung as East Sussex and Northern Ireland.

Our reason for dwelling on patterns of siting is to stress the fact that none of the community-oriented initiatives has occurred as a flash in the pan. None is so local in its origins that it has acquired situational or idiosyncratic features that make it incapable of being applied in other locations. Furthermore, all are examples of developments that are surviving, still evolving, and spreading to other territories. So far they have shown an ability to adapt themselves to local needs and conditions. The flexibility of organization and procedure this implies appears to be an abiding survival characteristic. Though we are not here concerned with plotting the reasons for this trend, it seems most likely that they are rooted in concerns about the inflexibility of conventional statutory services, the inability of these systems to cope with the rising flood of demand, the overriding influence of bureaucracy and red tape, the costs of institutional care, and the desire to find cost-effective community-oriented alternatives. It is to be hoped that the broadening experiences of these and other developing schemes will provide a solid base for the building of more complete and unifying models of community care.

ISSUES IN ADVANCING PARTNERSHIP

Perspectives of Statutory Providers

The schemes described are not the typical model of social service provision. Though currently closest to the community and thus referred to as a type of front-line unit (Smith, 1965), the conventional area team existing in most counties stands at the periphery of the larger social services department. While suggesting that there is general decentralization of the executive decision-making process from the center to the periphery of the organization, this has typically resulted in confusion between professional discretion and agency authority, the two sources of power often leading to clashes of interest and even open conflict. An individualized, single-case orientation remains a pervading characteristic of social work, and reports have drawn attention to the relative absence of teamworking approaches (Stevenson & Parsloe, 1978; Rees, 1978). Given the unseen and privatized nature of much social work, many agencies have developed defensive attitudes toward accountability, as exemplified by the proliferation of case review and caseload management systems and general red tape that apparently irreconcilable demands for care and control have placed on the social work profession (Satyamurti, 1979).

Detailed studies in a wide variety of settings, both urban and rural, and in teams of contrasting composition and organization, show that workers feel frustrated at their lowly position in organizational hierarchies and at their inability to modify inflexible structures (Stevenson & Parsloe, 1978; Black et al., in press). This is exemplified by workers' feelings of being excluded from planning processes, their frustration at having to define and arrange interventions and resource mobilization activity on the basis of fixed or unmoveable budget headings, their sense that theirs is not the job to innovate, due to the implied element of risk taking, and, permeating all this, their feeling threatened by organizational structures all too ready to display their mistrust. Whether intended or not, these seem to be the outward signs of a system typified by a bureaucratic organizational form of the Weberian type, which finds it difficult to adapt to change.

Against this background it is easier to comprehend a reluctance to seek the fusion of informal with formal care resources. The work of Black and colleagues just referred to has provided further indications of why this holds in territories with different potentials for mutual aid. In one economically marginal rural area, the social work team perceived informal care networks as something brittle which professional intervention might destroy, so their response was to distance themselves from this type of activity, despite the fact that reciprocal social relations were perceived as a common feature of many village and farming communities in the area. In another rural area, with a rapidly expanding population, workers were more ambiguous about the strength of social networks and the possibilities for creative social work. The seeds of doubt were sufficient to neutralize any inclinations toward interweaving. In a third area, lying in the heart of a large conurbation, it was adjudged that informal care was lacking, especially on newer council housing estates. It was considered, however, that mobilization of these natural resources required a more concerted community work approach, which was impossible, given the current level of referral bombardment on the team.

Beneath this objective gloss the writers also discerned, in professional workers, uncertainties about the responsiveness and reliability of care networks. Professional judgments about the caring capacity of communities appeared as if colored by experiences relating predominantly to crisis intervention or to problems that occurred because networks were overburdened or attenuated. That the vast majority of the elderly in the community as well as those who are social services clients cope most of the time without statutory help was not readily acknowledged. We disagree with those writers who suggest that statutory welfare systems subvert or destroy informal care in any direct sense (P. Abrams, 1980). Rather, prevailing formally organized social services seem to ignore or take for granted family and neighborhood care, thus leading to a kind of innocent neglect. What we can say, however, is that knowledge of natural helping resources is not generally encouraged, and as a result appropriate practice skills are not acquired.

Social policy in Great Britain is not helped by the lack of research into the operation of contemporary care networks for alternative at-risk groups. We have some statistical information about the overall structure or composition of informal care, but our knowledge of factors that govern the giving and receiving of care, of the rewards and satisfactions, obligations and sanctions, the decision-making processes for the key participants, and the constraints on informal intervention are questions largely unexplored. We lack studies with adequate longitudinal bases and thus remain ignorant of how stable care networks are, what factors disturb their equilibrium, or how people as givers and receivers of care adapt and respond to these changes.

The recently published Barclay Report (National Institute for Social Work, 1982), while urging a perspective for social work that is based on the community, acknowledges the need for more knowledge about the extent, nature, variety, and dynamics of care networks but at the same time calls for greater integration of statutory services with informal systems. Although Barclay calls for a basic change in ideological outlook, our view is that this needs to be accompanied by organizational change. This is taken up in the concluding section about prospects for change.

Informal Support

Writers in the social policy field have questioned both the existence of informal support networks (Parsloe, 1981) and their prevalence or reliability as providers of care (P. Abrams, 1980). Often, misgivings about informal care have been predicated solely on the proximity of immediate kin (M. Abrams, 1980). In this climate of uncertainty, recent shifts in policy emphasis toward greater reliance on informal community support have received mixed reactions.

The indications are, however, that commitment to caring is the norm in both urban and rural environments (Isaacs, Livingstone, & Neville, 1972; Townsend, 1965; Wenger, 1982), although there may be some variations according to the stability of the neighborhood (Warren, 1980), and different neighborhoods may exhibit different patterns of support (Leat, 1982). There is some indication that urban residents are more dependent than rural residents on family resources as opposed to other informal sources of care (Wenger, 1982), but differences are more likely in terms of degree or style than in terms of presence or absence.

Our research shows that approximately a quarter of the elderly receive help with routine chores and household maintenance. Most of this help comes from the family, but there are subgroups within the elderly category for whom family are less available. These groups rely to a larger degree on friends and neighbors and include the single, the childless, those who live alone or with elderly relatives (other than spouse), and those who have no close relatives. Only a small minority of the elderly (less than 5 percent in most instances) need help with personal care (bathing, toileting, moving around the house, and so on), and for them, most help comes from another member of the household, usually a spouse. The family figures as the major source of support in crises. Friends and neighbors, however, are an important source of borrowing things and transport. Our evidence suggests they also play an important mental health role as a "friendly ear" or confidant.

Help from friends and neighbors seems to be slightly different from help from families and is frequently based on affectual or expressive linkages. While this is not to suggest that family help is not also based on affective bonds, there is a clear cultural expectation of responsibility on the part of the family. Friends and neighbors may "hold the fort" in crisis until family support can be mustered. The more serious the problem or the more dependent the elderly person, the more likely it is for family to be involved. Help from friends and neighbors is typically less regular than help from family, but this probably reflects an expectation of family intervention where regular help is necessary. At the same time, it appears that neighbor help is commonly underestimated. For various subsets of the elderly help from this source is, as we have noted, more common than that from the family.

In a microstudy of one street in a South Wales town, Bytheway (1979) found that where family were involved in caring for the ailing elderly, neighbors deferred to the family and were uninvolved, but where there was no family involvement, neighbors stepped in. Those without family to care were thus more integrated into the street as cooperation between neighbors developed. Contrary to fears of social workers, our research suggests that neighborhood involvement continues after social service intervention, and clients still turn to informal sources in crisis. The continued involvement of informal carers suggests that their care may shift from a predominantly instrumental pattern to a more expressive but equally life-enhancing mode when less effort is dictated.

It was found that fully one-third of elderly people were actually committed to helping their neighbors in one way or another, however irregularly. Others commented on their willingness to help if the need arose. Asking about help given by the elderly proved to be an emotive subject. Many respondents who were no longer able to help in any instrumental way felt this loss keenly. Supportive listening or advice giving appeared to be undervalued by the giver, despite the high proportions who turn to neighbors as a source of expressive support. The existence of natural helpers also became apparent; the names of neighbors recurred in the support networks of many of the elderly. Frequently these were younger retired people in the community, who could, given a community perspective by social workers, become a potential nexus for the coordinating of neighborly and statutory help.

It is important to remind oneself that most of the elderly are competent people requiring no help. Many of them are able and willing to provide help to others, thus helping themselves by compensating for role loss. Despite the stereotype of the unmarried daughter as carer, a higher proportion of the carers for the elderly are themselves the contemporaries of the elderly spouse, brother, sister, or friend for whom they care. In many instances the less frail or less ill partner cares for the other. In the study mentioned, one in ten of the elderly was caring for a relative who was completely dependent on him or her, usually another elderly person or in a few cases a disabled or handicapped younger relative. With the demographic shift toward greater longevity, the adult child caring for an aged parent is more likely to be over 60. Carers of the dependent elderly continue to carry large burdens of responsibility; consequently, breakdown of personal carers is a frequent cause of institutionalization of the frail elderly (Isaacs et al., 1972; Townsend, 1965; Pope, 1978). However, the direct support of carers by the statutory services is an area of social work that has been largely ignored, and even instrumental help seems to be offered only in extreme circumstances.

What is clear is the high level of interdependence at the informal level. Not only do the elderly rely significantly on their families for help, support, and reassurance but, for significant subgroups, needs and demands are met by friends and neighbors. The informal web of supportive reciprocity takes care of the majority of help and care received. The indications are that statutory or formal services are called upon only when for some reason informal carers are not available or can no longer cope with the burdens of their responsibilities. The need to develop relationships among the informal, statutory, and voluntary sectors, which our knowledge of informal care suggests, is more likely to be possible in the kinds of community-based innovations we have described.

The Locus of Initiative in Community Care

Although caring responsibilities are distributed unevenly across statutory, voluntary, and commercial agencies, quasi-formal neighborhood groups, and informal carers, each group can claim some special knowledge, expertise, or authority of relevance. Also, the nature of mutual dependencies between these groups raises many questions about what model of welfare pluralism is supposed to hold sway (Webb, 1981). Do we expect the statutory sector to complement or perhaps supplement informal care? What scope should there be for some deliberate duplication of activity? Whatever mix we end up with, community caring will demand coordinated or integrated modes of action, but it also raises questions about who should be taking the initiative. Being responsible for defining the framework of social policy, governments have an obvious part to play. What lines of action might they pursue?

A first consideration might be to offer incentives to local authorities, voluntary agencies, quasi-formal groups, and individuals to build collaborative bridges in their care activities. Incentives could take the form of cash payments like straight grant aid, subsidies, indemnity against operating-cost losses, loans, leasing arrangements, or payments in kind such as access to research resources. The principle of joint financing established between social services and health authorities could be extended to a wider spectrum of bodies, including the whole of the voluntary sector. Alternatively, methods could be found to reward agencies who demonstrate both a preparedness to experiment and a quality of leadership in innovative action. Nonfinancial rewards such as guarantees of publicity or use as an advisory resource may be just as relevant as financial rewards. A second possibility would be for government advisers to take a stronger lead in publicizing exemplary community care practices and in organizing gatherings where experiences could be shared with a wider public. The emphasis therefore would be on collating experiences and coordinating action. Third, some of the existing public research budget could be used to set up comparative studies between different experimental schemes or to stimulate replication. Care initiatives so often acquire features reflecting their situational context that it is difficult to know how far their organization, working methods, and therefore outcomes are generalizable to other settings. Greater emphasis on collaboration between researchers therefore seems a necessary and desirable objective for this last goal to be achieved.

At the same time, the priming of care initiatives could be going on in every community or neighborhood; it does not have to be dependent on pump priming from central government. Although social services departments disburse small grants to voluntary agencies that can often respond more quickly or flexibly to particular presenting needs, how many local authorities offer them direct professional or administrative advice and support? How many draw voluntary bodies into consultations about forward planning and research developments? That we do not know the answers to these questions is an indication of our compartmental thinking and concern with preserving the status quo. To break through this natural inertia seems to require policies encouraging some calculated risk taking and a preparedness to experiment at all levels.

PROSPECTS FOR CHANGE

The natural helping networks of the elderly described earlier have several identifiable characteristics that contrast with the predominant service delivery model. They consist of networks of individuals known to one another; they are recognized by others outside the network (that is, they are relatively visible); they are flexible and responsive to changes in need; and they are accessible to those whom they serve. These principles appear to underlie the successful functioning of a good part of community care. If we look at social services from this perspective, we can see that the innovatory schemes described earlier attempt to recognize these factors and take them into account. They are more in tune with what the Barclay Committee had in mind when they stressed the need for "the development of flexible decentralised patterns of organization based upon a social care plan which takes full account of informal care and mobilises voluntary and statutory provision in its support" (National Institute for Social Work, 1982, p. 13.3).

The innovations described in this chapter have been possible without wholesale reorganization of the personal social services. They appear to provide a more visible, familiar, and accessible service to the community. There is a strong suggestion in the case of neighborhood care and patch schemes that this leads to earlier intervention, but we await more research findings to confirm this and to see whether the effectiveness of outcome is raised. In all three types of scheme, natural carers are more readily targeted and provided with support.

Brokerage and enabling roles for professionals appear to be a natural outgrowth with implications for encouragement of mutual aid within the community. In the case of Gofal, this has developed spontaneously, husbands and children of helpers becoming involved in helping relationships and helpers providing support for one another. It could be said to represent what Bayley (1980) has called "sensitive interweaving" of the informal and formal sectors. We should acknowledge, however, that the path to greater integration of formal and informal care is not easy, so we should air some of the objections raised by proponents of the conventional service delivery model.

Opposition has been voiced in terms of accountability, confidentiality, and concerns about the role of professionalism and deskilling. If statutory services are to enter into partnership with informal provision and provide flexible and appropriate services, differences in resources between areas will be inevitable, and resource-rich areas are likely to be able to provide a better standard of care than less favored areas. The fear is that decentralized services will demonstrate a high degree of variability, but this can also be seen as an advantage if provision is appropriate to local needs. However, the debate about resource-rationing models as against decentralized systems has yet to be resolved. Devolution of more authority and responsibility on area teams would seem to require a broader conception of supervision, monitoring, and forms of budgetary allocation that allow the vision and priorities of individual teams to be reflected to a far greater degree than at present. We are, therefore, talking about organizational as well as ideological change as necessary and interdependent.

If interweaving of formal and informal care is to be promoted, social workers will find themselves working with indigenous nonprofessionals, like family members, neighbors and volunteers, but where does accountability to the agency fit into this picture? Although this traditional form of accountability will still be important to social workers and agencies alike, the development of a working partnership with the community assumes a willingness to respect the import of accountability to clients and community. Though this will place varied and often conflicting pressures on professionals, the indications from the Gofal experiment and its sister schemes give rise to some optimism in this regard. There is an urgent need for further experimentation so that other models that embody hybrid accountability processes can be put to the test. Empirical proof rather than supposition would be the best way of convincing skeptics.

The problem of confidentiality is one that is closely allied to accountability. For the professional attempting to work through such networks, ethical and statutory constraints may impede progress. Social workers are also members of the culture, and while informal helpers act intuitively and discretely, formal helpers must observe agency rules and procedures. Delegated bureaucratic authority allied to professional discretion would seem to offer conditions allowing workers the elbowroom to negotiate with those in the informal care system how respective responsibilities for care and support should be explored and subsequently subdivided. In this way, anxieties about breaches of confidentiality seem more likely to fade.

The indications from the Gofal and neighborhood care schemes are that financial inducements may need to be offered both to recruit and to maintain committed carers. An immediate implication of this for good neighbor schemes would therefore be a need for greater financial backing.

However, the use of cash incentives to attract lay helpers will undoubtedly test even the most discerning professional worker, for there is always the risk that this will lead to a commercialization of community care. We should remind the reader that cash disbursements are only used in Gofal-type schemes where the frailest and most needy elderly require intensive or demanding care of a type that could not be expected from an unpaid volunteer.

There is also a strong suggestion that the fostering of interdependencies among helpers or volunteers, as exemplified by Gofal's rota system, is a key ingredient in supporting the most needy elderly. Besides spreading the onus of responsibility for care, it affords helpers greater security and cues them into someone local who can be used as a sounding board at times of decision. Unpaid volunteers often require security that may not be found in their relationships with individual clients, so mechanisms providing for nonfinancial support to volunteers require attention from those seeking to bring formal and informal care closer together. The provision of relevant rewards for volunteers is another subject requiring further study. A reasonable start could be made by exploring more systematically the reasons people help, following the lead shown by Qureshi (1979).

Enhancement of care in the community appears also to require a greater commitment to teamwork. Privatized methods seem largely antithetical, even though they are prized and offer security to workers in the conventional statutory services. From what we can judge, workers, whether lay or professional, qualified or unqualified, derive both motivation and satisfaction from being able to draw on the strengths of each other. Not only does this rest on a condition of trust being present, but the more open relationships implied would seem just as likely to sustain this as a necessary underpinning to community care practice. They may also offer some reassurance in terms of accountability.

In some of the experiments we have discussed the limits of caring roles undertaken by volunteers, neighbors, or paid helpers remain indistinct. This arises less from woolly-mindedness in thinking about role definitions and more from an acknowledgment that these groups possess varying needs and degrees of resourcefulness that make it inappropriate to lay down strict guidelines for practice. In the Gofal scheme, for example, many of the tasks undertaken on behalf of the frail elderly are of a quasi-nursing type, thus potentially usurping the role of community nurses. The practice, however, has been allowed to continue because it falls in the "grey area" of responsibility between the separate health and social services agencies and because it has a legitimate support function for clients. In working out possibilities for collaborative action, especially in the roles of professional and lay staff, a degree of blurring at the edges seems necessary to offer scope for adjustment and maneuvering on all sides. The trouble is that this seems untidy. If we cannot distinguish where responsibilities begin and end among family, helpers, neighbors, volunteers, paid helpers, professionals, and those who have multiple roles, then confusion and chaos will be the order of the day. We would argue that it is the professional community social worker's role, backed by agency mandate, to fix or negotiate the parameters in each case.

Lest our argument so far be misunderstood, let us spell out clearly what is envisaged and particularly what interweaving is not. Interweaving is not about shifting responsibility from statutory services onto informal providers. Neither is it about co-opting and colonizing informal systems (Froland, 1980) or about superimposing existing packages of care on the community. If interweaving is to work well, it must start from a perspective of the community or locality as a caregiving system by seeking to reinforce and optimize existing resources and creating resources to fill gaps in provision. It therefore requires familiarity with family and neighborhood networks; consultation with network members as well as clients; development of partnerships with other social services, such as doctors' practices, schools, churches, and voluntary organizations; and, as Seebohm and Kilbrandon envisaged over a decade ago and Barclay has recently reiterated, a requirement to view the entire community as both needing and offering support. This raises important questions about the training and skill requirements of social workers. It implies that social work education must include attention to the sociology of groups and communities and the whole area of community organization as a central part of the social work role. More than that, it demands a greater commitment to the sharing of professional and administrative skills with clients, lay helpers, and voluntary agencies. It also assumes that other professional groups, notably doctors and community nurses in the case of the elderly, will be similarly disposed toward this type of interweaving. We have reason to believe that interorganizational relations between statutory bodies may yet prove to be the major stumbling block in effecting a transition. This caveat aside, communication, entrepreneurial, brokerage, and organizational skills will then become essential attributes of the successful community-oriented social worker, coexisting with the more traditional caseworking or counseling methodologies. The optimal division of labor in the community social work team is still, however, open to question.

Bayley (1980) has emphasized that no one pattern of interweaving the formal and informal sectors will work in all instances. He urges a creative relationship between the two, which takes account of the specific context. As already noted, the increasingly persuasive thrust toward a working partnership with voluntary bodies and informal carers implies some quite radical changes in the management and organization of social services as well as in ideology. It is not surprising, therefore, that resistance is being experienced. There is an inherent tension in a system that seeks to adapt itself more readily to local needs and simultaneously provide a basic national service. No clear relationship between the generic local model and the need for professional specialisms has been proposed. At the same time, social services in many European countries have demonstrated a pendulum effect between centralism and localism, and this tendency has not yet been resolved (Wenger, 1979). The problems of management in a diffuse and flexible system seem to predispose policymakers toward more account-ability and control, while strong centralist systems stifle innovation and lead to demands for the devolution of power. It is therefore difficult to assess the current developments without considering whether we are wit-nessing yet another swing of the pendulum. However, the consensus seems to be that domiciliary services are best provided from the grass roots, and certainly the record seems to demonstrate that involvement from the community thrives better in a climate of local participation. The indica-tions are that a hybrid system might emerge—one with a locally organized generic base supplemented by specialist consultants covering wider areas. At present, innovations striving toward creative adaptation to community need demonstrate a refreshingly new level of involvement and capacity, but it is impossible to know how much of this is a side effect of their novelty or the charisma and commitment of the innovators. Time and more experimentation will tell.

REFERENCES

Abrams, M. *Beyond three score years and ten: A second report on the elderly.* London: Age Concern Publications, 1980.
Abrams, P. Social change, social networks and neighbourhood care. *Social Work Services,* 1980, *22,* 12-13.

Abrams, P., Abrams, S., Humphrey, R., & Snaith, R. *Action for care: A review of good neighbour schemes in England.* Berkhamstead: The Volunteer Centre, 1981.

Bayley, M. Neighbourhood care and community care: A response to Philip Abrams. *Social Work Service,* 1980, *26,* 4-9.

Bayley, M., Parker, P., Seyd, R., & Tennant, A. *Neighbourhood services project Dinnington. Paper No. 1: Origins, strategy and proposed evaluation.* Sheffield: University of Sheffield, Department of Sociological Studies, 1980.

Black, J., Bowl, R., Burns, D., Critcher, C., Grant, G., & Stockford, D. *Social work in context: A comparative study of three area social work teams.* London: Tavistock, in press.

Bytheway, W. R. *Care in the street.* Swansea: University College Swansea, Medical Sociology Research Centre, 1979.

Challis, D., & Davies, B. A new approach to community care of the elderly. *British Journal of Social Work,* 1980, *10,* 1-18.

Cooper, M., Normanton: Interweaving social work and the community. In R. Hadley & M. McGrath (Eds.), *Going local: Neighbourhood social services.* London: National Council for Voluntary Organizations, 1980.

Currie, R., & Parrott, B. *A unitary approach to social work: Application in practice.* London: British Association of Social Workers, 1981.

Froland, C. Formal and informal care: Discontinuities in a continuum. *Social Service Review,* 1980, *54,* 572-587.

Gandy, J. M. Scottish governmental reorganization and human service delivery by teams. In D. Thursz & J. L. Vigilante (Eds.), *Meeting human needs: Additional perspectives from thirteen countries.* Beverly Hills, CA: Sage, 1976.

Glastonbury, B., Cooper, D. M., & Hawkins, P. *Social work in conflict: The practitioner and the bureaucrat.* London: Croom Helm, 1980.

Goldberg, E. M., & Connelly, N. (Eds.). *Evaluative research in social care.* London: Heinemann, 1981.

Hadley, R., & McGrath, M. *Going local: Neighbourhood social services.* London: National Council for Voluntary Organizations, 1980.

Hunt, A. *The elderly at home: A study of people aged sixty-five and over living in the community in England in 1976.* London: Social Survey Division, Office of Population Censuses and Surveys, 1978.

Isaacs, B., Livingstone, M., & Neville, Y. *Survival of the unfittest: A study of geriatric patients in Glasgow.* London: Routledge & Kegan Paul, 1972.

Leat, D. *Report of a pilot study of informal neighbourly care of the elderly.* London: Policy Studies Institute, 1982.

National Institute for Social Work. *Social Workers, their role and tasks.* London: Bedford Square Press/National Council for Voluntary Organizations, 1982.

Parry, N., Rustin, M., & Satyamurti, C. *Social work, welfare and the state.* London: Edward Arnold, 1979.

Parsloe, P. *Social services area teams.* London: Allen & Unwin, 1981.

Pope, P. *Emergency admissions into old people's homes.* Cardiff: Mid-Glamorgan County Council, Social Services Department, 1978.

Power, M. *Technical report to Department of Health & Social Security.* Bristol: University of Bristol, Social Care Research Project, School of Applied Social Studies, 1978.

Qureshi, H. *Dimensions of motivations: Preliminary investigations of motivations taken separately.* Kent Community Care Project Paper 10. Canterbury: University of Kent at Canterbury, Personal Social Service Research Unit, 1979.

Rees, S. *Social work face to face.* London: Edward Arnold, 1978.

Satyamurti, C. Care and control in local authority social work. In N. Parry, M. Rustin, & C. Satyamurti, *Social work, welfare and the state.* London: Edward Arnold, 1979.

Smith, D. Front-line organization in the state mental hospital. *Administrative Science Quarterly, 10,* 1965, 381-399.

Stevenson, O., & Parsloe, P. *Social services teams: the practitioner's view.* London: Her Majesty's Stationery Office, 1978.

Townsend, P. The effects of family structure on the likelihood of admission to an institution in old age: The application of a general theory. In E. Shanas & G. Streib (Eds.), *Social structure and the family: Generational relations,* Englewood Cliffs, NJ: Prentice-Hall, 1965.

Warren, D. I. Support systems in different types of neighbourhoods. In J. Garbarino & H. Stocking, *Protecting children from abuse and neglect.* San Francisco: Jossey-Bass, 1980.

Webb, A. *Collective action and welfare pluralism.* Occasional Paper No. 3. Essex: Association of Researchers into Voluntary Action in the Community, 1981.

Wenger, G. C. *Report to D.H.S.S. on European Symposium on the Elderly and the Care System, Jadwisin, Poland, 21-25 May, 1979.* Bangor: University College of North Wales, Social Services in Rural Areas Research Project, 1979.

Wenger, G. C. Ageing in rural communities: Family contacts and community integration. *Ageing and Society,* 1982, *2,* 211-229.

Westland, P. Neighborhood delivery and national policy in England. In D. Thursz and J. L. Vigilante (Eds.), *Reaching people: The structure of neighborhood services.* Beverly Hills, CA: Sage, 1978.

Williams, B. The Gofal service in practice: An initial discussion. Appendix C. In L. Tarron (Ed.), *Caring for dependent elderly people in rural areas by means of enhanced forms of community support.* Working Paper No. 20. Bangor: University College of North Wales, Social Services in Rural Areas Research Project, 1981.

2

REBUILDING REFUGEE NETWORKS

ALICE COLLINS
United States

In the spring of 1979, I was asked to train some of the refugee staff of the local Indochinese Center so that they might assist their compatriots with the difficult problems facing all the refugees as they attempted to become acclimated to the United States. The Center, located in a western city, had been organized in response to the needs of the first waves of Vietnamese refugees as a central place where they could find sympathetic understanding, specialized services, and referral to other resources being mobilized to help them. Supported by a combination of private and public funds, the Center was one of the first in this country to offer services not only to the Vietnamese refugees but also to the Laotian, Mnong, Cambodian, and Mien people, and later, to the "boat people." Classes in English, employment services, training in the use of public transportation, and preschool programs were undertaken with considerable success. After a time, however, it became evident that while these services were helpful to many, there were individuals and families whose past experience and present difficulties in resettlement were overwhelming to them.

A mental health counseling program was therefore instituted. It was based on the traditional American model of the establishment of an ongoing relationship between a mental health professional and a patient. The plan at the Center was not only to help the individuals with problems but also to train selected refugees as paraprofessionals so that they might eventually move into the community and find permanent jobs in that capacity or go on for full professional training. Like mental health services in general, the Indochinese Center soon experienced the paradoxical dilemma of being swamped by its own success. As its ability and willingness to help the emotionally disturbed became known, it was pressured to increase its service far beyond the limits of financial and staff resources. It seemed urgent that some way be found to meet the need, preventively and amelioratively, within practical limits of time and money. It was decided to experiment with the comparatively new concepts of working with natural networks.

NATURAL HELPING NETWORKS
AND THE INDOCHINESE

I was asked to undertake the task of training the Indochinese counselors because I had been working with the theory and practice of consultation with natural networks for some time. According to one typology (Froland, Pancoast, Chapman & Kimiboko, 1981), natural helping networks are one of five different kinds of helping networks. They are considered to be made up of those linkages that already exist in a community, often centering on one person who sees himself and is seen by others as a resource for information and support and who initiates linkages between people who can be helpful to one another. The relationship between such central figures, or natural helpers, and the professionals who work with them is collegial, a partnership rather than a directive approach. This was the model I hoped to introduce to the counselors, since it seemed especially well suited to the needs of the Indochinese community and the counselors' positions in it.

I was glad to accept the invitation to train the staff for a number of personal and professional reasons. It seemed to me that the counselors who would act as consultants would have no difficulty in identifying central figures, since they knew so many of their compatriots, both from contacts in their native countries and in the refugee camps, where they had lived for varying lengths of time. Therefore I would not have to spend much time—as was often necessary with American trainees—to convince the Indochinese counselors that such central helpers existed. I reasoned that they must have observed many instances of this kind of natural helping and that some of them were themselves natural helpers in the terrible life crises of their journey and resettlement. Certainly the issue of confidentiality, which had often proved a stumbling block for American counselors, would not be a consideration to people who had survived the forced intimacy of the camps and the endless public screenings for entrance to this country. It seemed to me that these shared experiences could be expected to facilitate the collegial relationships between the counselors and the natural helpers that would be the basis for the program. I looked forward to contact with the Indochinese, especially the large numbers of Mnong and Mien refugees, because I had enjoyed two short stays in Thailand in the early 1970s, where I had become especially interested in what little I could learn about the hill tribe people who had lived undisturbed in the inaccessible mountains of the "golden triangle" between Thailand, Burma, and Laos until the Vietnam War had forced them out of the stone age and into the world of deadly weapons. I had admired their artifacts and was intrigued by the history of these Tibetan-Chinese-Indian ancient nomads. Indeed, the week before the request to train the counselors had come, I had read a book by a French ethnographer about a Mnong village where he had spent a year in 1955 (Condominas, 1977). It was hard to believe that a considerable number of the refugees in this western city were possibly some of the same tribespeople whose relatives had fought to extinction for the U.S. military forces. It was staggering to realize that some of the children pictured nearly naked at work and play in the remote jungle villages might now be trying to bring up their own children in tiny, isolated apartments in a large modern city, shut away from the natural surroundings that had been their world, had given them their religious beliefs, and had provided their food and shelter for countless generations. The prospect of firsthand acquaintance with them was an exciting one for me.

PREPARING FOR THE MEETINGS

After a brief talk with the director of the assimilation program, who had invited me to do the training, I agreed to try to do what she asked. It appeared that what was needed was help for the counselors, who would, in turn, act as supports for the central figures. I thought it likely that some of the counselors were natural helpers themselves, and I would try to get them to expand their roles and include strangers as well as acquaintances in their networks. I saw my task as helping the counselors understand what they could do, increasing their knowledge about the behavior of those who needed their help, and providing them with information about referral resources.

We prepared for weekly meetings with the counseling staff, which comprised from ten to fifteen individuals, by having a lengthy conference that included CS, the director of the counseling program in the mental health service, the director of the assimilation program, and me. CS and the other members of the counseling staff, I learned, had been selected because of their level of education, their command of English, and their status in their communities, which was based on their experience in government or the military in their own countries. As I came to understand this, I began to question my assumption that they would be natural helpers, since their experience had been more directive than collegial.

CS explained that the Center needed my assistance in teaching the counselors how to reach the many people who needed help but did not ask for it, taking into consideration that the counselors were already working night and day to keep up with the demands made on them for help. The counselors were chiefly involved at present in helping refugees deal with existing social agencies. CS said that in his country there were no social agencies and no need for them. It was the duty of the extended family to look after its members, no matter how distantly related. Whatever help, personal or financial, was needed, was provided within the family and was not discussed or disclosed to outsiders. To do so would be to bring shame to all family members for failing in their duties. But now families were broken up. Probably every one of the refugees had lost family members or had been widely separated from them. They had to turn to strangers for their most basic needs—a difficult task for all, but for some evidently so distasteful they would not do it. CS pointed out that although the Vietnamese refugee group was the largest and presumably had the greatest problems, they rarely came to the Center for help and were the least cooperative with the counseling staff who tried to reach them. It was proving very difficult, according to CS, to find a Vietnamese man willing to act as a helpful counselor. I was not surprised to learn, in answer to my question, that CS was himself a Cambodian and had held a high government post in that country. CS's views about the Vietnamese could be more clearly understood in light of the long history of unfriendly relations between Cambodia and Vietnam.

The director asked me to tell something about my own background—perhaps because she could see that CS's account had shaken me out of some of my preconceived ideas. I thought it useful to describe my early settlement house experience with European immigrants, my work with other social agencies to help other immigrants, and my hope that this would prepare me for work with the Indochinese. My remarks were met with the polite silence I came to recognize as the Oriental equivalent of violent disagreement. CS closed the meeting by saying he looked forward to my teaching the counselors "networking."

COMPARISON OF INDOCHINESE
WITH OTHER IMMIGRANTS

Reviewing that meeting in my mind, I faced the fact that I had made several unwarranted assumptions. First, for the Indochinese, confidentiality was a deeply ingrained necessity; second, these immigrants did not resemble those I had known and described. The cliches about this country as a "melting pot" of immigrants had obscured the differences between these people and the European immigrants. Unlike those earlier immigrants, these refugees had not come eagerly to this country to find the opportunities denied them in their native lands. There were no groups of earlier immigrants, now settled and prospering, who would help in their rapid acclimatization to their new country. For the most part, the skills they utilized in their native countries had no place here. To "native" Americans, the children and grandchildren of earlier immigrations, these new immigrants were totally unfamiliar in appearance, in language, and in religion, not to mention lifestyle. Few Americans had been in their native countries, and those who had been there were inclined to regard them unsympathetically. I had to admit that they seemed to be strangers in a strange and unfriendly country to a much greater degree than any immigrants since those first few who were driven out of their native England.

MEETING THE COUNSELORS

Ordinarily I would have planned some exercises for an initial training session to clarify the existence of natural networks and their universality. I would have asked the trainees to diagram their own natural networks, including family, friends, and acquaintances and their degree of closeness to the trainee and to each other. But this approach, it seemed to me, would serve here only to emphasize how disrupted the counselors' natural networks had been. It seemed more useful for me to try to learn what the counselors were already doing in their jobs at present before proceeding to talk with them about natural networks.

The first meeting with the counselors was postponed several times, due to various emergencies and reorganizations in their work. When the day came, final preparations for my work had still not been completed, perhaps reflecting some ambivalence on CS's part. The question of a meeting room had to be settled, and it was explained that two of the counselors were absent because of emergency requests for help. CS took his place at the head of the table and began the introductions. I asked each counselor to spell his name for me, correct my pronunciation, and tell me how he preferred to be addressed, since some of the names were made up of two and some of three syllables. They were agreed that first names were customarily used, and I responded by telling them my name and suggesting that they use my first name, too. Each counselor had come in carrying a large yellow pad on which each now wrote "Mrs. Alice Collins."

I went on to explain that I had only a very general idea of what their work consisted of, and would appreciate it if they would tell me about recent cases in which they had been involved. After a brief silence, CS explained to me, in almost the identical words he had used at our earlier meeting, that there were no social agencies in their native countries and all helping activities took place within the extended family. He then went on to discuss, in detail, his many interventions in the case of a psychotic woman for whom help had to be mobilized from a number of social agencies, a time-consuming and frustrating task. CS felt she would have been much more expeditiously and successfully cared for in his country within her native family system. He also felt strongly that if the agencies here had recognized his abilities and had involved him in their efforts, he could have helped her more then strangers could.

PH followed at once with an account of his experience with a hospital outpatient clinic, to which he had accompanied an anxious and frightened compatriot. They had had a long wait, which concerned PH, since many other people were expecting him. Then he had been used solely as interpreter, the hospital taking over the treatment without any explanation to him or asking for his help in explaining procedures to the patient. He said he looked forward to learning from me how networking would save him time and how it could reach those people who had already had humiliating experiences and would not ask for needed help because they wanted to avoid repeating painful losses of dignity. In his country, there would have been someone in the family who would have contacted a healer, and whatever ceremony or other treatment was deemed necessary would have been carried on without being divulged to outsiders.

OBJECTIONS BY COUNSELORS

I tried to build on what he said by noting that it had been found that there were people in all communities who acted as though they were family members, and that what I hoped we might do together would be to identify such people in the Indochinese communities and discuss ways in which they could be mobilized to expand their activities, thereby lightening the burden on the counselors. Several counselors said, with as much anger as they could permit themselves, that there were certainly no such people in their community, only families so broken by loss and dislocation that the helping people within them no longer were functioning. The rest nodded in agreement with them.

KR, a Laotian who had held the most important post of any of the counselors, went on to explain that even if such people were found to exist, they would not wish to intervene in the lives of other individuals. It was a wide-spread belief that to do so was to interfere in a person's karma—his preordained life plan—and that anyone who did this remained responsible for that person forever. He explained that the counselors, with their higher education and greater understanding of the customs of this country, did not act on this ancient belief but that "ordinary people," which he understood I had been describing as natural helpers, might be seriously hindered by it. He went on to say that he wished that my ideas *could* work—he himself felt unable to do what needed to be done. For example, he had recently been appealed to by a middle-aged compatriot who wanted him to get her a divorce from her physically abusive husband. The hour ended before he could finish his account, and the counselors left, their yellow pads still blank except for my name.

The next meeting was held as arranged, but with two of the first group missing and the addition of a Vietnamese woman who had taught English in a Vietnamese high school and a beautiful young Cambodian woman. It was explained that the missing members had "found jobs." I understood that the basic objective of the program at the Center was to prepare all those working there to enter the open job market, but it was still disconcerting to be conducting a "training course" that would have a changing population.

I asked KR to tell us more about the case he had begun the previous week, and he said he was glad to do that, since he had been working on it all week and felt that he had accomplished nothing. He had worried about the woman because he knew that the husband, who had been the bodyguard of a province chief, was known for his violence, and he feared for her life. But when he made time to visit as soon as he could, he found the couple living together amicably. The wife withdrew her request, and the husband acknowledged his bad temper and vowed it would not flare up again. KR was too sophisticated to take the reconciliation at face value and was distressed at not knowing what to do to protect the wife, since he felt that the husband might well hurt or kill her next time.

I thought that this case might give me an opening to discuss the use of the natural system. I asked if the marital problems were known to the Laotians in the rest of the apartment building. Indeed they were, KR said, which was another reason he felt so worried, since if he did not solve the problem, he would lose the respect of all the others who knew about it. Hoping still to make my point, I referred to the case reported by PH, where after hours of waiting (which I explained were unfortunately often endured by all patients, not just the Indochinese) the counselor was used only as an interpreter. I suggested that perhaps there might be people, known to the patient, who interpreted for her in daily life and who would respond to an appeal from the counselor to accompany her to the hospital or perhaps find a mutual friend who would do so. PH replied that this would never work—the person asked to help would refuse on the basis that she would not do "for free" what the counselor was paid to do. The Vietnamese school teacher, AN, corroborated this and said that, unfortunately, in her country even families no longer helped each other. People had become so distrustful of each .other and so resigned to having buy favors that, while what I described would once have been a matter of course within the family, today it was every person for himself.

I was so thoroughly shaken by these negative comments that I did not try to respond to them but went ahead as I had planned to do, describing some of the natural networks we had learned about and the almost universal belief of natural helpers that they received as much as they gave and that payment in money was unnecessary. Fortunately for me, the hour soon ended, the counselors politely hoping I would teach them about networking soon, as their caseloads were becoming increasingly unmanageable. Their yellow pads remained blank.

I sought out the director and told her what I suspected she already knew, that I was not meeting the needs of the counselors and that we had established no working relationships because I had clearly not understood their situation and the insurmountable obstacles to a network approach. The director explained, with "face-saving" tact, that the counselors were confused at my approach, having expected to be *taught*. Indochinese teachers, she explained, even at the graduate level, maintained a distance from the pupils and lectured, giving specific assignments and checking on their accomplishment. She had also noted that the most difficult hurdle for the Indochinese counselors was the lack of respect they experienced from professional workers. The Indochinese considered the American workers as having a lower status than themselves and therefore were insulted by their behavior. They had been told that I was a social worker, which might account for some of the resistance I was meeting. On the other hand, as an elderly woman, I was in a position to command respect. The director reiterated her belief that the Center's counseling program must change in the direction of using natural networks if it was going to meet the enormous and constantly increasing needs of the refugees. My problem, she let me know, was part of the major problem of the Center— to help the Indochinese refugees to adapt to American life without abandoning all of their traditions.

A NEW DIRECTIVE APPROACH

I did some intensive thinking about how to make a new start and decided that since the counselors would have to work with social agencies, I might attempt to dispel their resentment somewhat. At the next meeting, therefore, I began by saying that since they were acting as social workers, I thought they should know something about the profession as it had grown up and was practiced in this country, and I had prepared a lecture about it for them. I was pleased to note, as I delivered it, that the yellow pads were filling up with beautiful calligraphy. I ended my speech, perhaps a little disingenuously, by describing the work on natural networks as a newly developed social work method, whose principles were being widely accepted, although the techniques for putting them into practice were still being developed.

I did not ask for comments or questions, remembering the director's description of Indochinese educational procedure, but did end with an assignment. Ignoring the objections raised in the earlier meetings, I asked that every counselor be prepared next time to describe a person known to him or observed who appeared to act as a natural helper. No objections were voiced. As the others left, the beautiful young Cambodian woman, who had said nothing at all previously, managed to stay behind. She closed the door and said she wanted to tell me that she *had* found natural helpers and made extensive use of them in her assigned job of settling unsponsored newcomers. She had found that she could ask some of their already well-settled compatriots to introduce them to American customs and help them find others from their home towns and villages. There was a sound of people coming into the adjoining room and she left abruptly in mid-sentence, evidently to avoid being overheard.

All the counselors came on time and stayed through the next session, except the director, CS. He was on a leave of absence, and it was explained that he was meeting with "important people" to attempt to improve the political situation in his native country.

At the next meeting, the first to respond to my request for observations was KR. With the first real smile I had seen in the group, he told of having met an elderly acquaintance from the apartment house where the marital problem existed. The old man was apologetic that KR had been involved— usually he himself had mediated the many quarrels in that marriage, because he knew that was what the woman's father had done at home. Unfortunately he had been away visiting a daughter at the time of the recent fight, or KR would never have been involved. He would see to it that KR would not be involved again in the future—unless, perhaps, if someone called the police; "Could he then ask for help from KR?" "Natural helper, yes?" KR commented with obvious pleasure—matched by mine!

AH reported that she had given several talks to the women's groups and had noticed that before and after the formal program, one lady, Mrs. N, appeared to be the natural helper type. She was constantly surrounded by groups of women who asked her advice about marketing, child care, and other domestic matters. AH had talked briefly to Mrs. N, who said she did indeed have lots of friends and she liked to talk to them "like a sister"— she had been the eldest in her family and the only one to reach this country, so it felt good to act like a sister again.

The counselor who had been kept waiting at the outpatient clinic said he hadn't exactly observed anyone, but when a call for interpretation had come from the hospital social worker to which he could not possibly respond, he had told the social worker about several high school students who lived near the patient and who might be willing to volunteer to interpret if the social worker asked them to do so as a great favor. He grinned when he said he had waited at the phone expecting the social worker to call him back and berate him because he had passed on her request for help instead of responding to it himself. Since that hadn't happened, he thought that maybe he might try now to find a few more young people who would be willing to serve as occasional interpreters.

The young Mnong man said it was the young people who worried him the most—and all his observations had only increased this feeling. The Mnong Tribal Council, elected as soon as the immigrants had arrived in the United States, successfully managed most of the affairs of the tribe in the traditional ways, setting up kinship networks in the usual pattern. But they did not know how to deal with the young people who were refusing to accept the Council's decisions. For example, the Council, after careful deliberation, had set an average bride price of $800 as equivalent to the worth of the livestock and household goods that constituted the bride price in the hills. But the young men ignored that and in fact were imitating American customs—were living in communal arrangements and consorting with girls, American prostitutes, or, worse, some Mnong girls who flouted age-old customs of sheltered propriety before marriage. He recognized that there were certain young men who encouraged the others and encouraged these illicit arrangements. Maybe these relationships could be called networks, but certainly they were not helpful. I suggested that he himself appeared to be a natural helper—a central figure in his community's network. Perhaps in that capacity he might broach the subject with the young Mnong men and girls and at least offer them the understanding of a more sophisticated person than their elders, which might have some effect. He brightened a little and said he could approach the young men, although he did not believe this would be much help, but he could under no circumstances talk with the girls. It would be so improper for him, a young man, that in doing so he would forfeit the respect of his whole community.

I was puzzled by the response of the young Cambodian woman to my request that she repeat for the group what she had told me of her use of natural helpers in resettlement. Looking both terrified and angry, she denied doing or saying any such thing. She said I had clearly misunderstood her, no doubt because of her poor English. As a matter of fact, she spoke English very well. She did not speak again in any group session. When I asked the director later what I had done to bring on this agitated denial, she explained that the young woman had come to this country with her sister and her young child, her husband being unable to accompany them. He had told her to assume that he was dead if she did not hear from him within a year and to feel free to remarry. PH, in our group, a fellow pilot of her husband, had promised to look after her and was strongly urging her to remarry, which she did not wish to do. I had interfered with her effort to make herself as inconspicuous as possible whenever PH was present.

At the next meeting, CS returned and without preamble launched into an attack on the whole notion of making use of networks and, by implication, on me. He announced that he had held discussions with some of the highly placed individuals with whom he had been meeting and they were agreed that he and they were already acting effectively through their traditional positions and were meeting the needs of their friends and colleagues and such other refugees who deserved their help. In fact, he thought that the Center ought to pay for all the food and drink he had supplied at the friendly meetings with his colleagues and subsidize what was *really* needed—a pagoda like those in his country, where people could come to worship and then enjoy a neighborly kind of picnic at which heads of families could discuss mutual concerns and plan to meet the needs of their many kinfolk. Without such a religious center he could see that the community was irrevocably splitting up into cliques that spent their time opposing and plotting against each other. No one could expect to do any useful networking in such an atmosphere.

He was listened to politely by the other counselors and then, almost as though he were invisible, they went on to tell what they had done in their work with natural helpers since our last meeting. KR had taken on the problem of a 14-year-old boy who was in an American foster home and was reported by the school as failing in spite of good intelligence and language skill. He seemed to be influenced by an older school dropout. KR had talked the problem over with an elderly aquaintance, and between them they had made a plan whereby this man would try to establish a relationship with the boy as though he were his grandfather, a well-regarded role in his native culture. The two men agreed that the boy must be looking for some relationship with an older person, since he had lost his entire family under terrible circumstances on his trip to this country. The men agreed to confer now and then, and KR volunteered to keep in touch with the school.

The Mnong tribesman had discovered that his wife had struck up a friendship with a girl in the next apartment and that she and some of her friends often spent the afternoons visiting, talking to his wife about their confused feelings. On one hand, they wanted and meant to have the freedom of American girls. On the other, they knew and regretted the shame and depression their behavior brought to their elders. The counselor was clearly pleased to discover his wife's skills and to tell the group about her functioning as a natural helper.

AH reported that she had asked Mrs. N to talk informally about the necessity for inoculations for their babies with the women who talked to her. Mrs. N had at first protested that she was too ignorant to talk about such matters, but AH had quite easily persuaded her that she could do it with AH's help in preparing her. Several other counselors cited instances of observing natural helpers and of plans to contact them. It seemed as though the counselors were ready to work with natural networks and needed only some support from me.

Unfortunately, subsequent meetings had to be interrupted and postponed, due to the move of the Center into larger quarters and the celebration of American and Indochinese holidays. Eventually, it was decided to suspend the meetings and reconvene later to learn if and how the counselors had made use of natural networks. This meeting was never held, because heavy funding cuts made it necessary to assign the counselors to other duties.

HINDSIGHT

Although I was not able to follow up with the counselors, I had time to look back and review what I had learned that might be useful for myself and others working with refugees. I had had some of my convictions about natural networks confirmed, if painfully at times. I realized that I had made an initial mistake, which I had often warned others to avoid. I had assumed, from a secondhand impression gained from reading, not actual contact, that I understood the culture of the networks; actually, this understanding could be reached only by interacting with the counselors themselves. In one respect the counselors had turned out closely to resemble the American counselors I had previously trained in their skepticism about the existence of natural networks, the feasibility of finding and using them, and their capacity to help. Their pleasure and surprise when they had finally tried out the idea and found it to be relatively easy and rewarding were also typical.

More important for me, perhaps, are the glimpses I received of the refugees' daily lives, their attitudes and feelings about their surroundings, and their untapped capabilities. "Windows" into the functioning of natural systems have always seemed to be one of the most important benefits of working with natural networks. With the refugees, some interesting if somewhat disturbing observations were provided. Hindsight suggests that what CS had angrily said about the community's ability to manage its own affairs might have some validity, which I had been too taken aback and defensive about to note when he brought it up. Perhaps some combination of approaches with other kinds of networks, adopted as an agencywide strategy, might be more appropriate? Mutual aid and community empowerment approaches, two others in the Froland et al. (1981) typology, would possibly have been more acceptable to the counselors; they might already have been involved in such activities and could have been encouraged to enlarge them rather than forced to become familiar with an alien idea. This would have left the natural helper approach for those to whom such a way of working came "naturally."

I recalled that when the first wave of Vietnamese refugees was brought to this country, some communities had set up services with a refugee as director. In others, where a sizable number of refugees with a common background had settled, the associations to which they had belonged in their native countries continued to function here. Although I had no firm evidence as to why centers directed by Americans and linked to existing social agencies had become the national model for Indochinese services, I guessed that the refugees' associations had used their native styles of procedure rather than the more efficient, accountable approach expected of American administrators. I also supposed that, with the advent of refugees from other Indochinese countries who were and had long been enemies of the Vietnamese, more energy was devoted to international and internal political disagreements than to service to those in need. Now, as agencies were more and more restricted in the services that they were able to offer refugees, the associations and national and regional clubs were joining together in efforts to deal with the many problems of their membership. Since the success of all types of network-based intervention depends on the support provided to the staff who are working with them, we have assumed that this support must be provided by an existing agency. There is, in fact, no reason why the leaders of the refugee groups could not offer their fellows support, which might well be in better accord with cultural customs than agencies can hope to be.

It is interesting to note that such an approach would bring us in this country to full circle with past experience with immigrants. Although I had vehemently rejected the idea that the Indochinese were just like the more familiar European immigrants of an earlier generation, there were in fact strong resemblances to the ways in which resettlement and assimilation were undertaken. The earlier immigrants had found their major support in the "old country" associations their compatriots had brought with them and in the new ones that they set up among themselves with the express purpose of assisting each other. Without insisting on perfect parallels, it might be useful to study the methods and the outcome of these early network ventures.

What emerged as a major lesson for me from my experience with the Indochinese counselors was the conviction that there are many ways all refugees might be helped to make use of their networks and that the task of American professionals is to help them to become aware of these resources and to value them.

REFERENCES

Condominas, G. *We have eaten the forest.* New York: Hill & Wang, 1977.
Froland, C., Pancoast, D. L., Chapman, N., and Kimboko, P. *Helping networks and human services.* Beverly Hills, CA: Sage, 1981.

3

NETWORK INTERVENTIONS ON THE MARGIN

A Service Experiment in a Welfare Hotel

CARL I. COHEN, ARLENE G. ADLER,
and JOAN E. MINTZ
United States

Studies over the past two decades have pointed to a number of ways in which informal networks can affect help-seeking behavior: (a) by buffering the experience of stress, which obviates the need for formal assistance; (b) by providing material and affective support that can likewise delay the need for formal services; (c) by influencing individuals as to when and where to seek formal services; (d) by transmitting values, attitudes, and norms that facilitate or discourage the use of formal help (Gourash, 1978). These studies, along with the concomitant expansion of health and social services into the community in the late 1960s, provided impetus for extensive experimentation with and the examination of potential benefits derived from the partnerships between formal and informal helping systems. The diminution of public monies in the 1970s further enhanced

AUTHORS' NOTE: *The study was funded by grants from the Ittleson, New York, and Van Ameringen foundations and the National Institute of Mental Health's Center for Studies of the Mental Health of the Aging, No. 1-RO-MH31745. The authors thank Henry Rajkowski, Jay Sokolovsky, Jeffery Draisen, Steven Sperber, and Community Research Applications for their assistance.*

interest in natural support systems as a low-cost alternative to professional services. Consequently, this orientation received an official imprimatur in the form of several governmental policy statements that called for the development and strengthening of partnerships between formal and informal systems (National Commission on Neighborhoods, 1979; Task Force on Community Support Systems, 1978).

Agency programs involving work with informal support systems have encompassed a broad array of activities and foci: families, ex-mental patients, the elderly, day-care families, alcoholics, and residents of inner-city hotels, to name but a few. Comprehensive reviews of the relationship between professional and natural support systems are adequately dealt with elsewhere (Collins & Pancoast, 1976; Froland, Pancoast, Chapman, & Kimboko, 1979; Mitchell & Trickett, 1980; Swenson, 1979; Trimble, 1980; Turkat, 1980). Most relevant for our present discussion has been the paucity of empirical data that exist on the efficacy of interventions with natural support systems (Hirsh, 1980; Knight, Wollert, Levy, Frame, & Padgett, 1980). Most reports have been descriptive, anecdotal, retrospective, and noncontrolled. In a review of helping programs developed by thirty services agencies across the United States, Froland and associates (1981) observed that "many of the effects of strategies for working with informal sources of care were difficult to measure and most programs had not made systematic assessments of outcome." Those agencies that had formally assessed impact used outcome measures that assessed client satisfaction, emotional well-being, deinstitutionalization, and levels of isolation. While these are important outcomes, we were particularly interested in determining to what extent formal/informal partnerships could help accomplish specific material and emotional tasks. For example, can an agency assist a client in obtaining food through a network intervention? Can clients who come for emotional support have their needs rechanneled into their networks?

This chapter describes an experimental network service program that was conducted in a large single-room occupancy (SRO) hotel in midtown Manhattan. Network interventions were carried out using methods developed by Collins and Pancoast (1976) and Cohen and Sokolovsky (1979). Our aim was to answer the following questions:

(1) Which types of presenting problems can be more successfully dealt with solely through a network intervention?

(2) Which characteristics of clients are conducive to network successes or failures?
(3) What are the factors that serve to hamper network interventions?

DEFINING HELPING NETWORKS

A major impediment to the systematic evaluation of network intervention has been the imprecision in the definition of helping networks. In the literature a wide array of approaches have been included under the same rubric. For example, highly structured mutual aid groups such as Weight Watchers and informal caregivers such as advice-giving bartenders are commonly combined under the same broad heading. Froland and associates (1979) have made significant strides toward resolving this problem. They have classified natural networks on the bases of whether they are preexisting or fostered, and on the particular foci of intervention, individual or family, circumscribed population group, or larger community (Figure 3.1). This typology not only has assisted in specifying the category of network intervention that is being examined, but also can be a valuable adjunct in evaluating these techniques. In this chapter we will be describing intervention techniques included within categories I, II, IV, V.

NETWORK ANALYSIS AS A
CLINICAL AND RESEARCH TOOL

Our network approach was derived primarily from an anthropological perspective, and therefore it is theoretically linked to the early work of Barnes (1954) and Bott (1957). This theoretical approach views networks as "a specific set of linkages among a set of persons with the . . . property that the characteristic of these linkages as a whole may be used to interpret the social behavior of persons involved" (Mitchell, 1969).

Operationally, investigators have divided networks into interactional and morphological characteristics. Interactional criteria include the frequency and duration of interaction, the direction and flow of aid, and an analysis of transactional content. With regard to the latter, "uniplex" relations, in which links representing one type of content (such as conversation, loans, and medical aid) are differentiated from "multiplex" relations, which contain more than one content area. Morphological criteria comprise size, density, and clustering. "Density" is defined as the ratio of

Source

Basis	Existing	Created
Individual and family	I personal network of individual client or family	II linking helper to individual client or family
Population	III mutual aid network	IV linking similar individuals for mutual aid
Locality	V central figures in neighborhood network	VI organizing community representatives

FIGURE 3.1   Types of Helping Networks

actual links in a network to potential ones. "Clustering" refers to compartments of networks that have a relatively high density.

We endeavored to create an instrument for mapping networks that would have both research and therapeutic applicability. Indeed, the experimental service program was designed to be integrated with a network research program that was operating concurrently with the hotel. With respect to research, this instrument must be able to generate empirical comparative data and qualitative behavioral information. Concerning its therapeutic usefulness, it must be able to chart accurately and expeditiously a client's personal network; and it must be flexible enough to be utilized by persons from varied backgrounds. As an outgrowth of our fieldwork with released mental patients and elderly residents of SRO hotels in midtown Manhattan (Sokolovsky & Cohen, 1981), we developed the Network Analysis Profile (NAP; see Figure 2 for an illustration). The profile is made up of six fields of interaction: tenant-tenant, tenant-nontenant, tenant-kin, tenant-hotel staff, tenant-agency staff, and tenant-social institution. In charting an individual's network within each parameter of interaction, the extent of the content of the relationship is delineated, as is the frequency, duration, intensity, and directional flow of the link. The totality of the profile encompasses what Jay (1964) calls the "activity field." The interrater reliability is high: .83 to .92 on various subsections of the profile.

DESCRIPTION OF THE PROJECT

In 1978 the project received $45,000 from a consortium of three private foundations. The experimental service program was to be guided by the following principles:

(1) The project staff must make an initial attempt to deal with all problems raised by clients through a network procedure rather than through direct assistance.

(2) The worker was to employ network techniques that were developed in previous community research (these are described in detail below).

(3) Careful records were to be kept as to whether a network intervention was actually attempted and, if so, whether it succeeded or at what point it failed.

From the outset it was decided that the service program would be conducted within an SRO hotel. To those unfamiliar with these hotels this might appear to be a peculiar choice of locale. However, previous research and clinical work (Cohen & Sokolovsky, 1979; Shapiro, 1971; Sokolovsky, Cohen, Berger, & Geiger, 1978) had revealed that SRO hotels offered several advantages to those attempting network strategies. For one thing, SRO hotels could be viewed as small urban villages. Within the decaying walls of these hotels existed extensive informal network systems that integrated individuals who had a variety of mental, physical, and social pathologies. Second, despite the great needs of this population, they generally distrusted and underutilized formal services, such as medical facilities, social agencies, and the like (Ehrlich, 1976; Erickson & Eckert, 1977). Traditional modalities for reaching the SRO population have had only mixed success. Although some residents avail themselves of services at local agencies, those most in need rarely appear. Even in those instances in which agencies conduct outreach visits into the hotels, many of the residents remain unreceptive. Furthermore, traditional methods focus on deficits and pathology. This orientation tends to promote dependency, which can be an especially unfortunate outcome for individuals who adhere to an ethos of autonomy and self-reliance. It was our contention that the techniques developed with this difficult population could serve as a model for provision of services to other at-risk urban groups.

Beginning in the spring of 1978, a social worker and subsequently a social work student began servicing the Martin Hotel (a pseudonym), a 452-room hotel in midtown Manhattan. The hotel manager agreed to have an on-site project because he saw this as a vehicle for dealing with some of his difficult tenants. However, the manager also acted as an impediment to the project. He provided no private work space or access to a private telephone. The project staff were forced to make initial contact with clients in the hotel lounge, street, or adjoining coffee shop. Telephone calls had to be made at public telephones in the hotel lobby. Only after some trust had been established would tenants invite the workers into their rooms, which were the only available private spaces.

The workers' initial referrals came primarily from two sources: neighborhood agencies that had clients in hotels, and the manager and desk clerks. Although many hotel lodgers had knowledge that social workers were in the hotel, it took several weeks before people would engage in conversation. Limits and boundaries were eventually established. Initially there were many requests for money, cigarettes, and the like. Many did not want to be part of social work activities. Among those who were familiar with social work, some were chagrined to discover that the project social workers would not provide direct services.

One of the early tasks was to identify the indigenous tenant leaders. Leaders were seen as a key to the entry process, since they were sources of information, support, and power. Leaders were identified in several ways:

(a) Self-identification: An individual would begin to talk to the workers and reveal knowledge of others, request assistance in helping a friend, or offer information.
(b) Identification by hotel staff: Desk clerks or management would observe that "everyone knows the person in room 509."
(c) Identification by others: When tenants suggested persons join groups or provide network support, the same tenant would be identified by several people.
(d) Identification by network analysis: Network mapping by the social workers and the research team would reveal the same individual in several networks.
(e) Identification by observation: Observation of the social patterns in the hotel lobby and at the hotel entrance pointed to persons who were the foci of much activity.

A second method for gaining entry into the hotel's social world was through the establishment of several groups. These groups had multifold purposes, including the promotion of increased social interaction and the potential for being sources of social support for some lodgers. They also enabled the workers to learn more about hotel and personal problems as well as about individual and group social interaction. Moreover, the groups served to develop the workers' credibility as resource persons and as trustworthy individuals. A final part of the entry process was for the workers to establish linkages to the formal service system in the neighborhood. Their aim was to encourage permanent direct services to the hotel population as well as to familiarize the community with the needs and lifestyles of the SRO world.

NETWORK TECHNIQUES

The active phase of the service program was guided by a variety of network strategies that had been developed previously in work with former mental patients and the elderly living in SRO hotels (Cohen & Sokolovsky, 1978, 1979, 1980). These techniques were further tested and refined during the course of the project. Below, we have outlined the principal methods.

Strategies at the Overall Planning Level

Sensitization of Service Workers. Network analysis can be particularly valuable in sensitizing service personnel to the notion that their clients, on the average, have viable and complex network formations and are not incapable of engaging in emotional interactions. For example, the findings of the on-site research study showed the social workers that residents of the Martin Hotel had a mean network size of 9.4 contacts, more than half of which involved multiplex ties and nearly two-fifths of which involved the exchange of sustenance items (food, money, and medical assistance). The findings also alerted the workers to the diversity in network magnitude and intensity. Networks ranged in size from 1 to 25, and although 7 percent of the tenants had no multiplex relationships, 17 percent had 10 or more such relationships.

Assisting Staff to Comprehend Behavior in the Context of Systems. The focus of community treatment has been chiefly on the individual in need of help. Although community practice has expanded to include an inter-

DIRECTIONAL
CODE: 1. EGO TO OTHER
             2. OTHER TO EGO
             3. RECIPROCAL
N.A. : NOT ASCERTAINED

FORM A: HOTEL CONTACTS

INTER-CONNECTIONS	NAME	ROOM NO.	RACE	OCCUP STATUS	LENGTH OF LINK
Write: form letter/ person number	1. Male 2. Female Age_____	or address	1. Wt. 2. Blk. 3. Hisp. 4. Other 9. N. A.	1. Work 2. S. S. 3. SSI 4. Welf. 5. Pension 9. N. A.	(years)
A₂	1 Eva, 2 6 8	Rm. 705	2	3	6

CONTENT OF RELATIONSHIP

	VISITS ROOM	MEET IN LOUNGE	INFORMAL CONVERS'N	ADVICE	MONEY/ LOANS	DRINKING/ DRUGS	FOOD AID
	Direction 1, 2, 3			Direc. 1, 2, 3	Direc. 1, 2, 3	Direc. 1, 2, 3	Direc. 1, 2, 3
	Frequency 0. None 1. 1x/mo. 2. Less 9. N. A.	Freq. 0. None 1. 1x/mo. 2. Less 9. N. A.	Freq. 0. None 1. 1x/mo. 2. Less 9. N. A.	Freq. 0. None 1. 1x/mo. 2. Less 9. N. A.	Freq. 0. None 1. 1x/mo. 2. Less 9. N. A.	Freq. 0. None 1. 1x/mo. 2. Less 9. N. A.	Freq. 0. None 1. 1x/mo. 2. Less 9. N. A.
Direc.	3			3	3	3	3
Freq.	1	1	1	1	1 $2-5	1 drink beer	1 cook for each other

FIGURE 3.2   Network Analysis Profile Completed for Hotel Sector

disciplinary approach, new problems are still commonly viewed as an individual matter, and little emphasis is placed on the total set of systems surrounding the person (Auerswald, 1968). Network analysis is a "system" theory: "Symptoms, defenses, character structure and personality are regarded as terms describing the individual's typical interaction which occurs in response to a particular context, rather than as intrapsychic entities" (Jackson, 1969). Thus, network analysis has taught staff members to comprehend behavior in terms of clients' location within a network system.

Case Illustration

Mr. C, a 65-year-old man, periodically came to the project staff at the end of the month asking for loans so that he could purchase

FORM A: HOTEL CONTACTS (continued)

CONTEXT OF LINK	LAST SAW	VISUAL CONTACT FREQUENCY	TELEP. FREQ.	TIME OF DAY OF CONTACT	CHANGE: MONTHLY SEASONAL
1. Work	1. Yester./	1. Daily	same	1. Day	0. None
2. Friend	Today	2. Few/wk.	code	2. Night	1. Monthly
3. Kin	2. Past Wk.	3. 1x/wk.	as	3. Day	2. Seasonal
4. Hotel	3. Past Mo.	4. 1x/mo.	prior	or	3. Yearly
5. Senior	4. Past 6 Mo.	5. 2x/yr.	box	Night	
center	5. Past Yr.	6. 1x/yr.		9. N.A.	
6. Other	6. Past 5 Yr.	7 1x/5 yr.			
9. N. A.	7. Plus 5 Yr.	8. Less			
4	1	1	0	3	2-gone 2 weeks in summer

CONTENT OF RELATIONSHIP (Continued)

	MEDICAL DIA	OTHER AID	EAT OUT TOGETHER	OTHER SOCIAL OUTINGS	GLOBAL IMPORTANCE	FRIENDSHIP	SHARE INTIMATE THOUGHTS WITH
	Direc. 1, 2, 3	Direc. 1, 2, 3		(parks, movies.)	1. Not import. 2. Important 3. Very import. 4. Most import. 9. N. A.	1. Not a friend 2. A friend 3. A good friend 4. Best friend 9. N. A.	1. Yes 2. No 3. N. A.
	Freq. 0. None 1. 1x/mo. 2. Less 9. N. A.	Freq. 0. None 1. 1x/mo. 2. Less 9. N. A.	Freq. 0. None 1. 1x/mo. 2. Less 9. N. A.	Freq. 0. None 1. 1x/mo. 2. Less 9. N. A.			
Direc.	3	3			4-depend on when I "feel crazy"	4	1-"Don't hold any-thing back from each other"
Freq.	2 care for when sick	2 emotion-al aid	2	0			

FIGURE 3.2   (Continued)

food and other necessities. Mr. C admitted that his budgetary diffi-culties stemmed from his gambling at a local betting parlor. Initially, staff concentrated on Mr. C's problems with impulse control and his seemingly immature personality structure. However, upon mapping his social network, it was discovered that his entire social world revolved around the betting parlor. Moreover, many of his contacts frequently provided Mr. C with loans, food, and other assistance. In delineating Mr. C's network, his behavior was reformulated in terms of a social context with strengths and weaknesses rather than as psychopathology.

Allocation of Resources. The advantages of network analysis versus nonempirical approaches to natural groups are most apparent in the organizing of service programs. A network survey of a target population will enable personnel to be more appropriately assigned on the basis of risk categories, geography, and temporality. For example, a survey of those Martin Hotel residents aged 60 and over revealed that men had proportionately more contacts outside the hotel, whereas women had proportionately more within the hotel (hotel residents and staff). The findings reinforced the project workers' observations that attempts to influence male networks would require visits to betting parlors, taverns, restaurants, and the like.

A number of temporal patterns have been discerned. There are monthly patterns that revolve around the arrival of public assistance and social security checks. Shortly after the arrival of the checks, those who imbibe are especially at risk. Staff workers developed strategies to assist networks in providing support to those with a propensity to exhaust their funds on alcohol. Similarly, at the end of the monthly cycles, many lodgers would run low on cash, and networks would be pressured to lend money and to provide food.

Establishing Relationships Between Agency Personnel and Indigenous Leaders. Network research in the Martin Hotel revealed extensive clustering: 78% of the tenants were enmeshed in grouping that varied from constellations comprising three persons to quasi-families dominated by a "mother" who fed, protected, and set norms for 6 to 11 family members who met in her room. Other large configurations centered on gambling, drugs, and art. A number of natural helpers also worked independently of clusters, assisting other lodgers with shopping, errands, and advice giving.

Project staff attempted to identify leaders and stronger network members so as to furnish them with (a) informal supervision for psychosocial and health problems arising within their networks, (b) information regarding available community resources, and (c) backup services when the informal system cannot cope with a situation.

Use at the Client Level

Although the techniques outlined below are arranged sequentially, frequently they were handled simultaneously.

Using the Network Analysis Profile. The Network Analysis Profile should be completed comcomitantly with the standard intake data. It can be used to determine whether the client falls within a vulnerable, high-risk category, such as monthly cycles of debauchery. If not, less staff time may be required. It can also be used to assess strengths and weaknesses in the network. Many networks offer therapeutic protection, food, medication, and emotional girding independent of staff support.

Case Illustration

Mr. A, a 70-year-old man, had moved to the hotel several years ago after a series of heart attacks had forced him from a building that had no elevator. He had no family in New York. His former wife and children lived in California. He was very well liked by staff and residents of the hotel, and a support group developed around him. Although not necessarily friends with each other, this group provided an array of services that enabled him to remain in the hotel, rather than being placed in a long-term facility. Network members referred to him as a "special friend," and they would bring him newspapers, food, and social support. One of the maids would buy food for him, often purchasing foods she believed would be especially nutritious for him. As Mr. A became more frail, he recognized the strength of this help and his dependence on others.

When a client presents a problem, resolution can be sought first by utilizing network methods. The worker must initially ascertain whether a client's network is able to alleviate the difficulty. For instance, if the individual is not ambulatory, is there someone within his network who is available to supply the vital necessities? Or if a person presents a psychological problem, can her network be brought together to provide assistance and solutions to the problem (Speck & Attneave, 1973)? To cite an example, an elderly woman was causing disturbances by her episodic alcohol bouts. The workers attempted to convene her network together in order to attempt solutions to her drinking problem and thereby to forstall her eviction from the hotel. When no person is available within the client's network to furnish support, contact may be initiated with individuals who have been identified as indigenous leaders and service providers.

Case Illustration

Ms. K, an elderly woman, had been identified as a tenant leader. She was primarily involved with women on her floor, and the younger ones considered her an advice giver and a good listener. There was much affection for her, and network members said they would do anything for her. One of the newer floor residents was a depressed middle-aged woman who spoke of her "failing beauty" and her fears of growing old. The worker asked Ms. K if she would sit and talk with this woman. Ms. K agreed, and their relationship subsequently grew into an intimate and lasting bond.

Another approach may entail the involvement of "second-order" linkages. Second-order relationships consist of those persons who are not in direct contact with the client but who are linked to members of the client's network. These are potential contacts, and a large second-order zone is an important resource. Should the "friend of a friend" meet the client, there is a high probability they will become friends (Hammer & Schaffer, 1975). Thus, second-order contacts may possibly be tapped during periods of stress.

Finally, the tolerance level of the network must be determined. Some network structures may be able to absorb more stress and to offer more services than others.

Case Illustration

After the operation of an older woman, network members were concerned about the outcome and wanted to visit her. However, network members were unwilling to take the two buses necessary to get to the hospital. When the worker indicated that she would accompany the group, they agreed to go.

It should be ascertained whether any formal services under consideration interfere with extant beneficial services supplied by the informal support system. For example, offering to loan clients money may result in the discontinuance of ties with neighbors who lend them money along with considerable conversation and emotional support. An assessment of a client's network would also indicate whether any components are conflicting with each other. For instance, one agency may be advocating nursing home placement whereas a second agency may be encouraging community living.

For the frail or emotionally unstable client a rupture in network structure can be especially devastating. It is important to determine whether the client is enmeshed in a network vulnerable to disruption. Often the viability of high-density clusters is predicated on the presence of one key figure. Should this person become incapacitated or change his residence, the network may collapse. Similarly, persons engaged in small, fragile, low-density, star-like configurations can also rapidly lose their support. In either situation, external (agency) support must be available immediately to assist group members.

Case Illustration

Network analysis of Ms. G, a 76-year-old woman, revealed that she had only one contact. This was a close relationship with a frail elderly man who lived in the hotel. They frequently went on walks, ate out, helped each other with money and errands, and provided assistance to the other during illness. Because of the strong support she received, project staff saw no need for additional services, although they remained vigilant for a network rupture. When the man was finally compelled to move to a nursing home, staff acted quickly to provide emotional and material buttressing to Ms. G. The staff worked with her to establish new ties and sources of support.

When indicated, groups oriented toward specific needs or services should be created. For example, the art group served as a vehicle for many young unemployed hotel residents to share experiences and information. After the group terminated, several members remained friends.

EVALUATING THE NETWORK INTERVENTIONS

Description of Clients

The sample participating in the experimental service program was composed of 156 hotel residents who received network assistance during the period May 1, 1978, to July 31, 1979. Of these, 51 percent were aged 60 and older and 60 percent were male; the percentages having attended or graduated high school or college were 44 percent and 37 percent, respectively. Nearly nine-tenths of the sample was white, which was reflective of the overall hotel population as well as the larger community.

Examination of Table 3.1 indicates that the 156 residents presented with 505 problems (approximately three presenting problems per resident). The five most common problem areas identified, in descending order of frequency, were emotional support, physical health, income, hotel conditions, and information and advice. Slightly more than half of these problems were self-referred, and the remainder were primarily identified by significant others or by the project staff (Table 3.2).

A comparison of those under 60 with those 60 years of age and older reveals significant differences between the two age groups in certain problem areas. Employment and drug problems were more frequently cited as areas where assistance was needed for those under 60; in contrast, those 60 and over identified physical health and sustenance problems more frequently.

TABLE 3.1 Problem Areas for SRO Residents

Problem Areas	Number of Responses	Number of Persons	% of Total Persons	% Under 60 Years (N = 76)	% 60 Years and Older (N = 80)	x^2 (df = 1)
Income	65	56	35.9	33.8	38.2	N. S.
Hotel conditions	52	43	27.6	26.3	28.9	N. S.
Employment	32	29	18.6	28.8	7.9	11.2**
Drinking	28	28	17.9	15.0	21.1	N. S.
Drugs	8	8	5.1	8.8	1.3	4.4*
Other antisocial	13	13	8.3	8.8	7.9	N. S.
Physical health	84	69	44.2	35.0	53.9	5.7*
Mental health	32	31	19.9	21.3	18.4	N. S.
Sustenance	20	20	12.8	7.5	18.4	4.2*
Information & advice	38	37	23.7	18.8	28.9	N. S.
Emotional support	96	79	50.6	52.5	48.7	N. S.
New housing	27	27	17.3	16.3	18.4	N. S.
Other	10	10	6.4	7.5	5.3	N. S.
	505	156				

*p < .05
**p < .01

a. Because each resident might have more than one problem for which a network intervention was possible, the sume of the percentages shown will be greater than 100. (There are approximately three presenting problems per resident.)

TABLE 3.2 Sources Identifying Problem Area for SRO Residents

Source	Number of Problems	Number of Persons	% of Total Persons	% Under 60 Years (N = 76)	% 60 Years and Older (N = 80)	x^2 (df = 1)
Self	263	116	74.4	68.8	80.3	N. S.
Significant other	52	48	30.8	28.8	32.9	N. S.
Project staff	52	46	29.5	28.8	30.3	N. S.
Other professionals	5	5	3.2	2.5	3.9	N. S.
Group	37	33	21.2	26.3	15.8	N. S.
Management	18	13	8.3	5.0	11.8	N. S.
Other	35	31	19.9	16.3	23.7	N. S.
	462	156				

a. Because each resident had an average of three problem areas, the sum of the percentages shown will be greater than 100.

Results

Overall, 75 percent of the sample had at least one network intervention attempted. However, only 16 percent of the problems were successfully dealt with through a network procedure. Furthermore, for approximately half of the problems presented, no network intervention was attempted at all. On the positive side, of those problems that were treated with a network approach, one-third had successful network interventions (Table 3.3). A network intervention was defined as successful if a specific task was accomplished using a network contact. Certain problem areas such as sustenance, new housing, and information and advice had higher success rates, whereas drug and employment problems had lower success rates (Table 3.4).

Given our unremarkable success rate, we subsequently sought to ascertain whether there were any demographic, physical, psychological, or network characteristics of clients that were associated with intervention success or failure. Using data obtained from the research project that was undertaken concurrently with the service program, we were able to obtain extensive information on a subsample of 62 of the clients (N = 30 for those aged 60 and over; N = 32 for those under age 60). The subsample was comparable to the large sample with respect to sex, education, and racial characteristics.

Because of the relatively small size of the subsamples, it was necessary to conduct multiple regression analyses in stages rather than simultaneously. For example, the relationship between outcome and health characteristics was examined separately from the relationship between outcome and network characteristics. Furthermore, the age groups were analyzed independently, since the data sets were not identical. Rather, comparable variables were used instead.

Three large data sets were conceived: (1) demographic, (2) physical and mental health, and (3) social network. Each large data set was made up of three to five variables. For each client an outcome variable was calculated. The outcome variable was operationally defined as the number of successful network interventions divided by the total number of network interventions attempted. Three regression analyses were performed for each age group, with the outcome variable (percentage success) regressed separately on the three large data sets.

Overall, the regression analyses indicated that for both age groups, those clients who had the fewest physical, mental, educational, and social resources were the most likely to have a successful network intervention.

TABLE 3.3 Results of Network Intervention for SRO Residents

Outcome	Number of Problems	Number of Persons	% of Total Persons[a]	% Under 60 Years (N = 76)	% 60 Years and Older (N = 80)	χ^2 (df = 1)
Never attempted	269	130	83.3	85.0	81.6	N. S.
Successful	83	52	33.3	31.3	35.5	N. S.
Failure at outset	132	82	52.6	53.8	51.3	N. S.
Failure at contact	24	24	15.4	15.0	15.8	N. S.
Failure at task	11	10	6.4	10.0	2.6	3.5*
	519	156				

* p < .05

a. Because more than one network intervention was possible for each resident, the sum of the percentages shown will be greater than 100. (There are approximately three presenting problems per resident.)

TABLE 3.4   Type of Problem Presented by Outcome of Network Intervention

Problem Areas	% Success	% Failure	% Never Attempted
Emotional support	19.0	31.5	49.5
Physical health	17.6	32.4	50.0
Income	19.1	33.6	47.3
Hotel conditions	20.4	24.3	45.3
Information & advice	21.4	28.1	50.5
Employment	13.8	27.6	58.6
Mental health	17.5	30.6	51.9
Drinking	16.8	31.2	52.0
New housing	24.7	24.7	50.6
Sustenance	26.0	34.6	39.4
Other antisocial	17.5	24.6	57.9
Drugs	12.8	28.2	59.0
Other	17.0	34.1	48.9

This relationship was somewhat more powerful among the younger group and there were some minor differences between the groups with regard to which individual variables within the larger sets were most significant (see Table 3.5). For clients under 60, successful outcome was associated with lower income, more organic mental impairment, and smaller, less active social networks. For those 60 and over, successful outcome was associated with less education, ambulatory difficulties, and smaller social networks.

Discussion

Our findings suggested that network interventions are neither for every problem nor for everybody. Within a particular community, individuals are seemingly adept at providing support in some areas but not in others. Not surprisingly, it is those transactions that have long been part of a population's cultural world that are most likely to yield successful intervention outcomes. For example, the folkways of SRO hotels have involved the exchange of food or money, frequent gossiping and advice giving, and intense concerns about the deterioration of the hotel in a world in which fellow lodgers come and go. Hence, it followed that project staff were more successful in effecting network interventions in those areas such as

TABLE 3.5   Predictors of Success of Network Intervention

	Percentage Variance Explained	
Data Sets	Under Age 60	Age 60 and Over
Demographic	32.0	30.7
Physical/mental health	51.9	20.9
Social network	47.1	24.4

NOTE: Regression analysis using number of successful interventions divided by total network interventions as the outcome variable.

sustenance, finding new housing, information and advice, and hotel conditions. On the other hand, many hotel residents had poor work histories and were less comfortable and adept at helping others with employment problems. Similarly with respect to drug problems, most hotel residents tend to avoid drug abusers, who generally form a small subculture within many hotels. Consequently, interest in assisting the drug abusers was rather low. Restating our findings epigrammatically, service workers should not expect a population to undertake network tasks with which it is not already familiar.

Our second aim was to ascertain whether there are certain clients who are more apt to benefit from a network intervention. Interestingly, it was not the most competent individuals who had more network successes. Rather, it was those clients who had more social and health deficits. We believe that this was because the more competent individuals had exhausted their network resources prior to coming to the project staff. They expected and demanded that the project staff provide direct services. If a network intervention was attempted, it may have been done reluctantly within a network that was already burnt out. Conversely, clients with fewer personal resources were seemingly less certain that they had fully utilized all their social skills to obtain help for a particular problem. They were more willing to try to expand their networks or to attempt new approaches with their old networks. Hence, their success rates were higher than those who had more personal resources. In those aged 60 and over, although differences emerged between the success and failure groups in the areas of physical impairment, income, and size of network, both groups exhibited deficits in these areas in an absolute sense. This may have accounted for the smaller proportion of variance explained in the outcome variable for the older group in contrast to the younger group.

Finally, even when the problem area and client profile may be optimal for a network intervention, other factors may intervene to preclude success. We have identified several key factors that have emerged as impediments to attempting network interventions in lieu of direct services:

(1) Trust: Many clients were reticent about discussing their personal networks in detail with the project staff. In some instances they remained guarded because they perceived the workers as connected with governmental programs.

(2) Perceived isolation: Although our research in the hotel had uncovered an extensive informal network system that provided a multitude of supportive services, individuals were seemingly unaware of the supportive nature of their social ties. As one staff member observed, "It all added up for the worker to be in a sense searching for something others couldn't perceive."

(3) For some clients certain areas (such as money) were considered private matters that could be discussed only with an "official" person such as a social worker.

(4) Problems frequently had to be dealt with immediately, and this did not allow sufficient time to work with the network.

We have argued here that successful network interventions are bound to the particular cultural and personal characteristics of the community being serviced. Interventions cannot be generalized to all problems and to all persons. A careful analysis of the mores of the population combined with an ongoing assessment of individual characteristics that are related to success can assist workers in selecting problems and clients that are most amenable to network interventions. Of course, these analyses should be conducted in concert with the further development and refinement of intervention techniques. In an era of diminishing funds for social services, it is imperative that we eschew pronouncements that tout the use of indigenous support systems as a panacea for service delivery problems. As the Task Force on Community Support Systems (1978) warned, we must guard against using natural supports to "justify public policies which could withhold from various communities and individuals the resources they need to obtain professional and formal institutionalized services."

REFERENCES

Auerswald, E. H. Interdisciplinary versus ecological approach. *Family Process*, 1968, 7, 202-215.

Barnes, J. Class and committees in a Norwegian island parish. *Human Relations,* 1954, *7,* 39-58.

Bott, E. *Family and social networks.* London: Tavistock, 1957.

Cohen, C., & Sokolovsky, J. Schizophrenia and social networks. *Schizophrenia Bulletin,* 1978, *4,* 546-560.

Cohen, C., & Sokolovsky, J. Clinical use of network analysis for psychiatric and aged populations. *Community Mental Health Journal,* 1979, *15,* 203-213.

Cohen, C., & Sokolovsky. J. Social engagement versus isolation: The case of the aged in SRO hotels. *The Gerontologist,* 1980, *20,* 36-44.

Collins, A., & Pancoast, D. L. *Natural helping networks.* Washington, DC: National Association of Social Workers, 1976.

Erhlich, P. Study of the St. Louis invisible elderly: Needs and characteristics of aged "single room occupancy" downtown hotel residents. Unpublished manuscript, University of Southern Illinois at Carbondale, 1976. (Mimeograph)

Erickson, R., & Eckert, K. The elderly poor in downtown San Diego hotels. *The Gerontologist,* 1977, *17,* 440-446.

Froland, C., Pancoast, D. L., Chapman, N. J., & Kimboko, P. J. *Professional partnerships with informal helpers: Emerging forms.* Paper presented at the meeting of the American Psychological Association, New York, September 1979.

Froland, C., Pancoast, D. L., Chapman, N. J., & Kimboko, P. J. *Helping networks and human services.* Beverly Hills, CA: Sage, 1981.

Gourash, N. Help seeking: A review of the literature. *American Journal of Community Psychology,* 1978, *6,* 413-425.

Hammer, M., & Schaffer, A. Interconnectedness and the duration of connections in several small networks. *American Ethnologist,* 1975, *2,* 297-308.

Hirsch, B. J. Natural support systems and coping with major life changes. *American Journal of Community Psychology,* 1980, *8,* 159-172.

Jackson, D. D. The individual and the larger contexts. *Family Process,* 1969, *8,* 211-234.

Jay, E. The concept of "field" and "network" in anthropological research. *Man,* 1964, *64,* 127-139.

Knight, B., Wollert, R. W., Levy, L. H., Frame, C. L., & Padget, V. P. Self help groups: The members' perspective. *American Journal of Community Psychology,* 1980, *8,* 53-65.

Mitchell, J. C. Concept and use of social networks. In J. C. Mitchell (Ed.), *Social networks in urban situations.* Manchester: Manchester University Press, 1969.

Mitchell, R. E., & Trickett, E. J. Task force report: Social networks as mediators of social support. *Community Mental Health Journal,* 1980, *15,* 27-44.

National Commission on Neighborhoods. *People, building neighborhoods. Final Report to the President and the Congress of the United States.* Washington, DC: Government Printing Office, 1979.

Shapiro, J. *Communities of the alone.* New York: Association Press, 1971.

Sokolovsky, J., & Cohen, C. Toward a resolution of methodological dilemmas in network mapping. *Schizophrenia Bulletin,* 1981, *7,* 109-116.

Sokolovsky, J., Cohen, C., Berger, D., & Geiger, J. Personal networks of ex-mental patients in a Manhattan SRO hotel. *Human Organization,* 1978, *37,* 5-15.

Speck, R., & Attneave, C. *Family networks.* New York: Pantheon, 1973.

Swenson, C. Social networks, mutual aid, and the life model of practice. In C. R. Germain (Ed.), *Social work practice: People and environments.* New York: Columbia University Press, 1979.

Task Force on Community Support Systems. Report. In President's Commission on Mental Health, *Report to the President from the President's Commission on Mental Health* (Vol. 2). Washington, DC: Government Printing Office, 1978.

Trimble, D. A. A guide to network therapies. *Connections,* 1980, *3,* 9-21.

Turkat, D. Social networks: Theory and practice. *Journal of Community Psychology,* 1980, *8,* 99-109.

4

SUPPLEMENTING TRADITIONAL
SUPPORT NETWORKS

ANGELA FINLAYSON
Scotland

Before describing some of the developments taking place in Scotland in relations between professionals and informal help sources, it may be useful to declare briefly my own perspective on this subject. Research into families where men had suffered coronary heart disease (Finlayson, 1976; Finlayson & McEwen, 1977) confirmed what my previous experience with young mothers had suggested: In crises or long-term difficulties, many people lack appropriate support from their existing social networks, especially when role change is required. New significant others can help to counterbalance older and rigid expectations. Although when I planned this research I was assuming that these new significant others might be medical social workers and rehabilitation therapists, by the end I had concluded that formal support might be less constructive than that of other people who had themselves suffered heart attacks, and members of their social networks, if these people had in the meantime seized the opportunity to turn crisis and aftermath into learning experiences through self-help techniques.

Simultaneous with research, I have at various times taught sociology to social work students, nurses, and medical students and always had difficulty in finding literature on the concepts of significant others and social networks that was readily seen as relevant to the everyday practice of these professions. More recently, I have been working with The Open University on a course entitled "The Handicapped Person in the Community," using material supplied and annually updated by a course team based in Milton Keynes, England (The Open University, 1982). This material effectively fills the gap that I had identified. Many of the students who undertake this course in their spare time are already working in the field of disability; they include nurses, social workers, remedial therapists, teachers, community workers, volunteers, disabled people themselves, and sometimes—although rarely—physicians. The approach of the course is interprofessional, encouraging students to step out of their professional roles and learn to understand the perspectives of disabled people, their social networks and the self-help organizations that increasingly are sustaining them.

Many of the concepts introduced by the course are entirely new to the students and point to gaps in previous training. Even when students are aware of the concepts of significant others and social networks, they often fail initially to see the relevance of these concepts to their current work. By the time that they have reached the course units concerned with planning goals for, and with, a person who is impaired, they are beginning to make much better use of the concepts. When they have had to justify their choices between alternative goals, to think through in sequence all the steps needed, and to ensure continued communication between all the significant others relevant to achieving that goal, then they have become much more aware of the dynamics of a social network. Such experiences also alert students to the value of self-help groups for caregivers as well as for impaired people, introducing new significant others to compensate for weaknesses evident in many networks. At the same time, students often realize for the first time just how restricted they may themselves have become by their expectations of significant others in their own professions, seniors on whom promotion depends, peers on whom they rely for support, and textbook authors on whom their training has been based. Exposed in tutorials to the conflicting perspectives not only of disabled people and their families but also to those of professionals from other disciplines, students find themselves participating in what are in effect self-help groups made up of new significant others from a wide range of backgrounds. This, in turn, enables them gradually to feel less threatened by the current shift in emphasis, led by self-help organizations among disabled people themselves, toward redefining the traditional roles between helper and helped in more egalitarian terms and pressing for services geared to the perceived needs of clients with decreased dependence on direct professional support.

DEVELOPMENT OF SCOTTISH SERVICES

A brief discussion of the development of formal services in Scotland will provide some context for appreciating the possibilities for professional collaboration with informal sources of help. Scotland has a disproportionately high share among Western nations of serious social and health problems, including particularly high rates of unemployment, emigration, alcoholism, tobacco smoking, solvent abuse, and coronary heart disease—signs of deep individual and social malaise and just such matters as require, among other measures, more effective links between formal and informal systems. Few would claim that, despite a complex structure of services and their considerable expansion in the last two decades, response to these and other problems is in any way adequate. Services have generally grown up in isolation from each other, each tending to focus on some aspect of individuals as dependent patients or clients with little thought of the social and physical environments in which they live and how altering them might reduce dependence. Few professionals are likely to find that time and resources to encourage the development of self-help groups have been written into their contracts or job specifications. This seems particularly difficult for social workers and health workers, whose caseloads have expanded at rates in no way anticipated when the services were set up. Junior personnel who initiate mutual aid practices among, for instance, young mothers or handicapped adolescents sometimes resort to doing this surreptitiously or in their spare time. This is particularly true if there is any likelihood of being seen to encroach on the preserves of the traditionally dominant medical profession, many members of which tend to distrust such enterprises. It sometimes seems easier for self-help practices to be encouraged by those professionals who are working part-time, which raises the related issue of whether more part-time professional employment and job sharing might not be beneficial all round.

The complexity of services has already been mentioned, and it is necessary to indicate in highly compressed form the background of those services specific to Scotland that are relevant to the examples discussed below. When Scotland's Parliament was removed by the Act of Union with the English Parliament in 1707, certain important social institutions were left intact. These include the legal system, based largely on Roman principles and thus differing widely from English case law, the educational system, and the Church of Scotland (Presbyterian as distinct from the

Anglicanism of the Church of England). Central government services concerned with social policy today include those administered by the Secretary of State for Scotland through the Scottish Home and Health Department and the Scottish Education Department within the Scottish Office; others are services common to the United Kingdom, including the Department of Employment and the Department of Health and Social Security the latter being responsible in Scotland for the payment of cash benefits but not health or personal social services. Health services are administered through the Scottish Home and Health Department in conjunction with fifteen Regional Health Boards. The local government system also differs from that in England and Wales, being based on nine Regional Councils having responsibility within their areas for functions including education, social work, youth employment, police, and transport. These nine cover the whole of Scotland except for the Western Isles, Orkney, and Shetland, which have all-purpose Islands Councils. Voting patterns in national elections differ markedly from those in England, and since legislative and economic power rests with the U.K. Parliament in London, in which Scots Members constitute a small minority, pressure for a greater degree of self-determination persists and has increased in recent years. (For further information on the Scottish political situation see Kellas, 1975; on social services, see English & Martin, 1979.)

Meanwhile, at the administrative level, services have undergone drastic reorganization in the last two decades with consequent upheaval among staff. In this process there has been little explicit official recognition of relationships with informal care systems, except insofar as previous dependence has been maintained on many existing services provided by voluntary organizations, particularly in the residential sphere. Inenvitably relations are uneasy. Voluntary organizations, including those run on self-help principles, increasingly need financial assistance from statutory agencies but fear a loss of independence; statutory agencies are put in a position of being required to monitor standards without discouraging enterprise. Voluntary workers frequently complain that their abilities are not being utilized, but the fragmentary nature of the voluntary sector has made for difficulties in achieving effective recognition from statutory authorities. Efforts are being made to improve this by improved liaison between voluntary bodies within regions. As elsewhere, the shift in social policy away from institutional provision to care in the community has meant in effect that the burden of care most frequently falls on one person, generally a mother, daughter, or sister, at a time when central government cuts reduce domicilary support services.

Despite the deficiencies of formal services, there is encouragement to be found at the informal level in surviving traces of a much older collectivist tradition, based on strong ties to family and birthplace. In the past these ties found expression in mutual aid customs, such as those embodied by the Highland clan system or the support afforded each other by Glasgow tenement neighbors. In addition, many of the emigrants forced out of Scotland by economic privation or political repression over the past few centuries moved in patterns of "chain" migration, earlier emigrants scrupulously sending back information and giving settling-in support to those who followed them. It is this sense of belonging together that can still be drawn on to adapt community support to the needs of today.

EMERGING INNOVATIONS IN LINKING
FORMAL AND INFORMAL SUPPORT

That Scotland succeeded in maintaining control of some social institutions, particularly the legal and educational systems, has sometimes proved an advantage in facilitating innovations that might not necessarily suit the whole of the United Kingdom. Similarly, it can sometimes be easier to innovate among a small population (five million, more comparable with the Netherlands, Norway, or Switzerland than with the population of England, ten times as numerous). The main features of two such innovations will be briefly described first, one of these being a statutory development that gives volunteers an important new role in a legal setting and one being a mutual aid group that operates in a highly informal context but that still maintains a sufficiently structured basis to qualify for some support from statutory sources. Finally, a relatively new profession based within the educational system will be discussed in some detail with particular reference to the ways in which it is adapting to local needs in different areas and notably to rural communities in the northern Highlands and Islands.

THE CHILDREN'S HEARINGS SYSTEM

The children's hearings system is a statutory development that Scotland has pioneered in social policy and that has attracted favorable attention from other countries, some of which have been considering similar measures. This was instigated by legislation following a report to the Secretary of State for Scotland from a committee under Lord Kilbrandon, which in 1964 recommended the removal from the courts of children committing less serious offenses. Under the new system, initial referrals of children in trouble are received by a reporter (an administrator with legal qualifications) who refers such children as seem to be in need of compulsory measures of care to a lay panel of three persons who meet in private with the child, his parents, the reporter, and a social worker. At any one hearing, the lay panel members are drawn from a pool of some 1,600 volunteers ranging from around 900 in Strathclyde to 10 in Orkney. They are appointed by the Secretary of State from a list of applicants nominated by a committee in each region, created for the main purpose of recruiting and selecting panel members. Preparatory training is given mainly by professionals in legal, social, and health services, and further training is available during each volunteer's three-year term of office (which may be renewed). There is concern over the difficulty of recruiting members from manual occupations, and it is not yet clear whether efforts to remedy this are meeting with success. It may be that it will prove easier to recruit more widely for the different task of helping with the supervision of children in the community after panel decisions have been made, a task in which volunteers as well as professionals are increasingly involved.

As well as having precipitated the establishment of generic social work departments within Scottish local authorities at a date earlier than occurred in England, and the setting up of a specialized Social Work Services Group within the Scottish Office, the Hearings system has opened up new kinds of collaboration between professionals and the volunteers who become panel members. In addition to providing training, social workers are responsible for making background reports on the children to the panel and for carrying out the panel's decisions. It is too early yet for analysis of this aspect, but a chapter in English and Martin (1979) describes the hearings and relevant legislation and literature.

THE SIX CIRCLE GROUP

To select one among many voluntary organizations is an invidious task, but two features particularly distinguish the Six Circle Group. First, it facilitates mutual aid among socially isolated individuals who would hitherto have been classified into, and restricted to, several different categories of disadvantage. Second, the group as such exists only in Scotland, having grown out of a camp organized in 1969 in the West Highlands by professionals from the prison service, who took a group of adolescent offenders from a training institution to share a camping holiday with a group of mentally and physically handicapped children brought by staff from a voluntary community home. Finding from the initial camp that the children had as much to offer the trainees in their needs as the trainees had to offer the children in theirs, they developed a system of interchangeable or mutual community service. As an emblem that explains their name, they adopted galvanized-iron interlaced rings from the nearby wartime boom defense net. They assembled them so that each ring intersected the other five, symbolizing the belief that "in meeting the needs of others, you meet the needs of yourself."

Now, with other summer camps held elsewhere in Scotland and local groups keeping activities going in the remainder of the year, the group sees its future as acting as a catalyst to specialist agencies, not expecting to take over their tasks but fostering communication between such agencies and designing projects toward this end. At the same time, they seek to change public attitudes toward those who are socially isolated or labeled in derogatory-sounding ways. Their belief that everyone, however much hitherto entirely preoccupied with the task of just surviving, has something positive to offer others is reflected in the structure of the Six Circle Group. In both local groups and camps, much of the serious decision making is carried out by members themselves, through their community meetings. Representatives of local branches can attend the association of local branches from which members can be co-opted to the national committee. In 1978 a full-time development officer was appointed with the help of a grant from the Social Work Services Group within the Scottish Education Department. The headquarters of the Six Circle Group is financially supported by the Scottish Office and by contributions from individuals, trusts, members's fees, and members' special fund-raising efforts. Local branches are self-financing and may obtain help from regional social work departments, in addition to raising their own funds and seeking local sponsorship. Some local branches include members who are professionals working in an unofficial capacity. Others contain no professionals, although some may include people with previous professional experience. In general, those branches with some professional membership may be able to get things done more quickly and effectively because of greater familiarity with complex systems, but an element of professional membership is not considered necessary. (For further information, see Six Circle Group, n.d.)

COMMUNITY EDUCATION WORKERS

It is interesting that the term "self-help" has become common in the literature and vocabulary of many professionals in the health and social services, although they may sometimes be restricted from promoting its practice. In contrast, the term is seldom explicitly used in official statements about the newer profession of community education, although in practice much of the time of its workers is spent in fostering self-help. This may in part be because social and health workers generally see individuals at crisis or transition points when the need for help is evident, whereas the purpose of community education in Scotland is defined as being "to stimulate people of all ages—individually and collectively—to use and develop the processes and resources of education, as a means of personal and community development" (Scottish Community Education Centre, 1981.) The same document goes on to state that "the essential element in community education is that it involves people and encourages them to participate and make their own decisions . . . letting them teach and support each other, develop their own programmes and organise their own affairs. It is only when people are involved that they gain the confidence to solve problems and to contribute to developing and improving the communities in which they live."

The contrast is thus between the therapeutic context, in which medical and social workers see their patients and clients, and the educational context, in which learning resources are available from which people can select those they need to help themselves and also those enabling them to support each other. It may be that this is also the setting most congenial in Scotland, with its tradition of emphasis on education. At the same time, community education offers one way of compensating for what has become the most criticized feature of the Scottish school system, namely, that it has concentrated unduly on a curriculum suited to an academically able elite—a disproportionate number of whom then emigrate because of lack of opportunities in Scotland—at the expense of the less able majority (a criticism well made by Donaldson, 1978).

Historically the roots of Scottish community education lie partly in youth work and partly in adult education, the former developing from voluntary enterprise in the last century and the latter going back further to scientific and literary societies in the eighteenth century. They were brought together as the result of a report of a committee set up in 1970 by the Secretary of State for Scotland under Professor K.W.J. Alexander (later Sir Kenneth Alexander) to consider voluntary leisure-time courses for adults, which were educational but not specifically vocational. This body took a wide interpretation of its subject and, reporting in 1975, recommended that adult education be regarded as an aspect of community education and, with the existing youth and community service, be incorporated into a community education service. Subtitling their report "The

Challenge of Change," the committee found it reassuring that "social responsibilities are still recognised and undertaken though not always by the individuals from whom earlier generations would have expected the response" (para. 53), which indicates recognition of the widening of social networks beyond the immediate family. In considering motivation, the committee claimed that there is now sufficient evidence to show that "adults will be more highly motivated to learn if . . . the content is related to the performance of everyday tasks and obligations and if the methods used take into account their accumulated experience of life."

Following the Alexander Report, overall supervision of the provision of community education in Scotland was added to the responsibilities of the Scottish Education Department, and the Scottish Council for Community Education was set up within the Department to advise the Secretary of State on matters related to community education, to promote its development, and to foster cooperation between the statutory and voluntary organizations concerned. In 1982 the Scottish Council for Community Education and the Scottish Community Education Centre, previously a semi-independent unit, merged to unify the functions of policy formulation and resource development at the national level. The Centre's main services include a resource library available to workers in the field. Staff deal with 10,000 enquiries annually and, besides other publications, produce a monthly newspaper, *Scan*, and a reference directory for individuals working in community education and related fields in Scotland (see Scottish Community Education Centre, 1981).

All twelve regional or island authorities have powers or duties under earlier legislation to secure the provision of adequate facilities for social, cultural, and recreational activities in their areas. Nine of the twelve authorities now operate community education services, the exceptions being the Central Region and Orkney Island councils, which operate youth and community services, and Shetland Island Council, which subsumes community education functions within the leisure and recreation department. In most instances, each service has a principal officer who is responsible to the assistant or deputy director of education.

Together, statutory and voluntary bodies employ approximately 1,000 full-time community education workers. The role of community education workers as "enablers" or "multipliers" means that their impact is out of all proportion to their numbers. These 1,000 are actively engaged in recruiting, training, and supporting a vast number of volunteers. For example, there are over 70,000 adults involved in part-time youth work (more than the total number of teachers in Scotland), while in preschool play groups over 40,000 mothers help with groups regularly attended by 43,000 children. These figures relate only to the more commonly needed type of provision, but they indicate something of the scale of operation and the usefulness of the multiplier approach. Other activities vary greatly according to the needs of the community and the particular interests of the worker but may include helping action groups to learn strategies of campaigning, aiding tenants' associations in designing constitutions and following committee procedures, making information available to enable individuals or groups to obtain financial or legal rights, recruiting local adults to participate in summer playschemes or to befriend vulnerable teenagers, providing facilities for established societies or setting up new enterprises such as health clubs, convincing ordinary people that they are needed on councils or committees, and encouraging others to take up educational opportunities. By continually extending their skills in negotiation and by acting as learning resources community education workers help people to cope with social and personal change so that they can use it constructively. The expressive side of community education is as important as the instrumental. By showing respect for a community's history, the community education worker can help people to build up community archives—record oral history and retrieve old photographs and documents leading to revaluation of the pressures on previous generations that have shaped the contemporary community. The traditional ceilidh—an informal evening of song and storytelling around the fireside—has not yet entirely died out in some areas. Scottish country dancing is strong in its social aspects, since dancers constantly interchange partners in sets of six or eight rather than being restricted to one. The revival of traditional song and music is evident in the proliferation of folk and traditional music clubs over the last few decades. Centuries-old local festivals have taken on new life, quickly absorbing new techniques from street theater and community arts.

IMPLICATIONS FOR PROFESSIONAL
ROLES AND TRAINING

The role of the community education worker as it has developed in Scottish communities offers many important insights into the challenges professionals face in linking into informal networks. A closer look at some of these challenges and difficulties reveals several implications for the shape of professional roles and the need for training with more general application.

For example, one important challenge faced by community education workers lies in their relationship with local schools and schoolteachers. School buildings and facilities have often been used in the past for community purposes. More recently, some new schools have included purpose-built community facilities, and other schools are increasingly claiming the title of community school, even without such amenities. Apart from the obvious economic advantages of shared provision, such a move toward integration can be justified on many grounds, but the different orientations of the two groups of professionals cause some difficulties.

These difficulties have been discussed by Nisbet, Hendry, Stewart, and Watt (1980) with special reference to the Grampian region, where they mounted a three-year research project focusing on five case studies of different arrangements between schools and community education. One case study focused on a rural secondary school (with 600 pupils, aged 12-18) combined with a community center serving an area of 40 miles along the River Dee, opened in 1975. The authors found a range of views among both groups of professionals, but in general a marked difference between the professional ideologies of the two groups:

> To caricature these somewhat, the teachers favour a service-provision orientation which implies the organisation and co-ordination of a programme of classes and activities. The community education staff, on the other hand, adopt a self-help orientation, on the assumption that it is more valuable for individuals to learn by being actively involved in organising a group themselves rather than being the passive recipients of a service. Most members of staff would acknowledge that both approaches may be appropriate, but the emphasis which they place on one or the other varies. (p. 43)

Sometimes misunderstanding of the distinction between the service-provision and the self-help approaches led to a virtual breakdown in communication between individual staff members. The head teacher is quoted as saying, "Self-help philosophy makes nonsense of years spent in professional training and in gaining experience and expertise. A self-help philosophy would in itself never have launched the Grampian Community Schools programme. It needed professional direction from above and this is in my submission what is lacking at local level."

The Nisbet study concludes that the existence of "two communities" within community schools is a major obstacle to progress. Each, they believe (and society at large) would gain from a better understanding of the differences in aims and objectives, training patterns, and work styles. A start toward a closer integration of the two philosophies could, they consider, be made during the preservice training of both sets of professionals. Obstacles to interprofessional cooperation have been studied by McMichael and Irvine (1983) who point out that it is to be expected that social and community workers who identify themselves with the poor, the disadvantaged, and the failures of the academic system should distance themselves from the school system and seek to establish other priorities. Comparing student teachers with student social and community workers, all studying at Moray House, Edinburgh, they note that in addition to the educational ideology of the student social and community workers being more radical than that of the student teachers, their postschool experience had been wider and their memory of school relationships less satisfying. These characteristics, they consider, "may well contribute to difficulties in understanding the more prescriptive and task centred role of the teacher. This role, when reflected in their own and their clients' experience, may appear to reduce autonomy, to stifle individuality and to crush further the already disadvantaged." McMichael and Irvine conclude that the differences nevertheless are those on a continuum of caring, all the professions under discussion being positioned at the same end rather than opposing ends.

Another challenge, which also has implications for training, lies in the relationship of community education workers to the local employment context. Among several colleges offering community education courses, Aberdeen College of Education has been notable for breaking down barriers between an academic institution and the work situation and for encouraging students to learn for themselves methods that subsequently they will encourage community groups to adopt. It is therefore fitting that a new project, in which nearly all the training in a three-year course will be at the trainees' workplaces, scattered throughout remote areas of the Highlands and Islands, has been launched in 1982 by the Aberdeen College in collaboration with Community Work North. The latter body is made up of all the major employing bodies in the north of Scotland, including five regional or islands councils together with educational institutions. Thus, for the first time, employing agencies will have an important role in training which will have direct relevance to the local community and the economic context. The project will enable local people employed in community work by regional authorities to continue in full-time jobs while gaining qualifications for high-grade employment of the kind previously filled by well-qualified incomers often ignorant of local culture.

The content of the course is being built around the experience of each trainee within a broad educational framework covering: economics, including community co-operatives; politics, with reference to the relationships between local government, central government, and the European Economic Community; social development; education, including the possibility of making the system more flexible in rural areas; culture and language; theoretical background to community work, including contributions from sociology and other relevant disciplines; social problems; and needs of particular groups within communities. Ten trainees have been enrolled in the first course. Four of the five working in Gaelic-speaking areas are themselves Gaelic speakers, and the fifth is learning Gaelic. Links with the college are being maintained by visits from tutors for further training and to check progress; telephone conference calls can also be used for tutorial purposes. On satisfactory completion of the course, students will receive a Diploma in Youth and Community Work from Aberdeen College of Education. The initial two-year phase of the project qualifies for 50 percent funding from the Social Fund of the European Economic Community and will be evaluated with special reference to its relevance to other, less favored areas of the EEC. This European commitment opens opportunities for renewing Scotland's older, direct links with continental Europe and the experience that professionals are gathering in the organizations considered here may interest other countries as well.

CONCLUSION

Particularly important is the increased awareness that communities must be seen not just as settings containing social networks and self-help groups but as roots from which both draw necessary nourishment. As Nisbet and his coauthors emphasize, "Structures for change may start on a basis of inter-professional collaboration, but unless they also include community involvement they will remain empty frameworks."

REFERENCES

Aberdeen College of Education. Information on courses. Hilton, Aberdeen.
Secretary of State for Scotland. *Adult education: The challenge of change. Report by a committee of enquiry appointed by the Secretary of State for Scotland under the chairmanship of Professor K.J.W. Alexander.* Edinburgh: Her Majesty's Stationery Office, 1975.

Donaldson, M. *Children's minds.* Glasgow: Fontana/Collins, 1978.

English, J., & Martin, F. M. (Eds.). *Social services in Scotland.* Edinburgh: Scottish Academic Press, 1979.

Finlayson, A. Social networks as coping resources: Lay help and consultation patterns used by women in husband's post-infarction career. *Social Science and Medicine,* 1976, *10,* 97-103.

Finlayson, A., & McEwen, J. *Coronary heart disease and patterns of living.* London: Croom Helm, 1977.

Kellas, J. G. *The Scottish political system (2nd ed.)* Cambridge: Cambridge University Press, 1975.

Kilbrandon Committee. *Report of the committee on children and young persons, Scotland* Edinburgh: Her Majesty's Stationery Office, 1964.

Martin, F. M., & Murray, K. (Eds.). *Children's hearings.* Edinburgh: Scottish Academic Press, 1976.

McMichael, P., & Irvine, R. Obstacles to inter-professional co-operation: A study of student responses to education, schools and teachers. *Scottish Educational Review,* 1983.

Nisbet, J., Hendry, L., Stewart, C., & Watt, J. *Towards community education: An evaluation of community schools.* Aberdeen: Aberdeen University Press, 1980.

The Open University. *The handicapped person in the community.* Milton Keynes: The Open University Press, 1982.

Scottish Community Education Centre. *Community education in Scotland.* Edinburgh: Author, 1981.

Six Circle Group. Annual reports and information. Glasgow: Author, n.d.

II

PROFESSIONAL RELATIONSHIPS WITH SELF-HELP GROUPS

5

AVENUES OF COLLABORATION

RICHARD WOLLERT and
NANCY BARRON
United States

Self-help groups, in which members share a common concern and assume primary responsibility for both organizational direction and mutual assistance, have emerged over the last several decades as a robust social phenomenon in the United States. It has been estimated, for example, that well over a half million self-help groups currently exist in this country (Katz, 1982) and that at least 14 million citizens are members of these groups (Academy for Educational Development, 1979). Professional interest, reflected in the number of books published on the subject, has also been keen in recent years (Katz, 1981). Finally, although comparative data are limited, the published literature reflects the fact that American self-help groups are internationally distinguished in terms of their longevity, size, and breadth of concerns.

Why have self-help groups flourished so extensively in this country? To answer this question, it is necessary to consider multiple factors operating at several levels. Table 5.1 presents a summary of variables that self-help researchers, including the present authors, view as significant develop-

AUTHORS' NOTE: *The writing of this chapter was supported by National Institute of Mental Health grant RO1-MH33671 to the senior author. The authors wish to thank Steven Andrews, Linda Dixon, Lucia Eakins, Cathy Tuma, and John Wadsworth for their substantial contributions to this project as research assistants. The support of the Regional Research Institute for Human Services at Portland State University is also gratefully acknowledged.*

TABLE 5.1   Summary of the Sources of Development of American Self-Help Groups

I.   Systemic or Contextual Variables.

   A. Mediated pressures for the creation of additional human services resources.
      1. Erosion in the capacity of traditional sources (family, friends, church) to meet the supportive needs of a rapidly changing society.
      2. Weak governmental support for the formal development of comprehensive human services programs.
      3. Inability of the public and private sectors to generate truly effective (timely, coordinated, inexpensive, focused) service delivery systems.
   B. Allowed for the elaboration of the self-help concept.
      1. Constitutional guarantees of freedom of speech and freedom of assembly.
      2. Sufficient standard of living to direct attention beyond needs for material assistance or cultural adaptation.

II. Values, Ideals, and Beliefs. Oriented potential members toward self-help groups and channeled group activities.

   A. Traditional values.
      1. Religious fundamentalism: expiation of guilt through self-disclosure, achievement of change through commitment to a higher power.
      2. Democratic idealism and egalitarianism.
      3. Self-reliance and autonomy.
      4. Pragmatism and empiricism.
      5. Populism.
      6. Distrust of human services professionals.
   B. Emergent values and attitudes.
      1. Expansion of the range of conditions identified as issues, concerns, or problems in living.
      2. Justification for assertiveness in mobilizing efforts toward problem resolution.
      3. Expectation of consumer participation in the problem resolution process.

III. Expected benefits constituted a source of affiliative motivation.

   A. To gain material benefits.
   B. To obtain information and guidance.
   C. To overcome social isolation.
   D. To build a supportive network countervailing nonempathic or judgmental reactions of the larger community.

IV. Conditions insuring maintenance and perpetuation of the self-help group approach.

   A. Many members perceive their self-help experience as effective and valuable, and are thus supportive of the general concept.

TABLE 5.1 (Continued)

B. Self-help members, through their group participation, are experienced and confident in operationalizing self-help concepts.

C. Resources are available for the development of groups.

D. Community acceptance and awareness exists of the self-help approach as a legitimate strategy for personal change and enhancement.

E. Governmental support exists for the development and utilization of self-help groups.

---

mental sources of these groups. *Systemic variables,* for example, mediated pressures for the creation of additional human services resources or allowed for the elaboration of the self-help approach as it was adopted in response to these pressures. Included in this category are such contextual conditions as the erosion of traditional sources of support, weak governmental support for comprehensive human services programs, and the inability of public and private sectors to generate adequate service delivery systems. Certain *values and beliefs* oriented potential members toward self-help groups and channeled group activities. Among these were ideals and attitudes stemming from traditional American culture: religious fundamentalism, self-reliance, and a distrust of human services professionals. Emergent values, such as the emphasis placed on assertion for resolving personal concerns, also played an important role in the continued development of self-help groups.

The *expected benefits* of joining a self-help group represented a significant source of motivation for affiliating with others sharing similar concerns and conditions. For many members, self-help groups were expected to provide help with a specific "problem." Others expected their groups to provide material assistance and information. Still others saw their group as a supportive network that would countervail nonempathic and judgmental reactions of the larger community toward themselves or the conditions they faced.

Finally, several *reinforcing developments* took place to support the growth of self-help groups in the United States. Self-help groups came to be accepted, for example, as a valid means of obtaining support and pursuing personal change, and a widespread readiness developed to join or organize self-help groups in order to resolve personal concerns. To a large extent, the groups themselves were originally responsible for achieving this status in that they introduced the concept of self-help to a great many people and provided significant benefits to their members in the process (Knight, Wollert, Levy, Frame, & Padgett (1980). Currently, however, their legitimacy is being further enhanced by a variety of governmental endorsements. The most recent report of the President's Commission on Mental Health (1978) has, for example, set forth several recommendations directed at recognizing and strengthening natural networks such as self-help groups.

SELF-HELP GROUPS AND
MENTAL HEALTH PROFESSIONALS

This analysis points up a set of factors that have influenced the past development of self-help groups and that in all likelihood will influence their future course. Assuming that most of these factors are relatively stable, self-help groups will probably continue to expand vigorously in the United States over the next several decades. Because of this expansion alone, professional service providers will be more likely in the future fortuitously to come into contact with self-help groups or members of such groups. Collaborative efforts between self-help groups and professionals, many of whom have shown a readiness to assist self-help groups (Borman, 1979), are consequently expected to increase. Furthermore, because of governmental encouragement of collaborative efforts in the form of potential grant funding,[1] many relationships between mental health professionals and self-help groups are also expected to be drawn with a planfulness and formality not evident previously.

The foregoing assessment suggests that very significant collaborative efforts are likely to be undertaken by mental health professionals and self-help groups in the future. To structure these relationships optimally, these participants must have an awareness of the diverse services available from professionals and those aspects of self-help groups that may be enhanced via professional intervention. Some discussions have appeared that are relevant to this issue (Caplan, 1974, Ch. 1; Gartner & Riessman, 1980; Toseland & Hacker, 1982), but their summary nature and high level of generality provide a limited perspective of the possibilities and pitfalls of collaboration that often become apparent in practice. Because self-help groups are so heterogeneous and multifaceted and the challenge to collaborative efforts so formidable, extensive analyses are also necessary to orient self-help group members and professionals adequately toward potential avenues of collaboration.

The following sections, based largely on the authors' experiences working with self-help groups as part of a three-year federally funded research project, point up several services that may be rendered by professionals to self-help groups and a variety of alternatives for structuring collaborative relationships. Taken as a whole, they represent an effort toward developing the breadth of perspective necessary to achieve fruitful collaboration.

Organizational Development Services

The type of service that professionals have most commonly provided to self-help groups is some form of organizational assistance during initial stages of development. Borman (1979) analyzed the characteristics of the founders and early supporters of ten self-help organizations, including such well-known organizations as Alcoholics Anonymous, Recovery, Inc., and Parents Anonymous. He found that encouragement from professionals was evident in all cases. More significant, professionals either founded the group with which they were associated or carried out other major organizational functions in six of the ten groups.

Organizational development services that may be provided vary in terms of their level of assumed responsibility and the generality of tasks that are involved. One of the most general functions a professional might serve is providing a focal point for organizational efforts. Although the authority vested in this role may lead to conflicts between members and professionals over group autonomy, several benefits may also be obtained from such an association. Where it is possible that negative community reactions may challenge efforts to develop a new group, such as a Parents United chapter for sexually abusive families, a focal professional may legitimize organizational activities (Wollert, Barron, & Bob M., 1982). Group members may develop small group skills by observing appropriate interpersonal behavior on the professional's part. The confidence of group members may also be bolstered by working with a professional who, while not having the perfect solution in hand to all organizational dilemmas, is nevertheless confident that an ongoing group may be formed and is committed to pursuing this goal.

Case Illustration

The experience of the first author in founding a chapter of Gamblers Anonymous (GA) illustrates this type of relationship. Serving as a clinical volunteer for a crisis intervention hotline in 1977, Wollert was telephoned by Mrs. K, a woman whose husband was a problem gambler. Mrs. K indicated that her husband had sought out profes-

sional treatments to stop gambling, including hypnosis and family counseling, but these proved unsuccessful in surmounting the problem. She challenged Wollert to tell her whether any other available treatment resources could be expected to produce positive results. When he asked her if her husband had tried GA, Mrs. K indicated that no chapter of GA existed within the local metropolitan area. At Wollert's suggestion, she expressed a willingness to found a GA chapter if Wollert helped organize the group.

Responsibilities were divided so that Wollert obtained information about GA from the national headquarters, while Mr. and Mrs. K identified a meeting location and recruited other potential members through newspaper advertisements and press releases. The first meetings were disappointing in that none of the initial members had attended GA before, and they did not have the background to follow the typical format of GA meetings. Even more disappointing were the numerous persons who came to one meeting and then did not return to others. At one point, Mr. and Mrs. K became sufficiently discouraged to discuss the possibility with Wollert of abandoning organizational efforts. Wollert empathized with their discouragement, but expressed a conviction that a viable GA chapter could be formed. Patience and continued organizational efforts were necessary, however. Fortunately, several persons who had been GA members for many years in another city joined the chapter at the next meeting. They guided the meeting according to the typical GA format and, afterwards, offered other members advice, based on their own experience, on how to "use the program."

Wollert withdrew from his organizational role shortly after this meeting, since his group commitment and encouragement were not as important for maintaining the members' confidence as they once were. By building the confidence of members during a critical period, however, he helped the chapter remain viable long enough to be joined by several members who, with the initial members, formed a critical nucleus for achieving ongoing status.

In addition to serving as an organizational focal point, professionals might carry out any of several specific organizational tasks. They could, for example, be asked to develop auxiliary self-help programs for the relatives of group members. Gamanon, for spouses of compulsive gamblers, and Sons and Daughters United, for sexually abused children, are two such programs. By recognizing that behavioral and personality problems of one family member affect the adaptive functioning of others in the family, and by reaching out to those who are affected, auxiliary programs greatly increase the scope and flexibility of the self-help approach.

Other types of valuable auxiliary programs that might be fostered by a professional working with a self-help group include support networks and sponsorship programs (Silverman, 1980, Ch. 7). The purpose of these systems, in which members help one another through informal "one-to-one" contacts, is usually to orient new members to their group, intervene during a crisis, or initiate an ongoing helping relationship. These informal interactions often do not stand out as powerful interventions when viewed in contrast to the meetings of a group. They complement group activities, however, in the opportunities they hold out for individualized attention and high levels of self-disclosure. They are also of great potential benefit to group members, as members have reported that much of the help they received was gained through contacts with group members outside of formal group meetings (Wollert, Barron, & Bob M., 1982).

Another aspect of self-help groups that may not stand out against the backdrop of group interaction is group "ideology." Antze (1976) adopted this term to refer to the belief systems and knowledge shared by group members which underlie the cognitive and behavioral changes they achieve and prevent the occurrence of relapse. Although Antze's analysis indicates that ideology is important from the standpoint of personal change, it is also of great organizational significance in that it facilitates communication about the group with external agencies and the establishment of chapters in other locations. It is noteworthy in this respect that professionals have played a direct role in formalizing the precepts and ideologies of a great many self-help groups (see Low, 1950; Mowrer & Vattano, 1976).

That such contributions have been made by professionals is certainly understandable when one considers the writing and conceptualizing skills that many have developed. Articulating the precepts and ideology of a self-help group, as long as adequate input is obtained from group members, is therefore an activity that may be of great significance to the group and one to which professionals are particularly well suited.

In some cases professionals assume primary responsibility for founding a self-help group and, as a result, implement a set of diverse organizational tasks. Many circumstances may lead to this situation, but it seems particularly likely to occur when a professional becomes interested in a certain target population not served by an existing self-help group. If it is possible to obtain complete guidelines from a national self-help organization serving the population of concern, as in the earlier example of Gamblers Anonymous, the task of forming the group is simplified. If such specific guidelines are incomplete or unavailable, general guidelines may be drawn from manuals that discuss organizational techniques for self-help groups

(Humm, 1979; Silverman, 1980). These manuals point up such important developmental tasks as deciding on an organizational model, articulating a clear statement of purpose, identifying and obtaining needed resources, recruiting new members, and developing small group discussion skills.

Natural histories of self-help groups (Katz, 1970; Bond, Borman, Bankoff, Daiter, Lieberman, & Videka, 1979; Wollert et al., 1982) also represent another source from which organizational procedures may be derived. These histories, which are being published with increasing frequency, are particularly instructive when their target population is similar to the target population for which a new group is being founded. In time, perhaps, an adequate number of natural histories will be published to permit the formulation of models that place developmental tasks within a historical perspective. If this occurs, it may then be possible to specify which tasks are most appropriately undertaken at different stages of growth.

Consultive Services

Consultation is another service that professionals are capable of rendering to self-help groups. Some consultive activities overlap the organizational activities just discussed. They are differentiated, however, by the circumstances that in consultation professionals typically deal with an ongoing rather than an embryonic group and that professional interactions with the group are relatively time-limited or intermittent rather than open-ended and constant. Since the role of a professional consultant is usually circumscribed by a specific issue, the chances are also reduced that he or she will assume major control over the group's functioning.

A primary focus for the consultive efforts of professionals has been the group as a whole. When this occurs, the purpose of consultive activities is often to assess and remediate program deficits.

Case Illustration

Wollert, Knight & Levy (1980), for example, undertook a lengthy consultive project with one chapter of Make Today Count, a self-help group for cancer patients and their spouses (Kelly & Murray, 1975). This chapter, founded by medical professionals without the benefit of formal guidelines, possessed several strengths in the personality characteristics of the members and their determination to form an ongoing self-help group. Several weaknesses were also apparent in the low percentage of cancer patients (20%) attending the group, the lack of success the group had in recruiting new members, and continuing difficulties the group experienced in resolving organizational questions and deciding upon a meeting format which would

*facilitate discussions of adjustive challenges. After a series of inter-
view and group discussions, the consultants summarized a set of
organizational recommendations at the group's request. These
recommendations articulated a group purpose which members
agreed in previous discussions was clear and would permit new
members to identify with the group. Other sections of the recommendations discussed administrative structure, meeting formats, and
facilitative techniques for small group discussions. The group
assumed responsibility for implementing these recommendations.
The resulting changes had a great impact in enabling the group to
recruit new members and improving group discussions so that events
of personal importance were discussed with a greater readiness than
previously. During a nine-month follow-up period the chapter not
only consolidated these changes, but also moved from a "problem
child" status with the national organization to being a model for
other chapters facing organizational difficulties.*

This case study illustrates how consultants may benefit a group by
sharing their formal knowledge (Gartner & Reissman, 1977) with group
members. Conceivably, a consulting approach could be adopted for achieving positive goals of the group as well as overcoming organizational
weaknesses.

Case Illustration

*The first author and an associate[2] explored the potential utility of
such collaboration by presenting a structured eight-session communications training workshop to members of Parents United. This topic
was of considerable significance for members of this group since
inadequate communications skills are a hallmark of sexually abusive
families and since the group members themselves requested the
workshops. More participants than could be accommodated in one
workshop volunteered for the series, and a true experimental design
was implemented to take full advantage of this development. Members were randomly assigned to either an experimental condition or
a waiting list control condition. In the experimental condition,
members received the workshop series instead of attending the more
generally focused self-help group meetings. In the control condition,
members continued to participate in these meetings. An eleven-item
self-rating inventory of communications skills was administered to
all members before and after the workshop to assess the intervention's impact. Analysis of the data indicated that the means and
standard deviations of the inventory scores for the experimental and
control groups were similar before the workshop. The post-work-
shop means of these respective groups, however, reflected significantly greater scores for those who completed the workshop.*

These results support the value of this potentially cost-effective approach, which emphasizes the enhancement of members' skills through formal training and the consolidation of training gains within the group itself.

Instead of having an organizational focus, consultive activities may be case-focused. This approach is useful when questions arise concerning such issues as psychological diagnosis, medical screening, or crisis intervention. The authors' observations of over twenty self-help groups suggests that individually focused consultations in self-help groups are usually informally structured. This may be a major reason why this type of consultive work is rarely published.

Case Illustration

Silverman (1970), however, outlined an apparently positive consultive association with the Widow-to-Widow program. This program relied on widows with natural helping skills to assist other widows to achieve an effective psychological adjustment to their spouses' deaths. The work of these aides was not directly supervised, but they did consult with Silverman on a regular basis to review their visits with widows and discuss their plans for further interventions. Although program plans did not initially include provisions for founding a self-help group, the aides were apparently instrumental in forming such a group and also a telephone counseling service. One reflection of the positive appeal of this multifaceted self-help program may be seen in the nationwide interest it has stimulated for the development of similar programs.

Ongoing Service Roles

In contrast to adopting roles that are time-limited, professionals may adopt roles of an ongoing nature. The views of group members on this topic provide considerable insight into some potentially available roles. Knight et al. (1980) asked eighty members of behavioral control and stress-coping (Levy, 1976) self-help groups to outline the roles they believed professionals could serve in their respective groups and to rate the present and potential future levels of professional involvement. Although members of the stress-coping groups (such as Make Today Count) were more positive about future professional involvement than members of the behavioral control groups (such as Parents Anonymous), both categories of members rated potential involvement more highly than present involvement. These findings support the view that many self-help groups welcome the participation of professionals (Lieberman & Borman, 1979). As a complement to these results, three ongoing roles were found to be specified among the five most frequently mentioned roles: sponsor, referral source, and member.

Organizational policy constitutes another frame of reference with respect to structuring ongoing roles. The policies of many groups, notably Alcoholics Anonymous and Recovery, Inc., expressly forbid the participation of professionals in leadership roles. Other groups, however, encourage professional participation in different capacities. Parents Anonymous, for example, advises each of its chapters to work with a mental health professional who has agreed to serve as a chapter sponsor (Parents Anonymous, 1974). Parents United, alternatively, has established a policy whereby mental health professionals co-facilitate small group meetings with group members (Wollert et al., 1982).

Because facilitator and sponsor positions are so widely mentioned as roles for professionals in self-help groups, it is useful to consider some of the activities and professional-group relationships implied by these terms. Both facilitators and sponsors, by their participation in a group, provide professional acknowledgement of the group and contribute to the credibility of the group's standing in the community. Sponsors, however, ideally defer the guidance of meetings to a group member-leader, although they may affect group meetings through their advice to the leader or be called upon to intervene during emergencies. Facilitators, by contrast, assume more constant responsibility for directing group interactions. Administrative decisions within the group may also be influenced to a greater degree by facilitators than by sponsors, particularly when, as in Parents United, several facilitators participate in an organization. Overall, then, sponsors are somewhat avuncular in the orientation to the group they serve and fulfill a "backup" role, whereas facilitators are more personally involved and fulfill a "front-line" role.

As the concept of self-help is applied to an increasingly wide range of issues in the future, self-help groups will probably be sponsored by agencies in greater numbers than they are now. In particular, agencies may step forward to sponsor self-help groups for populations with special needs. Among such populations may be those at risk for serious health complications, those who are severely handicapped, and those who have been institutionalized but are attempting to achieve an adjustment to a noninstitutional environment.

Although the possibility of partnerships between agencies and self-help groups is attractive from several standpoints, including flexibility and cost-effectiveness, it is important to recognize that professionals and self-help members do not hold the same values and perspectives. Professionals, for example, seek to preserve their status as "experts" and to exercise control over interventions with which they are associated. Self-help members, alternatively, desire to establish their own autonomy and achieve recognition for their own competence. Professionals also tend to view problems in living from an evaluative and theoretical perspective, while self-help members assume a more affirmative and experiential orientation.

As some reports of collaborative efforts have indicated, the strains arising out of these differences may be very destructive (Kleiman, Mantell, & Alexander, 1976). To overcome and manage these conflicts, it would be facilitative to designate a professional with self-help expertise to fulfill the type of advocate-mediator role presented in Figure 5.1. The responsibilities of the advocate-mediator would include observing the group and group members, and, in the process, identifying conflicts as they arise. For each conflict, the advocate-mediator would attempt to clarify alternatives for its resolution and to negotiate compromises acceptable to those concerned. For disputes which could not be settled, the advocate-mediator would submit a report containing his or her recommendations to a governing board for the group.

In addition to crisis resolution, this role and the organizational structure on which it is based yield benefits to both a self-help group and its sponsoring agency. The self-help group, on the one hand, is assured a major voice in policy determination through the activities of someone who speaks with the authority of a professional yet does so from the perspective of an advocate for the self-help approach. The agency, on the other hand, is enabled to decentralize decision-making procedures but to do so in a highly responsible manner. The role of advocate-mediator, although it has never been fully operationalized, therefore appears to be sufficiently promising to warrant its adoption and evaluation in future collaborative efforts.

Clearinghouse Services

The preceding sections have considered how professionals might provide beneficial services to self-help groups on largely a group-by-group basis. Some professionals are committed to promoting the concept of self-help more generally, however, and are consequently interested in developing methods of providing broad support to self-help groups and facilitating access to the use of self-help groups throughout a community. To address these goals they have initiated self-help clearinghouses in

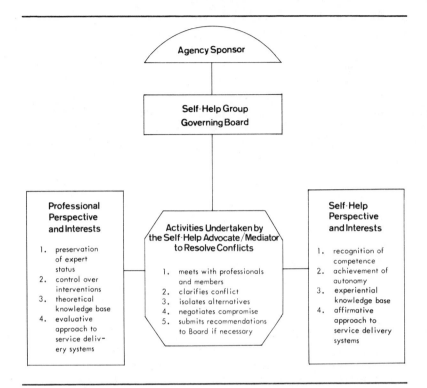

Figure 5.1: Structure of the Self-Help Advocate/Mediator Role

several metropolitan areas during the last five years (Borck & Aronowitz, 1982).

The major functions of these clearinghouses have been systematically to *collect information* about self-help groups and to *disseminate this information* to interested community residents through directories, newsletters, or telephone networks. In line with the goals of increasing self-help group use and accessibility, information systems focus on questions of concern to potential self-help group members. This requires developing capabilities to identify groups relevant to the needs of potential members and to provide information about their purpose, membership criteria, cost, and meeting locations and times.

The efficient operation of a centralized information system provides opportunities for realizing several other important functions. A *planning function* may be achieved, for example, when data about existing self-help resources are assessed in relation to the mental health needs of a community and the results of this assessment are shared with representatives of the formal mental health delivery system. A *coordinating function* is attainable when those interested in forming a group around an issue not yet addressed through self-help are linked with one another and, if desirable and possible, with professionals willing to provide organizational and consultive assistance. It is possible to serve a *resource mobilization function* by addressing the needs that groups often have for material support in the form of access to meeting places, babysitters, transportation, and printing materials. Finally, by providing valuable services, a clearinghouse may increase the readiness of self-help members to participate in studies of self-help processes and outcomes. This, coupled with the considerable access that professionals associated with a clearinghouse have to self-help groups, enables a *research function.*

Case Illustration

The authors' experience in developing Self-Help Information Service (SIS), serving the Portland Metropolitan area, points up several issues which must be satisfactorily resolved to organize a clearinghouse effectively. As initially conceived, the purpose of SIS was to disseminate information about local self-help groups and to generate research opportunities. Before a funding proposal could be submitted, however, it became apparent that interagency coordination was necessary to achieve local support for the project. This was accomplished by aligning SIS with the existing Information and Referral (I&R) Service, an arrangement which also minimized problems of logistics and service duplication while insuring access to expert consultation in the increasingly sophisticated field of information and referral.

After funding was obtained and the project staff selected, two information collection instruments were developed. A "Group Resource" Inventory was designed to collect information about local groups, and a "Potential Member" Inventory was designed to identify persons who were interested in joining a self-help group, but for whom no appropriate groups could be identified. Other self-help clearinghouses and information services were surveyed so that comparisons might be drawn between the SIS inventories and instruments adopted elsewhere. The responses received indicated that the SIS inventories were largely similar in format and content to other instruments in use.[3]

Two of the last tasks undertaken before placing SIS in operation were staff training and a publicity campaign to insure that the service would be utilized by the community. At first, project staff were placed at I&R on a round-robin basis for familiarization with community resources and training in information and referral tech-

niques. As the staff became thoroughly familiar with both SIS and I&R procedures, it was possible for them to withdraw from this placement and to train university students enrolled in practica courses to assume their responsibilities. This was particularly advantageous to the project in that more time could then be devoted by staff members to research goals. Eight hundred posters designed by a graphic artist were distributed to advertise SIS, and arrangements were later made for radio and television spot announcements to provide ongoing publicity. These efforts were very fruitful in that the number of requests for self-help information for the month after the publicity campaign was over 200 percent greater than for each of the previous six months.

In spite of the research constraints which molded the organizational structure and procedures of SIS, many clearinghouse functions were apparent during the course of the service's operation. Over 150 different self-help groups comprising approximately 20,000 members were inventoried within the metropolitan area, and the inventories used for the compilation of a self-help directory. Numerous consultations were provided by the project staff to self-help groups and, in one case, six persons who contacted SIS were placed in touch with one another for the purpose of founding a self-help group for persons with Altzheimer's disease. An assessment of the mental health needs of the community and available self-help resources, conducted by the second author, identified health disorders, emotional distress, unemployment, and sex role concerns as major issues which might be addressed through the formation of additional self-help groups. The staff assisted groups to gain access to needed resources by locating meeting places. Finally, through SIS, members of self-help groups were recruited to participate in research focused on group processes, the effects of group membership on adaptive functioning, and the contrasts between self-help and professional interventions.

SIS thus rendered diverse contributions to many self-help groups while being instrumental in achieving the research goals it was designed to support.

DISCUSSION

This chapter has presented an overview of services that mental health professionals may provide to self-help groups. It has also illustrated, through examples drawn from the literature and the authors' experiences in working with self-help groups, the varied nature of relationships that may be established between professionals and self-help groups. This framework, it is hoped, will assist agencies and individual providers to identify contributions they might offer to self-help groups. At the same time it may inform group members about the range of alternative services they might seek from professionals. The chapter at hand thus encourages efforts that incorporate elements from the formal and informal human service delivery systems and that reduce the existing separation between these systems.

Although collaborative efforts hold out great promise, an accurate appraisal of this potential requires that several presumptions be avoided. One such presumption is that collaboration will necessarily be successful. The vast difference between professional and self-help approaches (Gartner & Riessman, 1977; Lenrow & Burch, 1981) ensures that tensions will invariably arise between representatives of these perspectives. To resolve these tensions productively, it is important that professionals and members of self-help groups develop a basis of mutual understanding and knowledge, adopt constructive attitudes, set compatible goals for their efforts, and structure unambiguous role relationships that minimize struggles over competence and organizational control. The possibility of failure should be recognized where these criteria cannot be satisfied, and the feasibility of collaborative action evaluated accordingly.

A second misleading presumption is that self-help groups and their members are the sole beneficiaries of collaborative efforts. Although the structure of this article has precluded such a discussion, it is undeniably the case that self-help groups may serve professionals in a number of ways. They could, for instance, provide valuable training experiences to those interested in small group processes or assist professionals in expanding their clinical knowledge and formulating theoretical hypotheses. To obtain these benefits without exploiting self-help group members, however, it is desirable to establish working relationships between professionals and self-help groups that are based on the theme of reciprocity. This constraint clearly guided the operation of SIS, which provided an information dissemination service to self-help groups while it also allowed project staff to invite the participation of group members in research activities.

As funding sources recognize the utility and economy of the self-help approach, interest will undoubtedly increase in evaluating the interchangeability of this naturalistic approach with professionally based approaches. Some enthusiastic proponents of the self-help approach have already offered their own assessment of matters. Hurvitz (1970), for example, has claimed that more people have been helped by self-help groups than all psychotherapists combined and, applying features of self-help groups to professionals, has recommended that the services of psychotherapists be offered without such elements of a bureaucratic structure as fees, records, scheduled appointments, privacy, special settings, professional training, etc., except those which the participants themselves decide are helpful to them and which they want to assume to achieve their goals. (p. 45)

Such broad comparisons, eventuating in global conclusions about efficacy and calls for prescriptive actions, could have several negative effects. They could, for example, convey the impression that the two systems serve similar populations, work toward similar goals, and employ similar procedures, thus implying that they are alternate and mutually exclusive treatment procedures. This would be extremely unfortunate, because it would alienate professionals from working with self-help groups. It would also be misleading in that the few quantified studies from which comparisons may be drawn suggest that professionals employ more complex behavioral interventions and more intense interpersonal techniques than self-help groups (Lieberman & Bond, 1976; Wollert, Levy, & Knight, 1982). Furthermore, the extent to which the population of group members overlaps the population of therapy participants has not, from the standpoint of personality functioning, been determined. Finally, the implication that self-help and professional treatment are mutually exclusive is not supported by the reports of members: In a preliminary analysis of interviews of thirty group members also seen for psychotherapy, the authors have very recently found that self-help and psychotherapy were seen as adjuncts to one another and that therapy was particularly useful in raising issues for expanded discussions within a group context.

These considerations suggest that the thrust of future evaluations should be toward identifying the different contributions self-help groups and professionals offer to those with adjustive concerns, and constructing a service framework that emphasizes complementarity and cooperation rather than competition. If this stance is assumed it may be possible not only to expand the scope of mental health services, but also to do so in a way that utilizes existing resources for the benefit of both consumers and providers.

NOTES

1. A recent request for proposals distributed by the Office of Human Development Services illustrates this encouragement. This office requested the submission of concept papers in ten priority areas. Of these areas, by far the greatest number of

awards were allocated to proposals dealing with volunteerism, a topic which included specific references to self-help groups.

2. The assistance of Samuel Kimball in co-facilitating this group and also assisting with the data analysis is gratefully acknowledged.

3. Copies of these instruments are available from the authors.

REFERENCES

Academy for Educational Development. *The voluntary sector in brief.* New York: Author, 1979.

Antze, P. The role of ideologies in peer psychotherapy organizations. *Journal of Applied Behavioral Science,* 1976, *12,* 323-346.

Bond, G. R., Borman, L. D., Bankoff, E. A., Daiter, S., Lieberman, M. A., & Videka, L. M. Growth of a medical self-help group. In M. A. Lieberman & L. D. Borman (Eds.), *Self-help groups for coping with crisis.* San Francisco: Jossey-Bass, 1979.

Borck, L. E., & Aronowitz, E. The role of a self-help clearinghouse. *Prevention in Human Services,* 1982, *1*(3), 121-129.

Borman, L. D. Characteristics of development and growth. In M. A. Lieberman & L. D. Borman (Eds.), *Self-help groups for coping with crisis.* San Francisco: Jossey-Bass, 1979.

Caplan, G. *Support systems and community mental health.* New York: Behavioral Publications, 1974.

Gartner, A., & Riessman, F. *Self-help in the human services.* San Francisco: Jossey-Bass, 1977.

Gartner, A., & Riessman, F. *Help: A working guide to self-help groups.* New York: New Viewpoints, 1980.

Humm, A. *How to organize a self-help group.* New York: City University of New York, Self-Help Clearinghouse, 1979.

Hurvitz, N. Peer self-help psychotherapy groups and their implications for psychotherapy. *Psychotherapy: Theory, Research and Practice,* 1970, *7,* 41-49.

Katz, A. H. Self-help organizations and volunteer participation in social welfare. *Social Work,* 1970, *15,* 51-60.

Katz, A. H. Self-help and mutual aid: An emerging social movement? *Annual Review of Sociology,* 1981, *7,* 129-155.

Katz, A. H. Self-help and human services. *Citizen Participation,* 1982, *3*(3), 22-23.

Kelly, O., & Murray, W. C. *Make today count.* New York: Delacorte, 1975.

Kleiman, M. A., Mantell, J. E., & Alexander, E. S. Collaboration and its discontents. *Journal of Applied Behavioral Science,* 1976, *12,* 403-410.

Knight, B., Wollert, R. W., Levy, L. H., Frame, C. L., & Padgett, V. P. Self-help groups: The members' perspectives. *American Journal of Community Psychology,* 1980, *8,* 53-65.

Lenrow, P. B., & Burch, R. W. Mutual aid and professional service: Opposing or complementary? In B. J. Gottlieb (Ed.), *Social networks and social support.* Beverly Hills, CA: Sage, 1981.

Levy, L. H. Self-help groups: Types and psychological processes. *Journal of Applied Behavioral Science,* 1976, *12,* 310-322.

Low, A. A. *Mental health through will-training.* Boston: Christopher Publishing House, 1950.

Lieberman, M. A., & Bond, G. R. The problem of being a woman: A survey of 1,700 women in consciousness-raising groups. *Journal of Applied Behavioral Science,* 1976, *12,* 363-379.

Lieberman, M. A., & Borman, L. D. Overview: The nature of self-help groups. In M. A. Lieberman & L. D. Borman, *Self-help groups for coping with crisis.* San Francisco: Jossey-Bass, 1979.

Mowrer, O. H., & Vattano, A. J. Integrity groups: A context for growth in honesty, responsibility, and involvement. *Journal of Applied Behavioral Science,* 1976, *12,* 419-431.

Parents Anonymous. *Chapter development manual.* Redondo Beach, CA: Author, 1974.

President's Commission on Mental Health. *Commission Report* (Vol. 1). Washington, DC: Government Printing Office, 1978.

Silverman, P. R. The widow as a caregiver in a program of preventive intervention with other widows. *Mental Hygiene,* 1970, *54,* 540-547.

Silverman, P. R. *Mutual help groups.* Beverly Hills, CA: Sage, 1980.

Toseland, R. W., & Hacker, L. Self-help groups and professional involvement. *Social Work,* 1982, *27,* 341-347.

Wollert, R. W., Barron, N., & Bob M. Parents United of Oregon: A self-help group for sexually abusive families. *Prevention in Human Services,* 1982, *1*(3), 99-109.

Wollert, R. W., Night, B., & Levy, L. H. Make Today Count: A collaborative model for professionals and self-help groups. *Professional Psychology,* 1980, *11,* 130-138.

Wollert, R. W., Levy, L. H., & Knight, B. G. Help-giving in behavioral control and stress coping self-help groups. *Small Group Behavior,* 1982, *13,* 204-218.

6

HOW PROFESSIONALS VIEW
SELF-HELP

CHRISTIANE DENEKE
West Germany

We are at present witnessing a change in the provision of
health care in the United States of America and Western
Europe that may have far-reaching consequences. This
change has come about by both self-help activities of
people taking care of their own health, and the acceptance
by the professional of the positive role of lay self-care.
(Kickbusch, 1981, p. 1)

This chapter is concerned mainly with the question of the extent to which
professionals (here, social workers) in West Germany accept lay self-care in
its collective form—self-help groups—and what their attitude toward
cooperating with them is. To outline the context, the first and second part
will give a brief description of the incidence and development of self-help
groups and provide some information on the relevant sociopolitical
framework. The main part presents some of the results of a survey of
health professionals in Hamburg.

Little research has been done on the relationship between professionals
and self-help groups in West Germany, mostly because the phenomenon
"self-help group" has only recently been recognized in research here.
There had been no research about self-help groups in West Germany before
1975. The first comprehensive book, by Moeller, was published in 1978.
Larger-scale research (funded by the West German government) started in

1978. The first book on the role of professionals with respect to self-help groups, again by Moeller, was published in 1981.

A general political trend has to be taken into account when evaluating the research findings: Lip service to self-help has become very common, and it may be that the superpositive attitudes, or rather utterances, of policymakers and representatives of the medical professions are being reflected in the overt attitude of individual professionals. Their feelings and sometimes fears about the active patient, the independent client, and the possible loss of their jobs surfaced only in intensive interviews (Behrendt, Deneke, & Schorsch, 1981) and in additional remarks in the self-completed questionnaire.

THE DEVELOPMENT AND INCIDENCE OF SELF-HELP GROUPS

Looking into German history, the roots of self-help can be traced to the unions, the now compulsory health insurance system, and many welfare organizations. While the unions of the last century, for instance, could be seen as self-help organizations with a strong emphasis on advocacy, their growth and bureaucratization has left very little of this. Their present attitude toward any form of self-organization is ambiguous, but changing slightly toward seeing the positive aspects. In the field of health—or rather, ill health—groups exist for many chronic diseases, handicaps, and addictions. There are also various other groups that have some direct or indirect impact on people's health status: women's groups, groups for single parents, sexual minorities, or the elderly. But looking at the population as a whole, only 3.2 percent have ever participated in self-help group activities or consulted a self-help group for advice. Nevertheless, about one-third of the population feels that a self-help group could be of some help to them in case of need (Projektgruppe, 1981). This figure should be interpreted not as representing a potential membership for self-help groups, but rather as an indicator of a positive attitude toward the groups.

Our information about self-help organizations that are operating on a national basis is not comprehensive, especially concerning those organizations coping with social problems. The information is better for the health-related organizations because many of them are organized in the Bundesarbeitsgemeinschaft "Hilfe für Behinderte" (Help for the Handicapped), an umbrella organization whose members are organizations or groups for the disabled and parents of disabled children. We know of 35 such organizations, but whether all of them still function on a self-help basis is not yet known. The estimates for the total number of regional or local self-help groups are still quite vague, ranging between 5,000 and 10,000 groups for health and psychosocial problems, not including community action groups (Winkelvoss, Trojan, & Itzwerth, 1981).

Our definition of self-help associations is very broad; the different components are defined as follows.

The *health relevant* self-help associations are divided into five categories:

- associations concerned with *specific diseases* (for coping with a medically classified chronic disease or impairment);
- associations concerned with *life problems*, both social and psychological (women's and men's groups, groups for the lonely, associations of social security recipients, and the like);
- associations concerned with *public health or social services* (community action groups for the maintenance or installation of health institutions, patients' rights associations, and so on);
- *environmental* associations (for instance, fighting chemical pollution of the environment); and
- *alternative culture* associations (for communal living, collective working, where healthier living is an expressed aim, and so on).

Only the first two types of associations are subject to our empirical research.

Our defining criteria for self-help associations in health are:

- being affected by a shared problem;
- no or little involvement of professional helpers;
- no profit orientation;
- shared aims—personal and/or social change; and
- procedure emphasizing cooperation based on equality and mutuality of aid.

Associations comprise small groups and organizations, but for the empirical research we have limited the organizations to those where at least a subgroup meets at least monthly. Large associations, even though they might call themselves self-help organizations, are often not included, because the criteria of "self-help" are not met.

TABLE 6.1   Distribution of Self-Help Groups in Health

Category	Number	Percentage
Alcohol, including groups for partners	235	58
Other psychiatric	9	2
Internal medicine	35	9
Physically handicapped	68	17
Surgery, including cancer	12	3
Other diseases	16	4
Groups of relatives	29	7
Total	404	100

The comprehensive figures available are for the urban area of Hamburg, which is a city-state, the biggest city of the Federal Republic of Germany with 1.7 million inhabitants. Economically, Hamburg is one of the wealthiest areas of Germany with the largest port and much international commerce. We know of about 570 groups, out of which 400 are directly disease-oriented and 170 deal with social and psychological problems. Because of the less formal organization of many groups concerned with social and especially psychological problems, the number, 170, strongly underestimates the actual incidence. To give some idea of the distribution of groups concerned with health, Table 6.1 shows the figures for the different categories.

This distribution shows a very strong bias toward alcoholism, where groups are well established. Networks for certain afflictions are developing, but for the vast majority of health problems, very few groups exist. Even though few figures exist concerning the growth in the number of self-help groups in West Germany, the experiences in the local, regional, and national clearinghouses show a growing interest in groups, supported by intensive mass media coverage, and quite a few new groups. The increase in Hamburg has been about 33 percent in about 20 months (May 1980 to January 1982). This figure does *not* include those groups directly concerned with alcoholism.

Our findings about membership, motivation, and success conform with findings in other countries (Deneke, Kegler, & Slotty, 1981). Relevant in this context are the findings relating to the links between self-help and the professional system. Almost 90 percent of the somatic disease groups and the groups for relatives, and 25 percent of the addiction groups and groups for other psychiatric problems, have some contact with state agencies. Contact with professionals is also most frequent in somatic disease groups. Professionals are at least sporadically involved in 64 percent of all disease groups. These differences are mainly due to the different orientation of the groups, reflected in their aims. Those groups that see their function as complementary to state and professional services maintain a close cooperation with them. This is often true for somatic disease groups, where the medical treatment is left to the professionals, while the self-help group complements this with psycho-social services.

For many groups, professionals were (or still are) important, because they helped to found the group or stimulated its foundation. While for groups concerned with social and psychological problems, or groups for relatives, member recruitment through professionals is not very frequent, disease groups get quite a few of their members through professional referrals. This is due to the lack of appropriate professional services for psycho-social problems. Even though the deficiencies of the professional system are one of the main reasons to join a group, there is little antiprofessional attitude within the groups. Most members of self-help groups want to cooperate—but with professionals accepting their aims and their approach.

THE POLICY BACKGROUND:
THE HEALTH AND SOCIAL SERVICE SYSTEM

To understand the political implications and dependencies of self-help in West Germany, a short discourse on the West German system of health and social services is necessary. The West German constitution provides a legitimate basis for the field of social services as a "democratic and social federal state" (Art. 20.1), that is, a welfare state. This is broadly interpreted as a federal responsibility for all social risks. Practically all citizens are obligatory members of fully comprehensive health insurance schemes. The payments relate to income and not to risk. Old age, work accidents, and unemployment are similarly comprehensively insured. But there are citizens for whom this system does not apply (for instance, people who were never employed and are not related to someone who is employed). In cases of poverty, the state social security system is responsible. Thus, all members of society are—theoretically—protected in case of illness even when they are destitute.

The principle of subsidiarity, state welfare as the service of last resort, is important for understanding the relevant sociopolitical framework for collective self-help in West Germany and similarly organized societies. This principle implies the subordination of the state in providing direct social services. So statutory agencies are supposed to offer services only if neither the individual nor primary social networks, like the family, nor nonstatutory bodies have acted. This subordination encouraged the growth of large, influential voluntary welfare organizations, three out of the six largest being church-affiliated. There are 400,000 paid staff and 4 million volunteers who work in this section—in hospitals, homes for the elderly, counseling services, and the like; 35 percent of all hospitals and 59 percent of all old-age homes are run by welfare organizations (Dorrie, 1981). On average, 40 percent of all their funds are state-provided (Strasser, 1979). The larger ones participate in legislative procedures and other major decisions in the welfare sector. There is no clear-cut distinction between self-help organizations and welfare organizations in general; quite a few of these welfare organizations started as self-help groups. The *Lebenshilfe*, for example, started as a group of parents caring for their mentally handicapped children. Now it is one of the main providers of (professional) services for the mentally handicapped, the influence of the parents being fairly minor. Other self-help groups are spin-offs of larger organizations or are members of *Deutscher Paeitatischer Wohlfahrtsverband* (DPWV), a large welfare organization functioning as an umbrella for thousands of smaller ones.

The DPWV not only provides direct social services itself but gives advice to its members on funding, accounting, legislation, and the like. It represents its members organizationally and politically. The whole organization of the welfare sector, especially the rules for state funding, produces pressure toward professionalization and growth. The typical development is:

- foundation of a group, because no other agency provides appropriate services;
- contact with official agencies and pressure on them;
- attracting (and sometimes training) professionals, who do paid work;
- consequent dependency on financial (statutory) support and the respective qualification criteria; and
- successive and at least partial elimination of former representatives of the interests of those people directly concerned.

At this point, new groups may be formed by directly involved people because, again, there are unmet needs (Breeger, 1979; Itzwerth, 1979). Of course, there are groups that successfully fight this process of institutionalization (Breuer, 1979), but the pressure toward it is evident. Despite the official positive political orientation toward self-help groups, the relevant legislation discourages self-help and its support (Riedmüller, 1981). Even though self-help is specifically mentioned, it is understood as individual self-help, not taking part in any collective action. This might be due to the general individualizing orientation of the whole welfare legislation and the casework orientation of those professionally involved.

The provision of medical services is under general state control, but in practice it is under the control of medical associations alone. Specific to the West German system are the facts that there is no outpatient treatment in hospitals and that the financing system makes it profitable—from the providers' point of view—to provide few services in the ambulatory sector and instead keep the patient in the hospital. For changes in the medical system, the cooperation of medical associations and health insurances is vitally necessary. This system—where profit is privatized and cost socialized—is not only expensive (about 12 percent of all private incomes is spent on health insurance, not counting additional health services paid for by the state—that is, the taxpayer) but also rather ineffective, leaving gaps in unprofitable areas like consultative and preventive activities. Self-help groups are likely to be found in these unprofitable gaps, so the increase of self-help groups will not make the health care system less expensive, but possibly will raise the quality and thus lessen the increase of costs, making further professionalization of services superfluous (Trojan, 1981).

HEALTH PROFESSIONALS VIEWING
SELF-HELP GROUPS: A SURVEY

This survey is part of a study on the relation of health professionals to self-help groups from the point of view of the professionals. The study as a whole adopted an action research approach, aiming to facilitate cooperation if wanted. Thus, the purpose of the survey was twofold:

(1) to gather information on knowledge about, attitude toward, and cooperation with self-help groups by physicians, psychologists, and social workers in the health field; and

(2) to identify those professionals interested in further information about self-help and those interested in more cooperation.

TABLE 6.2   Form of Organization

	Percentage
Consultive services	38
Residential services	24
Hospitals	20
Day centers	10
Other	8
Total	100

TABLE 6.3   Institutional Affiliation

	Percentage
State	59
Church	15
Other welfare organizations	26
Total	100

The next steps were the distribution of information material and the organization of meetings of those interested in cooperation. These activities have not yet been evaluated.

The presentation of the results will focus on the social workers. The postal survey included all Hamburg social workers in the field of illness, handicap, or addiction. Four hundred were contacted and 152 responded, a response rate of 38 percent. Even though the response rate is fairly high for an eleven-page questionnaire in a postal survey, we can by no means assume that the respondents represent the whole of their profession.

The social work respondents work in different organizations with different institutional affiliations (Tables 6.2 and 6.3). The information given about the clientele reflects the real distribution but also different views of the same problem. For example, social workers assigned to a surgery ward define their clients as ill, while those working with people with similar problems in a rehabilitation center classify them as handicapped (Table 6.4).

The average social worker is 37 years old, has worked for nine years after qualifying, and has been four years in his or her (68 percent are female) present job. Not surprisingly, almost all the respondents had heard ente / HOW PROFESSIONALS VIEW SELF-HELP   133

TABLE 6.4   Clientele

	Percentage
Addiction	22
Disease	43
Handicap	34
Psychosocial problems	14
Total	113

NOTE: The total is greater than 100 because of multiple responses.

of self-help groups. Areas mentioned were diverse, but alcoholism was mentioned by 72 percent; second was cancer, with only 34 percent (in an open question). Asked about groups they know (more than their mere existence), 64 percent of the social workers knew at least one group—on average, three. Here again, alcohol was first, the group mentioned most often being Alcoholics Anonymous, followed by another group for alcoholics. The main sources of information (see Table 6.5) are colleagues (66 percent), self-help group members (63 percent), and professional literature (52 percent). Looking at these and the other sources mentioned, the predominance of informal sources is striking.

Even though the social workers know something about the groups, quite a few feel they do not know enough; lack of information about groups and their work was noted as one of the reasons for no cooperation by almost 50 percent of the noncooperating social workers. The lack of information does not seem to be only pretext, because the interest in further information is large. More than 75 percent of all respondents asked for additional information on self-help groups. We had offered a few articles on the subject, a bibliography, a listing of larger self-help groups in the area, and seminars to be conducted at a later date. The respondents had to fill an extra leaflet with their address and a list of "items" they wanted.

When self-help group members have such an important information-giving role, it is not surprising that so many professionals know of groups for alcoholics only: The chance to meet a member of one out of 235 groups for alcoholics in Hamburg is rather good, which cannot be said about some of the other groups, being quite scarce. The general attitude toward self-help groups seems positive (stated attitudes being very positive, 37 percent; rather positive, 60 percent; rather negative, 2 percent; very negative, 0 percent; and no answer, 1 percent).

TABLE 6.5   Problem Area of Mentioned Groups (percentage of respondents mentioning any group)

	Percentage
Alcohol	67
Other addictions	3
Handicaps	34
Psychiatry	16
Cancer	18
Other diseases	16
Groups for relatives	20
Other groups	23
Total	197

NOTE: The total is greater than 100 because of multiple responses.

We must take into account that this attitude is often based on the knowledge of groups of alcoholics only, the most accepted field for self-help. But social workers know far more groups than other professionals—and still think more positively about them. This might be due to various differences:

(a) A much higher proportion of social workers than doctors or psychologists work with alcoholics.

(b) Self-help groups are widely accepted among social workers and have a higher level of cooperation with them than with the other professionals in the survey.

(c) Social workers seemed to feel more pressure to produce "expected" answers. Knowing that we were doing research on self-help groups, they may have tended to give answers that would "please" us.

(d) While we had special support with the questionnaire from the local medical association, there was no equivalent support from the psychologists and social workers as a professional body. This support may have led doctors to answer the questionnaire even if they were not interested in or were opposed to self-help.

Leaving the general attitude for a while, let us look at the ideas social workers have about self-help groups—their function in service delivery, their role with respect to other health sources, and the aims they should have.

TABLE 6.6   Self-Help Groups Having a Function in . . .

	Percentage
Prevention	60
Treatment	38
Aftercare	93
Complementing the professional services	93

NOTE: The total is greater than 100 because of multiple responses.

While personal goals are generally accepted, social goals, like functioning as a lobby group or trying to influence the social roots of a given problem, are not accepted by all the social workers (between 60 and 70 percent agree). Asked whether self-help groups would have any function in the health system if there were sufficient professional services available, almost all affirmed this. The special health service functions are perceived as shown in Table 6.6. Thus, the unquestioned domain for self-help groups is aftercare, complementing the rather deficient rehabilitation system.

What is important for social workers about the setting of the groups if they want to refer a client? First ranks the acceptability of the aims of the group to the social workers, not necessarily the client (79 percent), and second, the fact that professionals should be involved at least sporadically (59 percent). Asked for important criteria on the client's side, more than 90 percent mentioned the willingness to accept help from co-sufferers, and as a basis for any help, no denial of the problem. The client has to take full responsibility for participation (79 percent), even though the social workers would send him or her only to a group of which they themselves approve (see Table 6.6). Other attributes often mentioned as prerequisites for self-help group participation—like verbal capacity, middle-class status, assertiveness, or previous group experience—were not mentioned often (none of them more than 7 percent), but it was thought that the client should not be too domineering (32 percent). Seventy-one percent of the social work clients were thought to have a problem manageable in a self-help group, and 40 percent of those were thought to be suitable for a group. These figures are more an indication of the attitude toward self-help than actual referrals, which are far less frequent.

Asked about the achievements of self-help groups, most agreed that self-help groups have the following effects: They

TABLE 6.7   Areas of Self-Help Group Achievements

	Percentage
Directly symptom or problem-oriented	44
Oriented toward the general social and psychological situation	58
Providing general help	52
Achievements with reference to the professional system	13
Political achievements	19
No reply	17

— lessen personal isolation (99 percent),

— complement the professional system (97 percent),

— help in a way professionals cannot (85 percent), and

— help their members become "responsible" clients (94 percent).

Similar effects were mentioned in an open question about achievements, but the relative weighting of the effects was different. For instance, some mention that, because of the closer personal contact and understanding between the members, there is a better chance of solving personal problems.

The negative effects (see Table 6.7) were not chosen very often (increasing social isolation, 9 percent; interfering with the professional services, 8 percent; others even less). But asked in an open question for possible negative effects, quite a few mentioned something. The most prominent apprehension was that self-help groups might provide false information and prevent appropriate use of professional services. The overt attitude of social work respondents (see Table 6.8) is not only on average more positive than the attitude of physicians or psychologists, but furthermore none of them refused to cooperate on principle or refused ever to refer clients to self-help groups (7 percent of the physicians and 2 percent of the psychologists could be classified as such).

More professionals than we had expected mentioned cooperation with self-help groups (see Table 6.9). The rate of frequent cooperation is much higher with social workers than with physicians (14 percent) or psychologists (7 percent), which is due to the large proportion of social workers working with alcoholics. The reasons given for no cooperation reflect lack

TABLE 6.8 Areas of Possible Negative Effects of Self-Help Groups

	Percentage
No reply	36
No negative effects	5
Negative effects in respect to the (use of the) professional system	16
Negative group characteristics	21
Ghettoization	21
Overrating the capabilities of the group	16
Other negative effects	4

TABLE 6.9 Factual Cooperation and Willingness to Cooperate (in percentages)

	Total	Addiction	Other
Frequent cooperation	24	61	14
Occasional cooperation	35	24	37
Cooperation conceivable	40	15	47
Cooperation out of question	1	0	2

of information (lack of information about the work of the group, 46 percent; no groups known, 28 percent), a lack of familiarity with this form of work (cooperation being uncommon in their institution, 42 percent), the lack of indication (not indicated for the majority of clients, 33 percent; no interest on the clients' side, 30 percent), and, last but not least, the lack of time (36 percent).

The forms of cooperation vary from permanent participation to more general information about the existence of groups. The form mentioned most often is personal recommendation of a group (36 percent). No less than 34 percent of the cooperating social workers are active in getting information about the groups for their clients and are in contact with group members for this purpose. Seven percent participate regularly, and 23 percent at least sporadically.

Most of the cooperating social workers were quite satisfied with it (85 percent); only one social worker was very dissatisfied. Quite a few wanted to increase the cooperation (52 percent), and only one wanted to reduce it. Not all the cooperators mentioned the groups with which they worked, but groups for alcoholics were predominant again—not only mentioned by those who specialized in working with alcoholics. Those who noted changes in their work situation because of the cooperation considered them to have been predominately positive (92 percent)—most often job enrichment and positive changes in their relation to their clients. Forty-five percent of the cooperators mentioned some obstacles, time and organizational problems being the main ones (leaders of self-help groups are not necessarily available on a 9-to-5 basis).

Since one of our aims was to develop support for cooperation with self-help groups, we tried to identify the typical cooperator, assuming there were rather clear distinctions between cooperators and noncooperators. For this purpose we compared those who reported "frequent cooperation" with the rest of the social work respondents. The greatest distinction is in the clientele: addiction (mainly to alcohol but to drugs as well) is highly overrepresented among cooperators, but there are still 28 percent working with other clientele. The cooperators have fewer clients to work with than others (average 31 versus 50). Consultation services are over-represented, but only because so many cooperators work in addiction, which involves a lot of consultation. The noncooperators are more likely to work in a hospital (33 percent versus 21 percent).

Not surprisingly, the cooperators know slightly more groups, and their information stems more often from self-help group members or personal participation and less often from other sources, such as the mass media. Their general attitude toward self-help groups is only slightly more positive, but they see their clientele to a much higher degree to be suitable for such a group (57 percent instead of 35 percent of the others).

The cooperators are much less oriented toward professional control of the groups than the others. Only one-third of them feel that professionals should be involved in a group to which they want to refer a client (two-thirds of the others), and another 31 percent feel there should be no professional involvement (compared to 17 percent of the others). Only 12 percent mention that they think the client should be under further professional supervision (versus 33 percent of the noncoperators). The frequent cooperators more often accept that self-help groups aim to function as a lobby for all sufferers and try to influence the social roots of the problem. They see more of a preventive function for self-help groups than the others (75 percent versus 56 percent) and assume that self-help groups can slow down the cost increases in the health sector. More of the cooperators feel that the professional delivery system should be not only improved but changed profoundly (38 percent versus 21 percent), not in size but in quality. Last but not least, more cooperators are in self-help groups themselves—not as professionals, but to cope with their own personal problems.

NEW PERSPECTIVES

Even though the general orientation of those social workers who are cooperating frequently seems to entail little danger of co-optation by them of self-help groups, we have to assume that there is quite a bit of pressure on them to do so. Especially in times of recession, there is strong pressure to prove one's own usefulness, more so in areas where professionalization has not yet been fully accomplished, as is the case with social work in West Germany. To accept self-help as largely equivalent to professional help might imply one's own superfluity. And criticizing one's own work or doubting its effectiveness might soon lead to losing one's own job, instead of helping to achieve the fundamental changes envisaged. So the great interest in self-help by social workers quite often turns out to be a search for personal alternatives; they see self-help as a means of examining their own careers and the possibilities for their own futures. In effect, some social workers look to self-help for what it will do for them rather than for their clients.

The survey has shown much more cooperation by social workers with self-help groups than expected. The expectations were based not only on literature (Moeller, 1981; Mellett, 1980), but also on the results of intensive interviews with professionals (Behrendt et al., 1981). We expected the personal and institutional conflicts to be so prominent, especially for social workers, that cooperation would be avoided rather than sought. Later work with social workers in counseling services for alcoholics brought up one explanation for this unexpected result. The crucial point was not the cooperation with self-help groups per se, but rather the question of whether they were just a means for aftercare, thereby maintaining the preeminence of professional institutions, or whether they could be seen as an alternative to professional treatment and thus as competition to the services provided by social workers.

The danger of co-optation does not seem to be as important as is often assumed (Behrendt, Deneke, Itzwerth, & Trojan, 1981). Those social workers who cooperate frequently seem to be less oriented toward professional control and the status quo of the professional system than the others. But there seems to be another danger: Professionals try to use self-help groups as a means to get rid of clients they don't know what to do with; they refer them to a clearinghouse, even though the client has no idea of what self-help is and is not motivated at all.

Another aspect worth considering might be a rising solidarity between certain professionals and their clients, both concerned with social and economic changes: The cuts in the social sector are becoming more and more frequent, even in "wealthy" West Germany. There is a trend not only toward public saving in the social sector, but also toward more autonomy in large sections of society. Community action groups have become an important factor not only for environmental problems but also in many other spheres. Even though we cannot talk of a real self-help movement in West Germany (Breuer 1981), self-help groups can be understood as at least partly an element of social movements in West Germany society, the women's movement being one of the most prominent ones. When some groups started, they were concerned only about the particular problems shared by their members, but they have begun to see their problems in the context of the community or society as a whole. Thus, collective self-help is not only a way of coping; it can also be seen as a way to gain new experiences, alternatives to what has been experienced before.

This might be true not only for the sufferers themselves but also for the "new" professionals. After a first *Gesundheitstag* (Health Day) in 1980 (Huber, 1981), 15,000 health professionals, self-helpers, and other people from all over West Germany gathered in Hamburg in October 1981 for the second *Gesundheitstag,* discussing self-help and self-organization in the health field. What started as a counterevent to a meeting of representatives of the medical associations became a focal point for a variety of alternative forms of treatment and care—professional and lay alike.

In the field of social services, a similar development can be foreseen. In 1981 a coalition of social service professionals and their clients began to work with other established groups, like self-organized kindergarten groups and the Grey Panthers, to fight cuts in the social sector in Hamburg. This example has been taken up in quite a few other German cities. It may be that these joint experiences will change the relation of "professional" and "client." Perhaps they will lead to more partnership in the future.

REFERENCES

Behrendt, J. U., Deneke, C., Itzwerth, R., & Trojan, A. Selbsthilfegruppen vor der Vereinnahmung? Zur Verflechtung von Selbsthilfezusammenschlüssen mit staatlichen und professionellen Sozialzystemen. In B. Badura & C. V. Ferber (Eds.),

Selbsthilfe und Selbstorganisation im Gesundheitswesen. Munich: Oldenbourg, 1981.

Behrendt, J. U., Deneke, C., & Schorsch, E. M. Hindernisse in der Zusammenarbeit zwischen professionellen Helfern und Selbsthilfegruppen. In I. Kickbusch & A. Trojan (Eds.), *Gemeinsam sind wir stärker. Selbsthilfegruppen und Gesundheit.* Frankfurt/Main: fischer alternativ, 1981.

Breeger, N. Selbstorganisationsversuche Behinderter am Beispiel des Club 68. In P. Runde & R. G. Heinze (Eds.), *Chancengleichheit für Behinderte—Sozialwissenschaftliche Analysen für die Praxis.* Neuwied: Luchterhand, 1979.

Breuer, R. Welle oder Bewegung? Zur Frage der Gesellschaftsveränderung durch "Selbsthilfe." *Neue Praxis, 1981, Sonderheft 6,* 208-218.

Deneke, C., Kegler, R., & Slotty, A. Selbsthilfegruppen aus der Sicht der Betroffenen. In I. Kickbusch & A. Trojan (Eds.), *Gemeinsam sind wir stärker. Selbsthilfegruppen und Gesundheit.* Frankfurt/Main: fischer alternativ, 1981.

Deneke, C. Selbsthilfegruppen und Sozialarbeit. *Neue Praxis, 1981, Sonderheft 6,* 199-208.

Dorrie, K. *Was leistet die freie Wohlfahrtspflege für die Gesundheit der Bürger?* Paper presented at the XVII. Kongress of the Deutschen Zentrale für Volksgesundheitspflege e.V., Frankfurt am Main, November 1981.

Huber, E. Selbsthilfe—eine Chance für die professionellen Helfer? In I. Kickbusch & A. Trojan (Eds.), *Gemeinsam sind wir stärker. Selbsthilfegruppen und Gesundheit.* Frankfurt/Main: fischer alternativ, 1981.

Itzwerth, R. Von der Selbsthilfegruppe zur Dienstleistungsorganisation. In P. Runde, R. G. Heinze (Eds.), *Chancengleichheit für Behinderte—Sozialwissenschaftliche Analysen fur die Praxis.* Neuwied: Luchterhand, 1979.

Kickbusch, I. People's health in people's hands. In *Health for all by the year 2000.* Geneva: World Health Organization, 1981.

Mellett, J. Self-help, mental health and professionals. In S. Hatch (Ed.), *Mutual aid and social and health care.* Arvac Pamphlet No. 1. London: Arvac, 1980.

Moeller, M. L. *Selbsthilfegruppen.* Reinbek: Rowohlt, 1978.

Moeller, M. L. *Anders helfen. Selbsthilfegruppen und Fachleute argeiten zusammen.* Stuttgart: Klett-Cotta, 1981.

Projektgruppe Verwaltung und Publikum an der Universität Bielefeld. *Selbsthilfepotential in der Gesundheitsversorgung der Bundesrepublik Deutschland: Einstellungen, Motivation und strukturelle Rahmenbedingungen. (2. Zwischenbericht).* Bielefeld: Author, 1981.

Riedmüller, B. Selbsthilfe ist unerwünscht—Zur Stellung der Selbsthilfe im Sozialversicherungsrecht. In I. Kickbusch & A. Trojan (Eds.), *Gemeinsam sind wir starker. Selbsthilfegruppen und Gesundheit.* Frankfurt/Main: fisher alternativ, 1981.

Strasser, J. *Grenzen des Socialstaats? Sociale Sicherung in der Wachstumskrise.* Köln, Frankfurt/Main: EVA, 1979.

Trojan, A. Selbsthilfegruppen als Ersatz für professionelle Leistungen? Uberlegungen zur Frage, ob Selbsthilfegruppen die Gesundheitssicherung verbilligen. *Demokratisches Gesundheitswesen, 1981, 4,* 20-21.

Winkelvoss, H. Trojan, A., & Itzwerth, R. Zur Definition und Verbreitung von Gesundheitsselbsthilfegruppen. In I. Kickbusch & A. Trojan (Eds.), *Gemeinsam sind wir stärker. Selbsthilfegruppen und Gesundheit.* Frankfurt/Main: fischer alternativ, 1981.

7

BIRTH OF THE MOVEMENT

Early Milestones

JAN BRANCKAERTS
Belgium

This chapter deals with self-help groups in Flanders, although it makes some reference to individual self-care and to the Belgian situation as necessary. The incidence, development, research, and government policy aspects are discussed. A preliminary section introduces Belgium as a social reality.

BELGIUM TODAY

Belgium lies in Northwest Europe and is bordered by France, Germany, Luxemburg, Holland, and the North Sea. On 11,780 square miles of water-laced land lives a population of about 9,868,000 persons (Ministerie van Economische Zaken, 1981).

Belgium is heavily urbanized, and the vast majority of its population are in families supported by industrial or commercial enterprise: Over 90 percent of the population is more or less linked to urban employment. On a world level, Belgium is among the most prosperous nations, but the recent economic crisis in Western Europe has reduced the growth of the gross domestic prodict (GNP) and has increased the unemployment rate.

Better than statistical data, studies and interpretations of foreign observers can provide an introduction to Belgium's social structure (Nuyens, 1980). In its March 1979 issue, *National Geographic* introduced Belgium as follows: "At history's crossroads, Belgium's vulnerable geography has suffered foreign intervention since Caesar. . . . Now Parliament has passed a plan to set up two individually governed regions—Flanders and Wallonia—with Brussels as a semi-autonomous third. A federal government would conduct foreign and fiscal affairs and control national defense. . . . Belgium is not inhabited by Belgians but by Flemings and Walloons, and it is more a broken marriage than a nation" (Cerruti, 1979, p. 316).

Belgium is currently in the process of federalizing its Dutch-speaking (Flemish) and French-speaking (Walloon) communities. On some policy matters, including self-help, the Flemish government thus already takes its own independent stand. The Walloon part, culturally oriented toward France, has not shown much interest in the phenomenon—a lack of interest that can be observed in the Latin European countries in general.

Roemer and Roemer (1977, p. 2), studying the Belgian health care system, point to another characteristic of Belgium: "The general economy and the associated culture are strongly oriented to free enterprise and individualism, with a relatively weak public sector—resembling in this respect the United States more than most other European countries." This basic ideology constrains "welfare state" concepts. Due to the strong private sector, the society as a whole is organized by the classic free market mechanism of supply and demand. This private sector—the arena for numerous interest groups with power, influence, and capital—limits the innovative capacity of the public sector. This free market model shapes the health care and welfare system and subsequently the self-help sector and related policies.

Belgium has been labeled not only a divided society and a free market society, but also a "frozen society." R. C. Fox, an American sociologist who has studied Belgian society for over twenty years, notes: "Each crisis has temporarily drawn the many subgroups and factions of Belgian society into several, antagonistic blocks. And in each instance when these "en bloc" conflicts and confrontations have escalated to a certain point, they have been negotiated and resolved in an extra-parliamentary way, by a commission or a conclave in a castle" (1978, p. 223). This is indeed the specific Belgian way of neutralizing, regulating, and solving conflicts—and conflicts are manifold because of the socioeconomic, ethnolinguistic, and, above all, cultural-ideological differences in the population.

Indeed, in addition to the conflicts between employers and employees (capitalism versus socialism) and the conflicts between the Dutch- and French-speaking parts of the population (Flanders versus Wallonia) there are also conflicts among what are called the Catholic, liberal, and socialist pillars.

Pillars are, according the Thurlings (1978, p. 12), parallel organizational structures or complexes of organizations that are segregated from one another, each with its own "religious foundation." Religious foundation must be interpreted here as "world view," since liberals and socialists are not religious in the common sense of the word.

Pillarization implies that in the same sector—education, health, or welfare—two or more segregated and competing systems can exist. The state organizes and administers schools, hospitals, and social service centers but at the same time—according to the principle of subsidiarity—supports schools, hospitals, and centers that are privately organized by the pillars or "ideological families." This private sector has a far-ranging autonomy but is paid for by the state, out of taxpayers' money.

This ideological division affects all sectors of social life, including industry, commerce, science, and the arts. There are not only the Catholic (Christian-Democrat), liberal, and socialist political parties; there are also separate trade unions, playgrounds, primary and secondary schools, universities, hospitals, factories, cultural organizations, libraries, social clubs, health insurance companies, and even funeral companies! Thus, one can be born, live, and die in one pillar without ever being confronted with others from a different pillar. This external pluralism of self-sufficient networks turns social and political life into an arena of conflicting interest groups representing the many divisions. Conflicts are neutralized in the above-mentioned way.

INCIDENCE OF SELF-HELP GROUPS
IN FLANDERS

The concept of self-help was introduced in the Dutch-speaking part of Belgium (Flanders) in 1979. It was taken from literature appearing at the time in the Netherlands, originating from Great Britain and the United States, where the term had become fashionable.

The introduction of the term in Flanders awakened popular interest in the subject, and self-help groups began to form. Some followed the idealized and even romanticized models found in the literature—for example, MOM (*Mens onder Mensen*), a group of persons having experienced nervous breakdowns, which was organized structurally and functionally along the lines of Alcoholics Anonymous. In addition, some groups that had already existed for a number of years began calling themselves self-help groups. Among them were *Similes,* a group for families of psychiatric patients, and organizations such as the "friendly societies" and the "brotherhoods of the blind, deaf, and the handicapped," which have a history of over 40 years. Still other self-help groups were formed by loosely organized groupings of patients in hospitals and by well-established organizations for health education and disease prevention, such as the national organizations for epilepsy and mucoviscidosis. These latter organizations either started claiming the name of self-help, or were labeled that way by others.

The term also came to be more widely known through discussion in scientific and commercial publications, through research efforts of individual students, and through attention to the concept in newspapers and on radio and television. In addition, social groups organized around other concerns began discussing the topic.

On the other hand, certain other groups which might be typified as self-help groups actively avoided using the name and continued to term themselves "action groups." An example is the Red Butterfly Action Group for Revolutionary Homosexuality.

It is clear from the foregoing that there has not yet been established a consensus on what "self-help" implies. It can be observed only that the introduction of the concept of self-help has caused a few new groups to form, solidified the organizational structure of some already existing loose groupings, and given a new sense of orientation or self-definition to well-established groups. In some instances, it has caused groups to change their names; at the same time, it may have prompted groups to change their ways of functioning, although there is no empirical evidence to support this claim. Perhaps the recently published inventory of existing and potential self-help groups will allow more groups to determine how they might adapt themselves to the self-help concept (Branckaerts, 1980).

To estimate the potential number of self-help groups in Belgium, reference might be made to the National Project on Primary Health Care (National Project in de Sociale Wetenschappen, 1979), whose eight-volume publication includes a listing of all groups or organizations specifically interested in the health or illness of their members or of the broader public. At the time the project was completed in 1976, it listed around seventy such groupings. Of these, about twenty concerned themselves with specific types of illness or handicaps. Most of them were organized as nonprofit (VZW) organizations, begun by private initiative but subsequently subsidized by the government. A few of them (about three) took the legal form of public utilities, instituted and funded by the government but operated as independent, decentralized services. The listing includes the Belgian Union for the Handicapped and the Belgian organizations for voice-defects, epilepsy, spastic children, mucoviscidosis, diabetics, myopathics, rheumatics, and hemophiliacs. Other organizations work to decrease usage of tobacco, alcohol, and drugs and to combat cancer. Still others are the Cardiological League and the Multiple Sclerosis League.

(Alcoholics Anonymous was not included, since it is organized locally and has only a centralized clearinghouse).

The aims of the organizations are uniformly to promote research, to gather and distribute information, and to provide personal services and reintegration of the afflicted into society through individual social care and group education. In general they have local branches and serve the whole of Belgium; they also initiate ad hoc groups on demand. Defined as organizations for health education and promotion, they are recognized by the Belgian National Ministry of Public Health's Section for Social Medicine.

A more recent inventory of self-help groups includes more groups and a greater variety (Branckaerts, 1980). The number of different kinds of groups dealing with various kinds of problems via self-help groups is estimated to be 55. This excludes groups concerned more generally with the health care system and self-help-promoting groups. The number of known and more or less organized self-help groups, including local branches and central secretariats (but assuming only one group per province) is estimated to be around 185. This is too conservative, since several local branches can be working in one province; if these and the self-help groups included in other institutions (such as centers for family planning and sex education) are taken into account, one easily arrives at about 300 to 500 self-help groups in Flanders.

As to the nature of the problems with which the groups deal, it should be mentioned that certain categories listed in English and American surveys do not exist in Flanders (for example, groups for the elderly, the young, or the "average woman"). This is due to the fact that the Flemish society is highly organized and has well-funded "cultural" organizations along ideological lines for such categories (the Catholic League for the Retired, the Socialist League for the Retired, the Liberal League, and so on). The division (pillarization) of Belgium into three ideological families has given rise to a network of services and organizations that covers almost every problem of every stage of life. New groups might be needed but surely would tend to parallel or compete with already existing groups.

THE DEVELOPMENT OF SELF-HELP

The development of the concept of self-help, although occurring rather rapidly, can be divided into three distinct periods. In the initial period, from 1979 to mid-1980, self-help groups publicly identified themselves as such. The second period, from the publication of the first directory of self-help groups in mid-1980 until the middle of 1982, was characterized by the formation of new groups, extensive media coverage, and increased public awareness. The third period, which continues to the present time, shows extensive social organization of the field and supportive attention from politicians.

The Start

The concept of self-help was introduced in Belgium by the publication of the Dutch book, *Self-Help: A New Way of Helping?* (Van Harberden & Lafaille, 1978). It was a compilation of mainly American literature on the subject, complemented with introductions and articles referring to the situation in the Netherlands. The editors were active in another way in promoting the concept: They induced a Flemish organization to organize the first self-help fair.

Thus, in 1979, this leftist organization for community development organized a study and information day on self-help in Alken, Limburg. Also in 1979, Bevema, a professional organization for social workers, organized a similar event in Antwerp. In the winter of 1979-1980, a leftist institute for continuing education at Leuven organized a cycle of courses in which self-help groups could introduce themselves and hold discussions with course participants. At the beginning of 1980, an event called Health 80 included a congress and a fair promoting aids to health, in which self-help groups participated. The congress, organized by the Christian Sick Fund and the Scientific Organization for Flemish General Practitioners, also devoted some attention to self-care and self-help groups. Finally, in mid-1980, the Flemish Humanist Organization sponsored a study day at Ostende, West-Flanders, on the possibilities of self-help.

Two comments can be made regarding these events. First, they included most of the Flemish provinces of Belgium. Second, they came about not from the initiative of self-help groups themselves but as a result of interest expressed by other groups. These observations lead to the question: What kind of organizations are interested in promoting and discussing self-help?

Such organizations might be grouped into three categories, each of which includes two of the cited events. The first category includes institutes for community development and continuing education. Both are interested in altering society, the first by structural and the second by cultural means. This perspective assumes that self-help is an emancipating power. The second category includes organizations that deal with professions, namely, social workers and general practitioners. Their interest in self-help can be seen to stem from the wish clearly to delineate professional responsibilities. The third category, Christian Sick Funds and the

Humanistic Organization, are, as their names indicate, organizations with ideological points of view. They are two of the three main organizational groupings along ideological lines in Flanders that provide services for their adherents (Socialists being the third); their interest may be considered indicative of a general trend of developing recognition by such types of groups.

In sum, then, it might be noted that diverse groups were paying attention to the phenomenon, although in this stage self-help groups were not themselves organizing their own forums.

Acceleration of Development

The publication by the Sociologisch Onde Zoeksinstuut (a research center at the Katholieke Universiteit Leuven) of the *Preliminary Directory* of Self-Help Groups in Flanders (Branckaerts, 1980) marked a change in public awareness. This directory had been compiled on the basis of existing data and on the basis of responses to published calls to self-help groups to present themselves to the general public. On publication, it received considerable attention in the newspapers. Moreover, it created a central information center or point of reference, since the public started to attribute clearinghouse functions to the research center. Simultaneous with the increased public awareness, the introduction of a commercial handbook on the organization of the health and welfare system in Flanders, including a chapter on self-help groups, introduced growing knowledge and acceptance in the professional world (Nuyens, 1979). These activities resulted in an acceleration of the development of self-help.

This phrase, "acceleration of the development of self-help," indicates the diversity and vagueness of the self-help-related events. An estimate of their significance can only be made in the long run, after it has become clear what they contributed to the current changes in the lay component of the care system.

One sign of acceleration is a remarkable proliferation of already existing groups. For example, the Huntington's League, formerly with only one central headquarters, started several local chapters around the country. New groups are forming for problems like sarcoidosis, Morbus Crohn, and Sudden Infant Death Syndrome. These groups seem to be able to reach not only a large proportion of the afflicted but also professionals involved in studying and treating the condition in a fairly short time.

Moreover, "self-help" has been discovered by the news media. An important leading newspaper regularly prints full-page stories about particular self-help groups and reports on research activities. Other newspapers have followed this initiative. In the beginning, reporters would contact groups to hear their stories and write about them. As the months went by, more and more individuals started to contact the media people to present their case and start new groups. Belgian Radio and Television, the noncommercial, state-controlled network with a monopoly on broadcasting which functions as a tool of information and cultural education, devotes a biweekly, one-hour television program to self-help initiatives. The radio started a weekly program based on the principles of lay expertise and mutual aid; persons with problems are given the opportunity to present their cases to the public via a phone call and receive, again by phone, answers from listeners all over the country. Both programs have recently been awarded a prize for "the best broadcast," an indication of the high esteem in which they are held by the public.

Furthermore, students and professional health workers are showing interest in the phenomenon. Social and hospital nurses include information on self-help groups in their postgraduate training, schools for social work stimulate students to explore the phenomenon, and divisions for social psychology conduct projects on specific groups from the point of view of social movements. Although these efforts mainly represent "lower-level" health workers, there have also been seminars on self-help groups in at least two medical schools.

In conferences, colloquia, and symposia, where scholars and health workers meet, reverential bows are made to "the lay health care system." This, of course, can be interpreted as sheer politeness or a nod to fashion. But since it is becoming obligatory, it seems to indicate that the lay care system can no longer be denied. In sum then, it is clear that the increased attention from researchers, media, and professionals is broadening the field of self-help.

Organization of the Self-Help Sector

In the middle of 1982, two new initiatives concerning the organization of the self-help sector were announced, the first on a provincial level, the second on a regional level.

The previously mentioned organization for community development in Alken, Limburg, initiated a Platform for Self-Help Groups in Limburg. After gathering information on existing groups in their province, the organization assembled representatives of these groups and started a nonprofit organization. The aim of this organization is to support and foster the development of self-help in health and welfare. This will be done by enabling and stimulating communication among groups and between groups and other self-help "relevant others," such as sick funds and professional organizations for health workers. In general, the Platform was to act as a clearinghouse, including such functions as publishing a newsletter; organizing a data bank and a "switchboard" to provide information and referral for the public; training of professionals in self-help and ways to work with self-help groups; encouraging, collaborating with, and organizing scientific research about the effects of self-help; and, finally, addressing professional and public policy audiences.

The first public manifestation of the Platform for Self-Help Groups was the organization of a study and information day on the topic of self-help and primary health care. Representatives not only of self-help groups but also of most of the influential interest groups in the health care system attended the meeting. The Flemish Minister for Health concluded the day with a speech in favor of self-help.

The second event was the start of Network Self-Help for Flanders. The above-mentioned television program on self-help featured the Berlin *Netzwerk Sellbsthilfe*. The program invited interested viewers to react and start something like it in Flanders. Several individuals and groups responded by starting a nonprofit organization. The target group, aims, and activities are broader than in the first case. The organization works for the whole of Flanders. It does not limit itself to self-help groups in health and welfare but includes socioeconomic and political projects based on the principles of self-help and mutual aid. The aim is to provide practical support—material and financial—and organizational guidance to its groups and projects. The necessary funds will be gathered by asking members of the Network to contribute 1 percent of their income to the fund for redistribution. The Network aims at starting a movement that could alter the cultural, political, and economic climate of Flemish society.

Groups that want to apply for funds must meet the following conditions: They must be organized in a democratic, self-governing way; they must develop alternative ways of living or working; they must socialize their profits; they must be prepared to collaborate with other projects; they must ensure continuity by adopting a viable organizational form; and they must aim at economic self-reliance.

It is too early to discuss the effects of these two new programs. It can be noted, however, that some of those who first called attention to self-help during the initial and developmental phases have gone on to seek the collaboration of self-help groups and have actively organized the self-help sector or enabled this sector to organize itself.

RESEARCH ON SELF-HELP

As in most other Western countries, including the United States, the self-help sector has been fostered by academic teaching and research centers (Waterplas, Branckaerts, & Nuyens, 1981). By discussing the phenomenon, presenting research findings, and even openly promoting the idea of self-help, certain segments of universities have contributed to its public constitution.

The Division for Medical Sociology of the Catholic University of Leuven has carried out and coordinated the self-help research in Flanders (Branckaerts, 1982b). In presenting the research projects, particular reference will be made to the findings concerning the relationship between self-help and professionals.

In collaboration with the Academic Psychiatric Center, Sint-Kamillus, two projects were carried out on specific self-help groups.

Similes

The first one involved families of psychiatric patients, who have organized themselves into a national federation known as Similes (Branckaerts, et al., 1981). The aim was to explore the self-help functions performed by this federation and by its local groups, to characterize the members, and to determine the relationship between the self-help groups and the hospitals with which they collaborate and/or compete.

One of the conclusions that emerged was that ward nurses and social workers in psychiatric hospitals play an important role in referring potential members to Similes groups and are crucial in the groups' efforts to expand their membership. A constraining factor in the contact between groups and ward personnel is the high turnover of the nurses, who are therefore hardly able to get to know the patients and the patients' families. Still another component of the groups' policy constrained the relationship: The groups usually establish firm relations with the directors of the hospitals and with the psychiatrists. While they might be in favor of the ideas of the self-help groups, they don't have to deal with the consequences. The debate on the more individualized approach to the patient, wanted by the families, versus the more universalistic approach, wanted by the nurses, influences in its implementation the professional behavior of the nurses and social workers and not of the directors and psychiatrists. Therefore, although the top was in favor of self-help, the bottom rejected the idea because it presented a threat to their professional way of working. Consequently they refused to inform families of patients about the existence of a self-help group.

As a result of the research project, the self-help group started to promote its image to a greater extent among nurses and social workers, emphasizing the potential advantages of collaboration.

Huntington's League

The second project involves the Belgian Branch of Huntington's League, an international organization of self-help groups for sufferers of Huntington's chorea and their families. Huntington's Disease (HD) is a devastating hereditary disease that causes progressive deterioration of mind and body and eventually results in death. It is difficult to diagnose, and no cure or predictive test is available at this time.

The aim of the project is to encourage prevention of HD based on empirical data on the psychological and social consequences of the disease as perceived by sufferers and by persons at risk. The preventive programs will be implemented by the self-help groups. Therefore, part of the research concentrated on the organization and functioning of these groups (Branckaerts, 1982a).

These groups are remarkable in that they collaborate closely with professionals. This close collaboration is based not only on goodwill but also on bare necessity. The afflicted depend on the medical professionals for palliative care, hospitalization, and eventual detection and development of a treatment. On the other hand, medical doctors who want to do scientific research on HD need a population for experiments to develop predictive tests and test new medications. Huntington's patients and those at risk are eager to participate in these medical experiments, since their success might result in the solution of the problem. This mutually beneficial relationship between laypersons and professionals does not, of course, preclude the existence of humanitarian motives on the side of the professionals. They understand that until there is a definite cure, daily care for the patient is crucial.

The groups are remarkable in still another way. In the literature on self-help a controversy exists about whether groups are started by laypersons or by professionals. The American Committee to Combat Huntington's Disease was clearly a lay initiative. The idea was taken over by a professional who introduced this lay initiative in Flanders and stimulated Flemish laypersons to do the same.

A Study of Self-Help in Flanders

A third research project was commissioned and funded by the Flemish government and carried out by the Sociological Research Institute. The aim of the project was to clarify the concept of self-help, to identify and study existing self-help organizations and groups in Flanders, and to present models for potential government policy, based on the experiences of foreign countries and on the recommendations of supranational (EEC) and international (WHO) organizations (Waterplas et al., 1981). During the first year, eighteen major self-help organizations were studied; the local self-help groups are currently being interviewed. Again, it is impossible to summarize the findings, but concerning the relation between professionals and self-help, the following observations, based on a gross cross-sectional analysis, can be presented.

As to the initiation of the organizations, the findings show that they are initiated as often by professionals as by laypersons concerned with the problem. But in each case, collaboration between both parties involved started soon after the take-off. All organizations mention referral by professionals as the primary source of new members—to a lesser degree, publicity by newspapers and, least important, their own advertising.

Professionals are also important in the functioning of the organizations. A large majority (70 percent) incorporated in their structures special commissions, staffed by professionals relevant to the concerned problem and aimed at providing medical, legal, social, or spiritual advice. The same percentage of organizations (70 percent) did not have paid staff; in the minority that did, they were underpaid or employed in one of the government's programs to provide jobs for the unemployed. Secretarial skills were preferred for possible future staff members in almost half of the studied organizations. In only one case each were general social work and group therapy mentioned.

All of the organizations have permanent contacts with other institutions and organizations of the health and welfare sector. Organizations for specific illnesses tend to establish more—and consequently more varied—contacts than others. In general, however, for all the organizations the hospital sector seems to be most contacted by self-help organizations—significantly more than primary health care centers or other voluntary organizations.

Another remarkable finding is that about half of the organizations expect support from professionals. They plead for more scientific research on their specific conditions in order to establish new therapies and for more advice and practical information from professionals like physicans and lawyers.

The picture that emerged from the total analysis of the data was clearly not that of the professional as "enemy number one" of the self-help organizations. On the contrary, except for those organizations, like Alcoholics Anonymous, who insist on their autonomy, the majority of organizations present themselves as complementary rather than as competitive. One should keep in mind, however, that there are different professions and in each profession different subgroups with completely different attitudes.

In conclusion, it might be noted that the Flemish research on self-help has in general presented a clearer and more nuanced picture of what self-help organizations and groups do. This has contributed to the acceptance of the self-help idea by the government, the professional world, and the public.

NATIONAL AND REGIONAL POLICIES
TOWARD SELF-HELP

The Belgian Constitution of 1831 established a parliamentary monarchy, which prevails. As in most other European countries, there are numerous political parties. The three most important correspond to the three main pillars: Christian-Democrats, Socialists, and Liberals. The first stands for personalism and solidarity, the second, for humanism and collectivism, and the third, for individualism and free enterprise. (It might be confusing to interpret "liberals" the same way as in the United States, where they are considered to be more or less progressive. In Belgium, on the contrary, the Liberal Party is a right-wing formation considered to be rather conservative.)

The Belgian political situation is at present clouded by the fact that the country is in the process of federalization. As a result, there is a lot of conflict in the authority and jurisdiction of government at various levels. For cultural affairs, Belgian government institutions currently center on two communities: Dutch-speaking and French-speaking. For economic matters, on the other hand, three divisions are planned: Flemish, Walloon, and Bruxellois. Until the economic arrangements are clarified, however, regional, cultural, and related matters cannot be fully delineated. Even then it will be hard to determine what kind of problem is under the authority of what kind of government.

In addition, partly because of lack of general agreement on these administrative issues, Belgium has undergone several changes of government in the past years. Consequently, different national policies toward health care have been enunciated. It is unnecessary to list the various coalitions between Christian Democrats, Socialists, Conservative Liberals, and French and Flemish language parties that gave rise to the different administrations. Suffice it to say that one administration supported self-care as part of cultural policy and that, after a confused situation, the next administration promoted health education and advancement. This second administration neglected to mention self-care as part of health policy, while the following one considered family health care to be essential. The present administration—governing without the obligation to consult the Parliament—is trying to fight the economic crisis and for that reason concentrates on economic and monetary matters, ignoring health and welfare policies except for budget cutbacks. These shifts in government policy indicate that self-care and self-help are not yet clearly defined in government policy formulations and that the health and welfare sectors are considered to be minor policy problems.

This apparent confusion in government policy is reflected in already existing administrative organizations. Social work, for instance, falls within the jurisdiction of at least three ministries: Public Health, Culture, and Justice. Health care, on the other hand, is within the province of the ministries of Public Health, Social Security, National Education, and others. Besides the relative lack of coordination among ministries, a coherent government policy toward health and social care also suffers from the fact that such matters are additionally represented by a number of powerful interest groups that the government must also take into account—for example, the sick funds, representing the patients, and "trade unions" of physicians, representing the professional and financial interests of specialists and general practitioners. Nonetheless, the Belgian government does have certain agencies that promote self-help. Within the Ministry of Public Health, there is a section for social medicine, which currently funds various organizations that could be termed as self-help groups. In the Ministry of Culture, groups that could be identified as "self-help" are funded as organizations for community development for special categories.

From all this, it is clear that self-help is not a distinct category in national and regional policy planning. However, the government has shown interest in the work such groups perform by subsidizing some of them and by supporting further research. Currently, it is providing financial support to the three projects on self-help research described in this chapter. It should be added that these projects have been coordinated through the efforts of interested university researchers.

As a consequence of this coordination, the research center has expanded to perform clearinghouse functions. The collaboration between the two research directors of the projects has also enabled the identification of policymakers and politicians who want to be responsible for self-help groups and lay self-care. The Regional Ministry for Welfare, which subsidized two of the three research projects, has accepted this responsibility. The Minister herself has already made statements in favor of self-help groups in public and is willing to develop a self-help policy.

During a conference organized in mid-1982 by a self-help group for women with mastectomies, the Minister announced the organization of a meeting on self-help in Flanders by her administration. She also commissioned the Leuven research institute to start a clearinghouse for self-help groups before the end of 1982.

However, a lack of clarity remains. Since groups deal with physical, psychological, and social problems, they are not only in the reach of the welfare department. Shouldn't the Regional Ministry of Health be involved? An answer to this question was recently elicited during the above-mentioned study day on self-help and primary health care in Alken, Limburg. There the Minister of Health was questioned about his intentions. He assured the group that his administration would implement primary health care as a priority, stressed the necessity to adapt the whole health care sector to the needs of the population, and supported the idea of individual self-care or self-help. The still powerful national government was defined as the major obstacle in the realization of these intentions.

To understand the consequences of these declarations, one must note that the Flemish government is a coalition of all the Flemish political parties. The Minister of Welfare is a Christian-Democrat, while the Minister of Health is a Socialist. Apparently they have divided the self-help sector by attributing self-help groups to the welfare department, while individual self-care is considered to be in the jurisdiction of the health department. To complicate matters even further, the national government is—for the time being—a coalition between Christian-Democrats and Liberals. As a result, a comprehensive and integrated self-help policy is not to be expected.

Besides national and regional governments, Belgian citizens also have provincial and local governments (community councils). Although the provincial governments in Belgium have some responsibilities toward health care, they are confined largely to giving small grants to selected groups. Local governments also give small grants to groups, but they deal with social and health care only indirectly, through public centers for social work, which are semi-official service organizations. An exploratory survey in the Leuven area has shown that most local self-help groups have contact with these public centers for social work.

In sum, then, government policies toward self-help are developed in a divided and confused way. On the most influential regional level there is a tendency to favor self-help groups and to foster individual self-care.

REFERENCES

Branckaerts, J. *Voorlopige inventaris van zelfhulpgroepen in Vlaanderen.* Leuven: Sociologisch Onderzoeksinstituut, 1980.

Branckaerts, J. A case study in the collaboration between professionals and lays in a self-help group: The Belgian Huntington League. In S. Hatch & I. Kickbush (Eds.), *Self-help and health.* Copenhagen: World Health Organization, 1982. (a)

Branckaerts, J. Self-help and research. In S. Hatch & I. Kickbush (Eds.), *Self-help and health.* Copenhagen: World Health Organization, 1982. (b)

Branckaerts, J., Kuypers, E., & van den Meersche, J. *Similes: Zelfhulpgroepen in de Geestelijke Gezondheidszorg.* Heverlee: Groeneweg 151, 1981.

Cerruti, M. Belgium–The nation divisible. *National Geographic,* March 1979, 316-340.

Fox, R. Why Belgium? *European Journal of Sociology,* 1978, *19,* 205-228.

Ministerie van Economische Zaken. *Statistisch overzicht van België.* Brussels: Nationaal Instituut voor de Statistiek, 1981.

Nationaal Project in de Sociale Wetenschappen. *Eerstelijnsgezondheidszorg* (8 vols.). Brussels: Ministerie voor Wetenschapsbeleid, 1979.

Nuyens, Y. (Ed.). Sectie D: Zelfhulp. In *De Welzijnsgids.* Antwerpen: Van Loghum Slaterus, 1979.

Nuyens, Y. *Health care in Belgium.* Leuven: Sociological Research Institute, 1980.

Roemer, R., & Roemer, M. *Health manpower policies in the Belgium health care system.* Washington, DC: U.S. Department of Health, Education, and Welfare, 1977.

Thurlings, J. *De wankele zuil: Nederlandse katholieken tussen assimilatie en pluralisme.* Deventer: Dekker en Van de Vegt, 1978.

Van Harberden, P., & Lafaille, R. (Eds.). *Zelfhulp: Een nieuwe vorm van hulpverlenen?* The Hague: Vuga, 1978.

Waterplas, L., Branckaerts, J., & Nuyens, Y. *Zelfhulporganisaties in Vlaanderen.* Leuven: Sociologisch Onderzoeksinstituut, 1981.

8

SELF-HELP
Wolf or Lamb?

BERT BAKKER and MATTIEU KAREL
The Netherlands

During the 1950s, everyone in the Netherlands was preoccupied with postwar reconstruction. In the 1960s, the welfare state, as it is now known, was formed. In the 1970s a reexamination of its underlying values occurred, caused in part by the 1974 oil crisis and the subsequent economic decline. During this period the first signs of stagnation and crisis were to be perceived, not only with regard to economic developments, but also in the functioning of the welfare state and overloading of the welfare system. It is against this background that the development of self-help groups should be seen, in recognition that the modern "providing" state cannot solve all our problems. Even if health care and other welfare services were universally provided, problems would remain.

The Dutch welfare state has virtually reached the limit of its possibilities. Further improvement can be only qualitative, and more room must be made for parallel helping systems such as self-help. In this chapter, we shall first review the phenomenon of self-help in general, then assess the impact of self-help on society, and finally discuss the role of the professional in these developments and the implications of self-help for existing provisions in welfare work and health care. The major question we will be discussing in this chapter is: Under what conditions can professionals in welfare work and health care support self-help in the population and the work of self-help groups? We shall go beyond the Dutch situation to explain some general principles for dealing with self-help as a professional.

DEVELOPMENT AND MAJOR CHARACTERISTICS OF
SELF-HELP IN DUTCH SOCIETY

In the modern welfare state all sorts of provisions have been made for those who are in trouble. An elaborate system of services to which the citizen can turn is statutorily guaranteed in case of unemployment, illness, poverty, widowhood, old age, or disability. However, all these services have not solved all human problems. On the contrary, they are in some respects the source of new problems. In the past few years, more and more developments point to an increasing emancipation of people from dependency on the Welfare State. Squatters take matters in their own hands in their search for living accommodations. Self-help groups are organized around physical health problems, such as mastectomy, or mental health problems, such as loss of a loved one and ensuing grief, to enable people to take charge of their own recovery. Men's and women's groups have arisen to explore new social roles and norms. These new provisions have taken concrete form in the appearance of information centers, meeting places, and facilitative services.

Development

In Dutch society in the early 1970s, many new small groups developed, people joining hands to cope with particular problems: because they suffered from an unfamiliar disease, because they were the parents of a handicapped child, or because they felt alienated from society. However, one can observe an underlying historical pattern in all these scattered public initiatives. Some organizations concerned with particular problems (such as deafness or blindness) have actually existed since the previous century. The long-established character of these groups, aimed at promoting the interests of their members, is changing slightly now because of the appearance of the new self-help groups. Increasingly, these older voluntary organizations are also using the term "self-help" to describe their activities or their character.

It is interesting to note that these self-formed groups are active in all parts of the welfare state: in health care and social assistance, in the educational sector, and in the field of social security and housing (see Kagie, 1979; Wolffers, 1978). By setting up their own services, the users of these facilities implicitly criticize how the welfare state is organized, although they do not reject the welfare state itself. In the largest sense, the protest is really directed toward the way problems and suffering are created for individuals in society, both in institutional settings and in private life.

General Contours

Most national self-help organizations are relatively young, having developed mostly in the period 1974-1976 (Bakker, Karel, den Ambtman, & Meyer, 1981; Bakker & Karel, 1980). The groups are situated mainly in the conurbation area in the western part of the country and are typically called foundations, associations, or unions. Membership appears to range from several hundreds to thousands of people, sometimes even considerably more. Commonly there are several dozen local branches; less typically, more than a hundred.

Self-help groups do not usually arise out of reaction or resistance to professional workers in health care or welfare work. In some instances government policy has actually initiated the organization—for example, by recognizing the lack of statutory provisions or by the publication of an official report in connection with a particular problem. Some groups are formed around well-recognized problems; others identify new needs. Some groups are formed by people who are dissatisfied with certain arrangements or institutions and aim to bring about alterations.

The objectives of the organizations (often formulated in rather general terms) are directed toward the physical and spiritual well-being of the members. This is given concrete form in tasks like advocacy and the acquisition of facilities. Attempts are also made to provide mutual support through services, companionship, advocacy, training, and information. Frequently, goals of emancipation, integration within society, or self-improvement are also mentioned. Occasionally, purposes such as overcoming the repression sensed in the environment or the rejection of a particular condition by society are mentioned.

Several descriptions and definitions of self-help organizations are current. However, we do not believe in an overexact, one-sided attempt to fasten down the context of this notion. Instead, we prefer to show different aspects in the Dutch situation. "Self-help" should be regarded as an open concept that can be applied in different ways. A good approach to an "open" description is to describe the dynamic meaning of the group for the members who are the direct users of the term. Thus described, the self-help group is often fitted to the local circumstances and to the problem around which people gather, with great variations among groups.

The volume of self-help in the Netherlands can be only roughly indicated. There are several indications that among a particular group (for instance, all disabled people in a certain region or all people in a town quarter who have a certain problem), about 10 to 15 percent participate in a self-help group. This implies a high degree of organization per problem group, although that in itself says little. Most of these people are probably also receiving help from other sources. Naturally, friends can also give their support and it is possible to combine with other aid and care systems, such as the general practitioner for medication.

However, unfamiliarity with self-help is still widespread. Since involvement is to some extent dependent on initial chance contact, the potential membership of self-help groups may be larger still. It is striking to note, however, that in the United States, where there is quite a different social and care infrastructure then in the Dutch welfare state, the same figures are given for participation in self-help groups. The duration of support in self-help groups is often much longer than would be possible in professional institutions. The added contribution of self-help groups forms a parallel structure to the formal welfare and health care systems.

For the remainder of this chapter, we will define self-help as all the activities of an organized group of people who have a similar problem and who collectively use resources from their own group and from their surroundings to improve their situation or solve their problem.

Silent Mobilization

Through the activities of self-help, as it has been described above, a "silent mobilization" has taken place in the Dutch population among groups concerned with particular problems or situations. Participants have been progressively enriching their own experiences and insights, and, at least possibly, having an increasing influence on the environment. The effects self-help groups would have on institutions, individuals, and professionals were unforeseen and are gradually increasing. Self-help groups work in "silence"; they are always fragmented and they do not launch large or expensive campaigns. But this "silent mobilization" has effected a number of changes in the attitudes toward personal problem solving, of which we will discuss three.

The first change is one of values, for a different way of experiencing problems and situations requires different interpretations. The impulse to seek a self-help solution can also be formulated as a step toward new values, once the principle of mobilization has been recognized—as a step toward a new ideology, toward changes in the concepts of reciprocity, friendship, kinship, and the like. This may even be regarded as a step toward an alternative culture or counterculture. The transition of individuals to a meaningful environment with a new pattern of values has been described as the development of "fixed communities of belief" and "systems of meaning" (Antze, 1979).

The second change is one of finding different ways of solving problems, since inadequate existing services are one of the conditions that promote self-help. For the individual, new provisions such as self-help must add something extra. To its members, a self-help group is not only a new *Gemeinschaft* but also a means to exert pressure on the environment. In addition, the groups make the process of redefining problems easier, often by choosing the paradox approach—for example, "fat is beautiful" in the Suzy Orbach groups, and "you will remain an alcoholic all your life" as a member of Alcoholics Anonymous. Such perceptions are formed or reformulated as members share their experiences in the group. Here, also, a process of emancipation or politicization may set in. Sometimes the environment responds quickly and favorably to the new initiative, but often enough the group may desire to work toward more understanding, influence, or room to move in its development.

The last change is one of temporal priority: Do it now; do not wait until later and do not wait for others. Part of the reason for the initiation of a self-help group is often to make changes in the way existing services are provided. In their desire to see quick results, the groups may force something and short-circuit existing provisions before they have the required knowledge and skills. However, group members exhibit the facility to learn quickly in new situations.

THE UNDERLYING MEANING AND
MOTIVATION FOR SELF-HELP

On the basis of a great many structured conversations with members of self-help groups, we have derived their connotations of the term "self-help." In their descriptions an associative network arises, in which the connection between existing provisions and self-created provisions is particularly stressed.

The themes that come up in analyzing this material fall into three areas (Bakker & Karel, 1980). The first three themes are related to desired changes in personal relationships: compensating for the modern scarcity of primary relationships, emphasizing reciprocal relationships, and developing a new base for sociability. Three additional themes concern institutional change of either a complementary or corrective nature: Completion of existing provisions of the welfare state, changing the way services are delivered, and influencing society and the environment are all ways in which self-help is influencing the institutional framework of society. Finally, there are the themes of social and political liberation: emancipation, interest promotion, and autonomy, all representing self-help as a liberating force in relation to social and political ideologies in society.

Changing Personal Relationships

Self-help groups are a partial substitution for such vanishing social structures as the extended family, the small village community, or the familiar town quarter. However, this modern adaptation replaces the old solidarity in living, life, and work only to a certain extent. The group lifts the individual who has a certain problem out of his or her isolation and thus brings something new to a deadlocked situation. Being a fellow sufferer, one feels allied with others who are in a similar condition. The group becomes a sounding board for private feelings and experiences, and it offers unexpected possibilities for daily support. In this way, self-help groups form a new, long-lasting support system replacing other, failing ways of finding support in life. It is not necessary to participate intensely; passive membership is sometimes enough to provide support.

Self-help groups also emphasize the recovery of reciprocity in interpersonal relationships. People must be able to provide effective assistance and support to one another on the basis of their common humanity. Thus, fellow sufferers in groups bring about a paradoxical solution. People who used to feel excluded from the social norms of reciprocity in society, since they were experiencing their problem alone, are freed from their isolation by the contact with fellow sufferers—their isolation is replaced by the security of the group.

Self-help groups are born not only of need and helplessness; there is also a very positive element in self-help. They stress reciprocity, something that nowadays seems to be lacking in day-to-day relationships among people. Through self-help people successfully enter into new situations as well as come to terms subjectively with the problem or deficit. By establishing a group identity, the reciprocity with society is restored, too. In addition to individual support, there is improvement for the group as a whole (see Antze, 1979).

Self-help groups are a clear example of the emergence in society of a new sociability built on situations, and problems. There is a quiet growth of these sorts of groups in the direction of an exclusive subculture. Alongside the whole structure of existing official welfare and health facilities. a new parallel infrastructure of self-formed groups and support systems is showing up.

The building of a network through self-organization is an approved and still effective weapon for powerless and suppressed minorities. What is new is the flexibility in the forms such organizations take and the proliferation of supporting activities: newsletters, clearinghouses, workshops, and so on. In the Netherlands, one of the currently most successful examples is the squatting movement, which, despite a rather loose organizational form, is able to mobilize large numbers of people. The feminist movement, too, has woven a fine fabric of activities, groups, houses, and pubs over the Netherlands. In many ways an activist society is revealing itself which, unlike that of former times, is organized into new networks in order to promote various interests, independent of existing provisions.

Changing Institutions

The social map of service provisions still exhibits unexpected blank spaces. Self-help groups plainly fill a number of these. People organize themselves around problems that are scarcely or not at all recognized by the existing institutions of social service. With respect to those facilities that are obviously lacking in the existing care frameworks, they form their own, additional provisions. In this case, self-help has not only a complementary but also an exploring and identifying function.

The self-help group acts as an advance post in the field of welfare work and health care. This is not strange, since the extension of welfare facilities is often attended by institutionalization and bureaucratization. Due to the resulting stiffness and slowness, welfare facilities are often behind social developments. Self-help groups, on the contrary, are still unrestricted in their potential to contrive and test new solutions to a problem or to develop a new social institution. The self-help group forms a flexible unit that can freely choose from the available alternatives. Widely divergent methods are developed for each group and problem.

Self-help groups also want to have more influence on the structure of existing welfare facilities and health care. They want to deal with the working methods of professionals and their institutions and with the effects of institutionalization and bureaucratization, which are felt to be damaging. The self-help group also strives for a different definition of the position of the individual client or patient—for instance, by fighting for better legal status, the right to complain, or participation in the treatment process. One way to achieve these goals is to gain access to professional workers and medical specialists. For the professionals, this means that they must react to the wishes and rights of groups of clients. In the long run, this may develop into a reorientation of the professionals, if these groups are truly acknowledged.

Thus, self-help forms not only an addition to but also a correction of existing services. A new form of control by users, external to the system, has arisen. Self-help groups have the potential to correct the "sick-making" side effects of health care (Illich, 1980). One could extend this observation and assert that the contours of a countermovement are possibly emerging. In any case, a more two-sided situation will arise instead of the usual one-sided influence of services on the individual.

Self-help groups also search for ways of influencing society as a whole and its treatment of individuals, which is often felt to be repressive. The groups seek to influence social norms and social practices. They oppose, among other things, stigmatization and societal oppression, which can be observed at present toward women, psychiatric patients, homosexuals, and children. Self-organized groups of immigrants try to find support among themselves against the norms of the dominating Western society.

The actions of the groups can be directed outwardly toward their rejection by society through the search for influence on the behavior of professionals and the functions of welfare institutions, but they can be aimed at the direct environment as well, such as the family or the different relationships arising from work or leisure. The groups attempt to bring about real changes in their own living environments instead of only minor adaptions of perception. This division recurs in the activities of the groups. On the one hand, they provide for mutual support and information. On the other, they also make demands, sometimes stridently. Then the role of the mass media can be of decisive importance for the success of the group's efforts.

Social/Political Liberation

Self-help groups strive for emancipation. They try to get more control over their own situation, both as a group and as individuals. Often the groups are part of a wider movement, as are women's groups, for instance.

In all sorts of experiential groups, long conversations are carried on about personal situations. This is unusual in most people's life experience and may give rise to a new, coherent vision of the various difficulties one has experienced.

Sometimes self-help groups broach subjects and taboos to which society is still rather sensitive, such as sexual intercourse with children, transvestism, sadomasochism, euthanasia, and suicide. Through discussions that are originally private, a group can transform a subject of taboo into one of public discussion. Occasionally this is attended by demands for social change. In the first place, a rejection of the existing social situation takes place. Then the individual's own expectations are reinterpreted in the group and a new, more significant meaning is given to the private reality. This is expressed in the creation of a new terminology and in a sensation of joint problem sharing. It is a dilemma for the group, though, that as soon as its ends are achieved, it must change its structure and purpose.

Through self-organization, self-help groups also create "interest promotion." Together, people are stronger. If they find that statutory regulations have to be enacted or altered, they are able to exert specific pressure on the national or regional authorities. Interest groups are playing an ever greater part in society. As the welfare state is nearing its completion, it appears that at the same time many different kinds of groups feel wronged. Direct promotion of interests is a way of short-circuiting legal proceedings, which are seen as too lengthy or prolix. However, the limitations on how much pressure can be exerted, in relation to democratic principles, are, as yet, not clear-cut. May we speak of "civil resistance" as well as the already accepted "civil disobedience"?

The large-scale character of our society appears not only in matters such as industry or provision of energy, but also in the social services. The groups that we have defined so far as self-help groups are all part of a movement that strives for smaller-scale and more humanistic techniques. Clearly allied with this movement are the efforts toward worker control of job situations in experimental workshops and factories (see Kagie, 1979). But there are also experiments with living situations—for instance, with handicapped people, who are trying to live independently. Thus, different social structures are sought in order to give assistance in problem situations (see Young and Rigge, 1979).

A transition takes place in which self-help changes from a temporary provision to a social attainment. Self-help groups do more than reveal an unacknowledged need. They offer solutions the professional worker cannot (or can no longer) give.

The total structure of self-help and similar activities is perhaps best described as an "exploratory movement," that is, searching for new possibilities, different structures, and the mutual connection of all these different activities. In our opinion, it is not yet possible to predict what the ultimate effect will be. The direction is clear, however: Provisions that are set up and directed by the people themselves, and function as an addition to and at least partial replacement of tasks that are now still performed by professionals, will remain and probably expand.

OPPORTUNITIES FOR PROFESSIONALS

We shall first describe two well-known types of self-help organizations: one for parents and one for patients.

Two Examples

Parents' organizations often aim to affect provisions for care of their children through discussions with professionals. Usually the members are fellow sufferers, although other family members and friends are sometimes involved. Some parents' organizations have widened their membership to include professionals, sympathizers, or the general public. Sometimes they apply directly to governmental authorities, seeking changes in the law or an administrative revision.

All of this may be supported by private publications such as newsletters, brochures, or pamphlets, and occasionally there is a documentation center. The activities undertaken depend on the facilities and strategies mentioned above. Among these activities are publicity services, giving advice to the authorities, arranging regional social days, and creating debating clubs. There are hadly ever any hired experts or staff (such as psychologists or educational workers). Members work under their own steam and on the basis of their experiences (Borkman, 1976). Sometimes an official institution is enlisted for administration, but such work is done mostly by volunteers from the organization, schooled or not.

The patient organization, on the other hand, often works with an advisory board on which medical personnel serve. This is not only useful for getting information, but also essential in order to have access to the closed world of health care. Occasionally, organizations have engaged professionals for a task like facilitating or setting up discussion groups. As regards finances, expenses are nearly always covered by the contributions of the members themselves. There are sometimes donations or bequests, but subsidy is hardly ever mentioned by the groups we researched (Bakker

& Karel, 1980). As for future plans, most groups want to bring about an expansion of their services to include such things as a telephone complaint line or a job-finding service.

What do we see from these examples? Self-help organizations maintain a carefully studied relationship with professionals in their environment. As a parent, one tries to keep contact with the professional who cares for one's child because one feels dependent on that person. Often we see what we call a selective resistance to professionals: One has a strong opinion about only those professionals with which one is confronted. People are also often very happy with a professional who did something very good or gave a helpful solution or a correct diagnosis. Such a professional can become a charismatic leader. In medical situations, the dependence of people is even stronger. They are uncertain and have to use "good" professionals even to gain entrance into this professional bastion. Hence, we have observed different reactions of self-help organizations to professionals. The guidelines depend on the particular circumstances.

What do people want from professionals? Because professionals are paid for their services, people expect them to do their work well. They feel they have a right to optimal professional support in a welfare state. Born in part of necessity—of the shortcomings of professionals—self-help groups want to be taken seriously by professionals, acknowledged as a valid natural helping system and allowed routine contact with the professional systems via such mechanisms as referrals back and forth.

The participants in self-help groups feel acutely the lack of reciprocity with professional workers. They feel objectified or made into a part of the problem that is to be treated. Self-help counters the social estrangement that results from the one-sided, individualized approach of the professionals.

Self-help organizations try to work on their own, so they first try to use the professional expertise among their own members. Furthermore, they try to maintain good relationships with some "good" professionals, who function to interface with the whole profession. They are also strongly aware of the power of professionals and try to influence them by giving information to them about their own situations. But professionals also initiate interactions with self-help groups, of which we will give some examples, mostly drawn from the Dutch situation.

Some Practices of Professionals

It is clear from the foregoing that self-help organizations, while they do indeed have a particular character, are similar in many ways to many other voluntary organizations. The magical qualities sometimes ascribed to them and the closed defensiveness they are thought to display to outsiders are largely the myths and folklore of the outsiders themselves.

A striking aspect of studies of actual practices is that several types of links have been made between professional welfare, self-help, and self-directed groups. From these connections new qualities arise. In cooperation with professional workers we have written a book on these experiences and findings (Bakker & Karel, 1979), of which we will give some instances here.

A refined and structured model of connections within the health care field has been developed by Bremer-Schulte (1979). She tries to effect a new balance between patient as caretaker and professional worker as caregiver by forming pairs, both of whom act as leaders for the groups, and by giving special training to the persons involved. Gradually, professional interference decreases as patient leaders develop. In her approach, Bremer-Schulte takes into account not only effects at the group level but also those at the institutional and societal level. She warns that integration of new features can evoke new tensions and also that, with projects of this sort, it is important not to neglect contacts with authorities, institutions, and colleagues and focus exclusively on the problem group.

Medaer, Gijbels, and Jansen-Lowet (1979) have developed a kind of self-help method that can be employed by professionals with patients suffering from multiple sclerosis as a meaningful revitalization of existing clinical care. As a liberating new force, the group is likely to agitate for better treatment.

Working step by step with psychiatric patients, Sanders (1979) is building up a new supporting system in a "lodge," which is gradually withdrawing from the institutional orbit of a mental hospital (see also Fairweather, 1980). Here, professional assistance must be redefined. Skills are transmitted to the residents, and they are fitted into their new roles in the lodge, which becomes a network and living community. With this program, both a new link to the community and an institutional innovation are achieved. Within the residential groups new rules can be established for dealing with deviant behavior. Thus, agreement among the patients as to whether someone is hallucinating or not is more important than professional diagnosis.

In the case of a psychotherapeutic advice service for German students, we see that initiating, training, and then stepping back from a self-directed group creates a new support system that relieves an overcrowded professional agency (Trojen, 1977). The role of the professional worker is gradually restricted to consultation and presiding at a forum that brings all the groups together.

A more far-reaching project with students and ex-psychiatric patients has been started by Von Schuckmann at the University of Leiden. She has developed a step-by-step model of connections that can be completely transferred to independent discussion groups once it has fully matured. Professional support takes the form of starting, describing, and testing different models of groups. A guide is available to groups with a common problem, based on the thematic interaction model of Cohn (1976).

Rieuwers (1979) supplies context-free, programmed instructions to teach social skills to any group. The program is similar to language courses on records. The advantage of this approach is that it is suited to groups that otherwise would not readily approach a psychologist. Instead of a leader, there is now a tape recorder, which the members can employ in any way they desire. Knowledge is transmitted about basic communication skills without being tied to a particular problem.

A necessary adjunct for problems professional services cannot fully address is provided by mastectomy groups, among others. The personal experience of such a problem can only be understood and felt well enough by fellow sufferers. From the analysis by DeBruyn (1979), though, it is clear that a link between fellowsufferers' groups and professional aid is necessary. DeBruyn argues that volunteers to lead the groups should be carefully recruited and trained, and she calls for further structuring and recognition of such groups within the health care system.

In a new professional field such as prevention work which, in the Netherlands, is hardly institutionalized, there are other opportunities to forge links among forms of assistance. Problems and attempts to arrive at independent support for problem groups are described both by Römer (1979) and Kaay and Verburg (1979).

Since the 1960s, alternative forms of assistance for youth have been a force for change in services to this difficult population. Hageboud (1979) describes a self-help method with professional assistance as one of the first steps in a much longer process aimed at independence for this group. Although runaways already receive help from child welfare agencies, a different professional institutional system has organized an aid system of its own. Thus, self-help appears in the formal system in one place as a compensation for defects elsewhere in the system.

Van de Sanden (1979), dealing with primary health care in a "health store" (Van Dijk, 1978), aims at the construction of a local network of support groups and at improving the cooperation among the various professional disciplines at the store.

As a last example, despite the innovations in the Dutch second-chance educational system for adults, self-help groups have also arisen in this area. Right after the Open School was created by the government, independent, spontaneous open school groups arose, visited mostly by housewives. They are more like self-help groups than schools, and they maintain contacts with professionals. This is an example of how, within new professional groups, possibilities arise for further emancipation of neglected groups in society, such as women and working youth (see Defilte and van Riet-schoten, 1979).

In all these instances, professionals have put their short-term activities temporarily at the service of long-term forms of support for people who are in a situation they want to change. Thus, the professionals integrate different elements of their practice into new, significant forms of welfare facilities. The idea of self-help plays an important part in these developments.

Principles

In the relationship between self-help and professionals we see the contact between two different support systems. Various options are open to them: to ignore, quarrel, refer, cooperate, or even to meld together. Also, principles belonging to the methods of one system can be used in the other system.

We view self-help/professional cooperation experiments as subsystems, belonging in part to both main systems. Such subsystems can satisfy quite different needs because they are relatively independent of the main systems. In these subsystems the relationship between self-help and professionals is one of equality, respecting the special opportunities of each. Other important criteria for the relationship are the educative, interactive, and integrative aspects of such a subsystem.

Professionals have to get used to working with a system that aims to provide long-term support—one that does not focus on immediate cures or improvement and sometimes works in a shabby or amateurish way. Professionals are usually directed toward motivating the client, rapid change, and short-term involvement. Self-help is directed toward experience, learning by doing, and mutuality. Often change is not the goal so much as support in a grieving process or adapting to new life circumstances. Professionals tend to influence self-help by giving professional notions such as "improvement in functioning" or "social support" or "screening of new members." However, in practice the situation is often more complicated. The form the relationship between professionals and self-help should take cannot be prescribed in precise guidelines, but we can give general principles.

One of the basic mistakes is to get involved as a professional in the first-order problems of the group members, rather than to provide second-order assistance to help the group develop and maintain itself. The most important thing for the professional is to decide what the outcome or quality criteria will be for the contacts with self-help. As some important ones, we suggest the following. The groups should ultimately become self-supporting, if they have been originally started by the professional, and a fixed date for this to occur should be set. Bargaining, negotiating, and working on the basis of a contract are essential elements for contacts between professionals and groups. The attitude of the professional should be to be at the disposal of the group, not to be its caretaker.

The professional should also make clear to the group his or her mixture of theories, working models, and policy options, as well as intentions. The knowledge and skills of the professional are resources to the group and have to be able to flow through him or her. This allows the independent functioning of the group. Group members are free to take over these skills. The professional should also be aware of the working models and practice developed by the group itself. An integrative working style implies an openness to mutual influence.

Activities of the professional must prevent individualization of the clients' problems. The sharing of experiences of other members ought to grow in importance. By using integrative methods, a consensus on the definition of the problem occurs for both professionals and group members, and this should not be divided again into subproblems by other professionals. For instance, psychosocial elements ought to be connected to physical problems and to societal situations. A consequence is less "patient behavior" and "patient compliance." "Clients" are able to use mutual help and, as group members, are less dependent on professionals. The central point in all these principles is that the professional has to be careful to avoid paternalistic control and supervision.

Other criteria for professionals develop out of the motives (relational, institutional, and liberational) mentioned above. Thus, for example, the new provisions should be complementary to existing institutions and compensate for shortages or gaps. They should be corrective and have an influence on these institutions, welfare work and health care, society and life environment. They should have elements of emancipation and social and political impact. Reciprocity and mutuality in the form of new, autonomous networks are final criteria.

It would help professionals who use this approach if they would define themselves as appropriately belonging in the background of self-help activities. The professional should maintain openness in relationships and tasks by using concepts that are amenable to modification by the groups with which they are working. The professional is only one of the users of a concept and should not insist on his or her own definition or let a particular interpretation become a barrier to group participation. Professionals must develop and use language that stays close to the people.

When using the framework of systems and intermediate connections mentioned above, the criteria involved should also be made explicit to both professionals and members. When using a concept, the professional should make some attempt to study its history and various connotations. When working with a group, the professional should give them information and get them involved in the performance of "professional" activities. It is useful to originate an "open" or "empty" intervention intentionally in order to support group members in their own insights.

In short, the professional needs a theoretical framework (which, for us, is the systems model) and some general principles for acting (which we call integrative methods).

IMPLICATIONS OF SELF-HELP
FOR EXISTING SERVICES

With regard to welfare services, several types of effects of self-help groups can be noted, which are partly a reaction to these services.

Changes in the Notion of Problems

Defining a problem is often left in the hands of a social worker, who legitimizes a complaint into a problem for which professional treatment is likely to arise. This may well lead to violation of natural, lay services (see Chabot, 1979). Professionals also create languages in which they can talk about the problems; thus, everyday troubles are made into problems, which they know how to handle. The problem descriptions in professional terms have a strong influence on society and on the public, as developments like psychotherapy indicate. The client easily adopts the vocabulary of the professional worker. This, however, is a serious problem, alienating the person from his own life.

In the professional form of assistance, the phenomenon of "fragmentation" arises. For different problems people are referred to different institutions. In the process, these persons' problems are broken apart into a number of partial problems; the situation is never dealt with as a whole.

Self-help groups start from a different perspective. From their own experience they know that a problem affects a person as a whole, and that this has an effect on the immediate environment. They are more concerned with the question of how the situation is experienced than with what caused it; sometimes the cause is even left completely aside. This means that they have a different, more complete, gestaltlike manner of approaching problems. This approach is clearly fostered by the groups. With this change of approach, changes in the use of language have occurred since self-help groups have come into existence. This is a significant development, because the experiences of people are related to their own, natural use of language. Thus, the obstacle of a complex professional translation can be avoided. Additionally, recognition by other people in similar situations is made easier, enabling individuals to come out of their isolation sooner.

A New Definition of the Professional Role

On the level of direct contact with professionals, a major question for self-help groups is how to involve professionals in such a way that they do not fully take over the new, self-formed aid system. A particular activity may be required from professionals, but they need not be in control of the assistance situation (an important distinction).

The activities of self-help groups serve to redefine the function of professionals in welfare and health care. It is no longer self-evident that a professional worker is the right person for support in a given situation. Others, such as the persons in question themselves, may be equally appropriate. This puts a different face on large parts of the welfare services, which have been brought into being with so much difficulty. Instead of improving or expanding these services, restriction in favor of self-provision is perhaps desirable.

A different relationship between client and social worker is clearly needed. In a discussion of the welfare state in practice, Van Doorn (1977, p. 7) says:

In fact the most desirable way is a redefinition of professionalism: a great restraint in offering services—and certainly no "marketing" of services—proceeding from less confidence in specialism and, particularly, in the benefits of the technically most developed remedies, and founded on the conviction that the relationship between professional and client ought to be truly "horizontal."

Professionals derive their status from their activities, but the clients have to surrender their independence to make that possible. There is no possibility of an equal relationship, even though social workers often state that they "learn so much from their clients." It is not easy to introduce improvements in the existing relationship of help seeker and help giver.

According to Bremer-Schulte, a new balance in health care should be sought, between professional worker and patient and between patients' associations and medical facilities. The protestations of the patients' associations makes the pendulum swing from medical domination to users' domination. Both parties, however, must learn a lesson from history and search for a new balance. Clients have expertise on the basis of their own experience of the problem; professionals have special supporting knowledge in the medical or welfare sphere.

We have already mentioned the development of self-directed groups in welfare services, which are one model for a new professional role (Bakker & Karel, 1979). These groups were started by professionals but later came to be independent. They are variants of the spontaneously formed self-help groups. In these self-directed groups, professional knowledge and skills can be passed on systematically. Also, in these groups a joining of short-term professional care and longer-lasting self-directed forms of support is achieved. The groups, in turn, influence the professionals through their experiences.

Innovations in Care

Self-help is a source of innovation in welfare work and health care. This comes about mainly via the professional variant of self-help mentioned above: the self-directed group. Here and there, ideas of self-help and self-care are being introduced into practice by professionals. In all probability, this trend will gain strength in the coming years.

Caution should be exercised, though, because various qualitative criteria are at stake with regard to the autonomy of the group and the interests of the users as well as to the content of the professional's work. Also, the essence of self-help can be threatened by too rapid or too risky a transplantation from self-help to professional methods (Van Harberden and Lafaille, 1978). An example of this is the propagation of so-called self-help techniques: professionals (particularly in the medical field) "prescribing" individual self-help techniques for their clients, losing sight of the essential distinction between the transmission of medical knowledge and the autonomy of the users.

Professionals in a number of different fields are looking for a new integration of activities. The reinforcement of the "front line" in health care (professionals who are available to the public without a referral, such as general practitioners or family doctors) is an instance of this. Self-help and self-organization can form a major source of inspiration in this search for integration. Self-help groups often give long-lasting support, but many times this long-term assistance is also required from the person's immediate environment.

The question is, then: In what way can short-term professional activities contribute to the construction of long-term support systems? Naturally, renewal of professional support is achieved in several ways. As far as self-help groups are concerned, the members, on the one hand, who are also users of professional services, draw the professionals' attention to the deficits and imperfections in their working methods and, on the other hand, call attention to the personal experience of the problem (as compared to an often far too technical and professional approach). Finally, these groups bring about improved contacts and referral possibilities. A one-sided emphasis on the antagonistic function of self-help distorts the truth (see Liebermann & Borman, 1979). Self-help groups and organizations of clients develop methods that are readily adoptable by professionals. From the feminist movement, for example, the so-called VOS courses (Housewives Focusing on Society) have been taken over by several professional institutions in the field of sociocultural work after being developed in and growing out of private homes. In the welfare and prevention sector, experiments take place with forms of group work assisted by laypersons, not professionals.

Shifts in Services

All of the preceding effects can have a great influence on existing service provisions. A restriction of professional provisions in favor of self-provisions has been mentioned. More far-reaching and sweeping changes can be effected if, through the rise of self-help, some of the existing services, which have been created by society on the basis of identified needs, prove to be redundant. Thus, we can see a shift from residential treatment in children's homes and mental hospitals to a more community-based sector of "intermediate provisions" in the form of independent living projects. Such a development may well result in progressively firmer control of clients and users of their environment, leading in turn to a decrease in staff tasks and more incidental or facilitative support of the self-help activities.

We present here an analysis drawn from our studies of changes in professional practices (see Bakker & Karel, 1980). Professional workers direct their attention more and more to configurations of problems rather than to individual problems. It is no longer established in advance what the professional's contribution will be to the solution of an identified problem. The activities of the worker have become dependent on the particular situation of the client and on the possibilities available to the problem group as a whole. From this point of view, old professional roles are no longer sufficient.

Increasingly, workers direct their attention to the relation between human beings and their environment. They take the line that different social support systems exist and that relations are possible among them. People find their way to spontaneous self-help groups or they can turn to professional workers. They may also turn to both at the same time. It appears that both professionals and citizens are taking this more and more into account.

There is a tendency to effect various links between different forms of support, as well as to bring about improvements in the separate systems. For instance, professionals can deliberately create a new means of support for a particular problem group by starting a self-help group. The purpose of this group, long-lasting support, goes beyond the possibilities of professional treatment.

In the so-called integrative approach to practical problems (Specht & Vickery, 1977), we may perceive similarities in the manner in which individuals, groups, families, and societies are approached. It is possible to draw parallels among interventions that are initiated on different levels, from local to institutional to national (see Leonard, 1976). Quite often forms of systems thinking are employed which have been used in family therapy, for example, for a long time.

With all the attempts at integration of theories and of different methods, the importance of a growing social consciousness of the client comes forward. Interventions aiming at the augmentation of this consciousness occupy an important place.

DISCUSSION

We have used a rather wide definition of self-help in order to show various aspects, reactions, and effects with respect to old and new service provisions because an open concept offers more inputs and points of view. Thus we have lingered on the connotations of the notion for the participants themselves.

With the formation of self-help groups, a new criticism can be observed of the provisions of the welfare state. Quality of care is much more at issue than it used to be. In the groups, people object to careless treatment, based on their own feelings and experience. Pinker (1971, 1979), in his analysis of social facilities as a system of exchange, states that any study of welfare situations should pay attention to the emotional aspects of human behavior. In the meantime, self-help organizations express their criticism explicitly. Criticism of provisions and professionals is not only heard from users. Critical comments can be gathered from a long list of publications (see, for example, the 1974 Knelpuntennota "Note on Bottlenecks in Welfare Work"). Van Doorn and Schuyt (1978) even speak of the stagnant welfare state.

The stagnation of the welfare state appears on different levels. Dutch authorities labor under legitimation problems and under too many demands; there are no good growth checks in their policy. Economic growth creates room for a more open-handed policy, but during recessions these possibilities shrivel up. The rather shortsighted theory seems to be that as long as there is money in the purse, we can talk about policy.

Professional institutions become more and more involuted. The organization increases in size but the output remains the same. External organizations, too, become a part of this involuntary process. It is said that many institutions function as "organized anarchies." During the past few years there has been a strong tendency toward increasing routinization and a proliferation of procedures in various welfare contexts. Democratization has not fared well in these developments. Existing provisions fail to meet the demands of the users.

The chief influence of self-help groups and organizations on existing services has been a process of conceptual innovation in notions of problems and the growth of the natural language. Welfare services are exposed to examination through the external control of users. Relations between clients and social workers are redefined in the direction of equality in rights and status, more input by the client, and a restriction of "expert" domination. Professionals appear to be recognizing this more and more. Possibly, these conceptual changes are causing structural modifications in welfare work and health care. But certainly this has not happened everywhere.

Criticism of provisions in the welfare state is not new and is really related to all levels of policy execution. Impersonal assistance to "strangers" produces even more complex relationship problems, for both users and providers. In self-help groups people appear to be able to find in themselves and each other the potential for true support, and that is no small advantage.

REFERENCES

Antze, P. The role of ideologies in peer psycho-therapy groups. In M. Lieberman & L. Borman (Eds.), *Self-help groups for coping with crisis.* San Francisco: Jossey-Bass, 1979.

Bakker, B., & Karel, M. (Eds.). *Zelfhulp en welzijnswerk: Ervaringen van professionals met zelfgeleide groepen.* Alphen aan den Rijn: Samsom, 1979.

Bakker, B., & Karel, M. Self-help groups and mutual aid in the Netherlands: A Survey Research. In B. Bakker, M. Karel, & I. Sewandono, *Vehicles in welfare achievement: Self-help, self-care and public care; three working papers.* Amsterdam: Inst. v. Wetenschapder Andragogie (Institute for the Science of Andragogy), University of Amsterdam, 1980.

Bakker, B., Karel, M., den Ambtman, P., & Meyer, F. (Eds.) *Zelfhulpgroepen, patienten-en belangen verenigingen, alternatieve woorlichting in de gezondheidszorg.* The Hague: Elvas Nederlands Bibliothech en Lektorn Centrum (Butch Library and Lecture Center), 1981.

Borkman, T. Experiential knowledge: a new concept for the analysis of self-help groups. *Social Service Review,* 1976, *3,* 445-456.

Bremer-Schulte, M. Werken in duo: meer genzondheidsbevorderend? In B. Bakker & M. Karel (Eds.), *Zelfhulp en welzijnswerk: Ervaringen van professionals met zelfgeleide groepen.* Alphen aan den Rijn: Samson, 1979.

Bremer-Schulte, M. (Ed.). *Samen beter worden: Nieuwe samenwerkingsvormen tussen patient en hulpverlener.* Alphen aan den Rijn: Samson, 1980.

Chabot, B. Het recht op zorg voor elkaar: En zijn onopgemerkte uitholling. *Tijdschrift voor Psychotherapie,* 1979, *5* (4), 199-216.

Cohn, R. *Von der Psychoanalyse zur themencentrierte interaktion.* Munich: Kindler Verlag, 1976.

DeBruyn, L. Lotgenotencontact voor vrouwen met borstamputatie. In B. Bakker & M. Karel (Eds.), *Zelfhulp en welzijnswerk: Ervaringen van professionals met zelfgeleide groepen.* Alphen aan den Rijn: Samson, 1979.

Defilet, M., & van Rietschoten, N. Ervarend leren. In B. Bakker & M. Karel (Eds.), *Zelfhulp en welzijnswerk: Ervaringen van professionals met zelfgeleide groepen.* Alphen aan den Rijn: Samsom, 1979.

Fairweather, G. (Ed.). *The Fairweather lodge: A 25-year retrospective.* San Francisco: Jossey-Bass, 1980.

Hageboud, R. Zelfhulpverlening aaan tehuisweglopers. In B. Bakker & M. Karel (Eds.), *Zelfhup en welzijnswerk: Ervaringen van professionals met zelfgeleide groepen.* Alphen aan den Rijn: Samsom, 1979.

Illich, I. *De professional: Vriend of vijand.* Baarn: In den Toren, 1980.

Kaay, H., & Verburg, H. Alleenstaande ouders: Een zelfhulpgroep als preventieaktiviteit. In B. Bakker & M. Karel (Eds.), *Zelfhulp en welzijnswerk: Ervaringen van professionals met zelfgeleide groepen.* Alphen aan den Rijn: Samsom, 1979.

Kagie, R. *Op eigen kracht: Zelfhulp en zelforganisatie in Nederland en West-Duitsland.* Bloemendaal: Nelissen, 1979.

Knelpuntennota. *Harmonisatie welzijnsbeleid en welzijnswetgeving.* The Hague: Staatsuitgeverij, 1974.

Leonard, P. Toward a paradigm for radical practice. In R. Balley & M. Brake (Eds.), *Radical social work.* New York: Pantheon Books, 1976.

Lieberman, M., & Borman, L. (Eds.). *Self-help groups for coping with crisis.* San Francisco: Jossey-Bass, 1979.

Medaer, R., Gijbels, M., & Jansen-Lowet, M. Zelfhulp: Een niuwe therapeutische mogelijkheid voor multiple sclerose patienten. In B. Bakker & M. Karel (Eds.), *Zelfhulp en welzijnswerk: Ervaringen van professionals met zelfgeleide groepen.* Alphen aan den Rijn: Samsom, 1979.

Pinker, R. *Social theory and social policy.* London: Heinemann, 1971.

Pinker, R. *The idea of welfare.* London: Heinemann, 1979.

Rieuwers, R. Leiderlozegroepen: De ontwikkeling van een zelfhulp cursus op geluidsbanden. In B. Bakker & M. Karel (Eds.), *Zelfhulp en welzijnswerk: Ervaringen van professionals met zelfgeleide groepen.* Alphen aan den Rijn: Samsom, 1979.

Römer, M. Het opstarten van een WAO groep. In B. Bakker & M. Karel (Eds.), *Zelfhulp en welzijnswerk: Evaringen van professionals met zelfgeleide groepen.* Alphen aan den Rijn: Samsom, 1979.

Sanders, D. 75 patients–0 professionals: The lodge program in community rehabilitation. *Attitude,* 1979, *1*(7).

Specht, H., & Vickery, A. (Eds.). *Integrating social work methods.* London: Allen & Unwin, 1977.

Trojen, E. *Porträt einer Grüppe: Aus der Praxis einer Selbst Hilfe Gruppe von Studenten.* Munich: Juventa, 1977.

Van de Sanden, W. De gezondheidswinkel: Het stimuleren van zelfhulp in een stadswijk. In B. Bakker & M. Karel (Eds.), *Zelfhulp en welzijnswerk: Ervaringen van professionals met zelfgeleide groepen.* Alphen aan den Rijn: Samsom, 1979.

Van Dijk, P. *Naar een gezonde gezondheidszorg.* Deventer: Ankh Hermes, 1978.

Van Doorn, J. De beheersbaarheid van de verzorgingsstaat. *Beleid en Maatschappij,* 1977, *4,* 115-128.

Van Doorn, J., & Schuyt, C. (Eds.). *De stagnerende verzorgingsstaat.* Meppel: Boom, 1978.

Van Harberden, P., & Lafaille, R. Van zelfhulpgroep naar zelfhulpmethodiek: enige kanttekeningen bij een riskante transplantatie. In P. van Harberden & R. Lafaille (Eds.), *Zelfhulp: Een nieuwe vorm van hulpverlenen?* The Hague: Vuga, 1978.

Wolffers, I. *Zelfhulpgroepen: Een nieuw fenomeen in de gezondheids zorg.* Amsterdam: Bert Bakker, 1978.

Young, M., & Rigge, M. *Mutual aid in a selfish society.* London: Mutual Aid Press, 1979.

9

VOLUNTARY ACTION IN THE WELFARE STATE

Two Examples

DAN FERRAND-BECHMANN
France

To speak about self-help or informal care is to speak about activities ranging from various types of self-care, on the one hand, to the kind of informal helping systems that prevail among families, neighbors, and friends, on the other. To analyze the relationships between each of these types of informal care and professional social work is a broad, and important, task. While this is not the sole focus of our research at the Centre d'Etudes des Solidarités Sociales, where we are examining many aspects of the relationship between voluntarism and the welfare state in France, we can draw from our research two examples that raise many pertinent issues and indicate the current situation in France: (a) the emerging role of the elderly as volunteers in social action, and (b) the Jeunes Femmes movement.

These are two examples of self-help, of populations who are taking charge of themselves, excluding the interventions of others or limiting them as much as possible. In a broader context, we could also have spoken just as appropriately of families. Among the lower classes and the upper middle class, families tend to take total charge of their own welfare. Other classes are more likely to use professional services. We could also have spoken of neighborhood care, which is important for some types of exchanges (Ferrand-Bechmann, 1980b).

But the examples we give of the relationships between professional and voluntary work are typical of the French situation. In the first example, the relationship is full of conflict and antagonism. In the second, there is no relationship, because the group itself became professionalized. In France, professionalization means the transformation of a task into one which requires a diploma and a certain number of skills to perform and for which one is paid.

HISTORICAL BACKGROUND

It will be useful to have some background on the development of social welfare in France before discussing our two examples. It is necessary in the French context to understand the different stages in the development of the state and of the social structure in order to explain contemporary sociological phenomena. Broadly speaking, mediating structures, those intermediate groups between the state and individuals, have had many ups and downs and have encountered a variety of opposing forces. Describing "associations"—the legal form of all groups in France—could be the subject of another book. Such a book could demonstrate the overrepresentation of the middle classes in such organizations, as well as the structural antagonism between such groups and professionals and trade unionists. Voluntary organizations are always a threat to the social division of labor and the leadership of professionals on specific tasks.

Partly because of the increasing price of petrol, partly because of new technologies that lead to more unemployment, and partly because of structural factors inherent in capitalism and in the welfare state, France, as many other rich countries, is experiencing an economic crisis. The need to create new jobs, in particular, has opened old sores. It is the position of the current, socialist government that social policy can create a new economic dynamic. Increased social benefits are promoted as a way to provide a higher standard of living for families and individuals and increase consumption. Such a philosophy is implicitly opposed to informal solidarities and voluntarism. But the obligatory limits socialism places on the dynamics of production should be contradictory to this new doctrine (Blum—Girardeau, 1981).

In spite of these sources of opposition, the history of solidarity, of mutual aid, is deeply rooted in philanthropy, especially of the churches and upper classes, who wanted to maintain the social order and thus were concerned to limit misery to an acceptable and tolerable level. In the nineteenth century, the owners of industries—for example, in cities like "le Creusot" and Mulhouse—needed to maintain an effective labor force. Therefore, they replaced the informal mutual aid of families and workers with industrial social welfare benefits such as housing, training, insurance, and pensions. On the face of it, these were workers' benefits, but they were also examples of social welfare policy made by the church, the state, and industries out of self-interest.

During the same period, informal mutual aid systems developed among paupers. There were utopian communities (Godin, 1979), and many other examples of mutual aid among the poor are described by writers such as Honoré de Balzac, Victor Hugo, Georges Sand, and Emile Zola. Mutual aid was the price of survival. Many social innovations emerged among the working classes and the poor that were then appropriated by the state bureaucracy and by paternalistic policies in industry.

The origins of social welfare policies are full of contradictions in both the upper and lower classes. Seen in terms of social values, there is a consensus on the importance of helping one's fellow human being, but the motives are different. In the upper classes the motives are increasing worker productivity and therefore profit and the maintenance of the social order. In the lower classes the motives are survival and the struggle for a better, more equal society. At many points in the history of France, this struggle has given birth to revolutions.

Radical changes have occurred whenever social welfare benefits have been the focus of working-class revolutions. An example occurred in 1936, when the Popular Front included the demand for paid holidays in their program, with the approval and enthusiasm of the militant workers, who had brought them to power. The choice of National Solidarity as the title of the new ministry of social welfare is also symbolic of the new government's desire to address the concerns of the working classes. But hidden conflicts and political disputes continue.

SOURCES OF SOCIAL WELFARE

Social welfare originates from three sources: professionals, volunteers, and mutual aid. All forms of interaction and social exchange, including mutual aid and informal care among families, neighbors, and friends, constitute a total system. However, this is not the perspective of professional social workers in France today.

Professionalism

Social welfare is now highly professionalized in France compared to many other countries. It is clear that France has created professional functions where informal helping and voluntary action still prevail in other countries. For example, eight-year-old Côme, who was asked, "Who opens a jar of jam for an old lady who can't do it for herself?" replied, "She goes to her neighbor—no, she calls the local authority."

Why this quick professionalization? Perhaps there is more of a tradition of charities and voluntarism in other countries. Certainly a combination of economic and political factors has influenced the growth of professional services in France. Due partly to an economic crisis and partly to a very strict legal framework, medical and social care is very tightly controlled by the state. Child welfare is particularly controlled, but care provided to the sick, to old people, and to families is also highly regulated. These controls and the self-protection of specialized social workers impart a particular character to the French landscape: high fences protect the territories of each group.

The departmental social services offices in France (of which there are ninety) have great power in social welfare concerns. Additionally, each professional group confines itself to a strictly defined set of tasks over which it demands a monopoly. It seems that every month more of the domain of informal care comes under professional control, chiefly through the granting or withholding of diplomas, a severe control. For example, to be an unqualified community development worker or to take a child in charge without a diploma is more and more difficult. A grandmother who wishes to take care of her grandchild during the day must now be declared, controlled, and qualified.

Professional social work has poor relationships with volunteers and self-help groups in France. Professionals tend to be jealous and to have low morale because salaries are quite low, even though professional qualifications are difficult to obtain.

In its relations with various forms of mutual aid, social work often has colonialist aims. When a new function is created through voluntary action or self-help groups, such as alternative playgrounds or community development work, qualified social workers or the Ministry of National Solidarity take immediate control. This has many negative consequences, such as the imposition of strong norms, the loss to the client of autonomy or the capacity for self-help, the stigma of being a "social case," and the creation of the need for assistance in perpetuity (Meyer, 1972).

T become a welfare client of the Ministry of National Solidarity is always dysfunctional compared to being helped by an informal network, volunteers, neighbors, self-help groups, and the like. Many in France feel that to become a welfare client is to be trapped, caught in a net. One can never go back to the deep blue sea!

Even though there has been an improvement in the standard of living and better social benefits, several official reports written after the change of government in 1981 have concluded that the current welfare system produces few positive results, achieves little success in increasing equality of opportunity, and undermines solidarity (Blum-Girardeau, 1981; Questiaux, 1982; Schwartz, 1981).

Volunteers

Voluntary action is not very popular in France. Although associations are numerous, they are legally prohibited from many of the tasks of promoting solidarity or social action. This is in spite of the fact that we have shown that this is a very creative sector, which has made numerous innovations. For example, it is the private sector that has originated actions to help prostitutes, young offenders, and mentally ill children, often through self-help efforts. Generally speaking, the voluntary sector has no finances, no buildings, no rights, and no insurance. The assumption seems to be that voluntarism has no costs. It seems clear, however, that even without support, voluntarism is expanding (Ferrand-Bechman, 1982). Among the volunteers are increasing numbers of militants who have social change objectives, and there are increasing numbers of young people, men, and recently retired people in their ranks. They have strong altruistic and mutual aid motivations and understand clearly the difficulties imposed by economic hard times and unemployment.

This brief sketch of the development and characteristics of alternative sources of social welfare in France provides the background to the two examples I shall now describe. In the cases of both the elderly and the Jeunes Femmes movement we shall see how the larger social and political context of social welfare in France influences the direction of self-help efforts. We shall also examine how individual patterns of involvement and motivation are associated with these broader social forces.

FIRST EXAMPLE:
ELDERLY PEOPLE AS VOLUNTEERS

Historical Background

The recent experience of the elderly clearly presents an example of a part of the population increasingly taking charge of itself; it is self-help in the most general sense. In the nineteenth century, the principle sources of assistance for and among the elderly were:

(a) families and neighbors (Weber, 1971),
(b) charity performed by upper- and middle-class women,
(c) religious orders (monks and nuns),
(d) mutual aid among the working class, and
(e) industrial paternalism.

We can give a short example of the condition of the elderly in this period from *The Black Town* by Georges Sand (1861, p. 209). Social solidarity was the key to survival.

The old man had never been so well, never been so happy . . . now that he doesn't work anymore, that no one blames him for not working anymore. Everybody cares for him. It is the pride of the lower town. He can enter any home, anywhere, poor and rich give him what is best to eat and drink. . . . He says, "Everybody loves me in the countryside, everyone takes pity, gives me what is necessary. A piece of bread in a peasant's hut, soup in the share-croppers home, a coin in the castle, wine in the pub."

After World War II, life for the elderly was quite difficult and impoverished. They feared retirement. The most resourceful of them, seldom the neediest, were Catholic on Monday, Protestant on Tuesday, and begged from office to office, charity to charity, town to town. The elderly were very poor, with help coming primarily from families and charities as it had in the nineteenth century. Upper- and middle-class ladies went from parish to parish offering to help or to visit.

A famous report by Pierre Laroque (1962) opened a new period. Old age became a social problem, the focus of social policy and action and the target of social work intervention. With great effort, gerontological policies and services were created. But certain dysfunctions accompanied this effort, among them professionalization, loss of autonomy for the elderly, and stigmatization.

Opportunities for Self-Help

What place remains for volunteers and self-help? Three factors lead us to think that a significant place remains.

First, as a civil servant told us, "Old age is a cake that everybody eats." This suggests that the control of the state is less important in the case of the elderly than in other areas, such as abandoned or neglected children, because of the broader scope of need or the wider population affected.

Second, the elderly population is healthier now and increasingly accustomed to self-management. The elderly are actors in creating social policies as well as beneficiaries of them. They see these two roles as interrelated.

Third, old people prefer to turn to volunteers because they are more accessible. Frequently they would rather discuss their problems with other older people who are volunteers rather than with workers from official services, who they fear will treat them as a case and will give them a "record."

Voluntarism offers the elderly a new identity, a new source of social integration, a new power that neither work (Sainsaulieu, 1977), youth, nor maturity can offer them. Self-help among the elderly is quite particular to this age group. One could analyze it in terms of reaction, resistance, throwback, or innovation—reaction or resistance against young volunteers or social workers, throwback to the happy ideal of ancient times, and innovation through a new model of social action.

With the new perspectives created by the free time available at retirement appear new motives for voluntarism. We do not agree with the hypothesis that the level of participation of an older person is a function of his or her participation when younger. Some begin a new life at retirement. Some who have had responsibilities in trade unions, associations, churches, or political parties maintain the same activities or become volunteers in new associations.

Three types of motivations are found among active elderly people: to occupy themselves, to further a cause, and to work for charity. These attitudes are more or less egoistic or altruistic. Individual variations come from life histories, social class, qualifications, and type of work before retirement. As the "third age" becomes longer and longer, we wonder if those poorer in chances earlier in life might not find new opportunities in old age.

Our findings about motivation are close to the concepts of self-help or mutual aid found by a Dutch researcher (Sewandono, 1980). In self-help, people have a problem and need to resolve it. At first an egocentric act, it becomes an altruistic one. Self-care is more preventative than curative, whether among a primary group (families, neighbors, or friends) or in a social movement engaged in collective action. Volunteering can also be a form of social therapy. Leaders of the volunteer centers told us that many depressed people come to them, and they decide whether to involve them as volunteers or as clients. One might begin to attend a community center, then offer to help, then cooperate in administrative tasks, and then fight for more funds for the center or better activities. In this way, many people are brought along slowly as volunteers.

It appears that the lower-class elderly are more numerous in voluntary groups or self-help activities than are lower-class young people. Likewise, elderly participants are more numerous in rural counties than in urban ones, especially in community work and the management and leadership of associations. In our research we did not find as many upper- and middle-class volunteers in old-age volunteerism as in other types. This age group's recruitment gives a better representation of social classes. For example, a retired laborer is now the president of a club's federation.

In the clubs (senior centers), the elderly are doing the administration. They are organizing activities and various forms of recreation, finding contacts and places to go, arranging for buses and parties. However, recruiting new volunteers for these clubs is not always easy. The same (gray) heads seem to remain on the board term after term. In a way, these gray heads are evergreen. They do not want to relinquish leadership. Sometimes they ask for professional help for the heavier tasks.

The "universities of the Third Age" are built on the idea of training retired people or those of similar age. A few of them are linked to traditional universities, but more commonly they are directed by the older students themselves. Various academic and practical courses are offered. These universities are quite popular with the middle class and also offer some assistance to other groups, such as housewives and the unemployed.

Another important area for voluntarism among the elderly is local affairs in rural villages, where many urbanites have second or retirement homes. It seems that rural villages offer a certain resistance to "foreigners" (Ferrand-Bechmann, 1975), but they welcome those who come to live in the village or have come back to it regularly. Besides political leadership, the elderly do very well in community work.

We have also noticed that here, as in England (Davies, 1979), retired social workers often chose to volunteer in the field of their former qualifications. Retired social workers have organized community centers for handicapped people, organized parties and tours, and set up activities for isolated, bedridden people in nursing homes (Kniebiehler, 1981).

These examples show that self-help among the elderly may slowly replace volunteerism by other age groups toward the elderly. Old people are more and more becoming self-managers and community workers among themselves. It is mutual solidarity. However, there may be a growing distinction between the third age (young old) and the fourth one (old old), which could create some impediments to this newfound solidarity.

Large-scale governmental action on behalf of the elderly is quite new in France. One negative consequence of this effort might be the fatal weakening of existing local mutual aid systems in the face of competition from the national welfare system. Old people acting as volunteers on their own behalf could provide a new way of preserving local structures.

Beneficiaries and actors at the same time, increasingly "younger" old people are playing their parts. They are joining together to meet needs that governmental action cannot fulfill—or that governmental action has created. Self-help is more possible in this area of welfare policy than in others which are more tightly controlled. There is less antagonism with professionals in areas where the territory of each is well defined, as in hospitals, than where one does the same work as the other, as in the senior clubs, where the older volunteers and the administrators take part in the same tasks. The conflicts are more complex, here, because by tradition the elderly person is a client of the club but is also an organizer or an administrator in a society in which a gerontocracy has left its traces. To chose the eldest as president or leader is to raise again the tradition of domination by elders. Perhaps there is also here an element of revolt against the founders. In many cases these services were started by private initiative and then came under public auspices. The pioneers who cleared the land clash with those who come to cultivate it.

Professionals criticize volunteers for their absenteeism, their lack of seriousness (in effect, the lack of a "professional attitude"), for taking work away from others, for not accepting criticism, and for being power-hungry. Volunteers criticize professionals for under- or overutilizing them, for not thanking them enough, and for being paid to do what they do for free. But the older volunteers are not really competing for the professionals' jobs, so a potentially crippling source of antagonism is removed.

With newly found leisure time, created in part by the industrial crisis, self-help has found a place apart from work, apart from production, and removed from constraint or compulsion. Will self help among the elderly have the same negative consequences as governmental action? Or will there be a return to the past, when elderly people enjoyed high status and power, particularly in rural areas? This will be the topic of further research.

SECOND EXAMPLE:
JEUNES FEMMES

A Protestant women's group, acting outside the church organization to meet the needs of its members, Jeunes Femmes (which disbanded in 1981) evolved into a permanent educational movement over its thirty-five-year history. Its roots can be traced to women's voluntary service in missionary work in the church and to the dissatisfaction of women relegated to the home after the new independence of the war years.

According to the first article of their constitution, the Jeunes Femmes came together to help one another exert their individual and joint responsibilities and to take action that would encourage people to acknowledge the dignity of the human being. Starting from their own experiences in life, they compared their doubts, their convictions, their hopes. Out of joint reflection and education came a variety of activities directed toward self-improvement and the improvement of women's condition.

Patterns of Involvement

The involvement of women in Jeunes Femmes seems to have been an alternative to paid employment. Among the women active in the organization, one finds four patterns of involvement:

(1) no paid employment, only voluntary activity;
(2) voluntary activity first, then employment;
(3) employment, then voluntary activity; and
(4) employment, a period of voluntary activity, and then the resumption of professional employment.

Among the eleven relatively detailed case histories we have in our possession, the first and second patterns occur only once each. On the other hand, the third and fourth patterns describe respectively five and four women. It seems therefore that participation in Jeunes Femmes generally followed professional experience whether or not it led to a resumption of professional employment. It was a process, a passage. As one of the women (Mrs. J) says, "The women who are capable of being national leaders [in the movement] are also those who are ready for paid activity, which makes it increasingly difficult to find leaders."

The women volunteers whose case histories we draw upon were very important in the Jeunes Femmes movement. They were often "permanent" workers, devoting significant amounts of time to the organization without remuneration. Among them, one finds again and again the same course of involvement: taking part in various youth movements, becoming a member of a local group of Jeunes Femmes, regional engagement, and then national involvement. Two of these women were involved in the international activities of the organization. It is not surprising, therefore, that many people regard their involvement as work, even if it is unpaid. "The work called 'voluntary' requires as much *competency* and quality as the work called 'professional' " (Mrs. I). "I have always thought that a volunteer, serious and competent in his responsibilities, is as socially useful as a paid person, assuming that the latter is also competent and professionally serious. A salary is by no means a guarantee in this respect" (Mrs. G). The notion of "competency" is frequently used to suggest the seriousness of the involvement and the usefulness of the activity. "They speak of a kind of professional conscientiousness" (Mrs. G). With such a perspective, voluntary work is not seen as merely something to do. It is distinguished from "charity work."

"I was a member [of Jeunes Femmes] doing volunteer work occasionally, but not very much" (Mrs. J). "To me, voluntary work was not like a professional involvement because it was occasional. Many other members wanted it to be even more temporary than I did" (Mrs. I). "On the other hand, when I was on the national board of Jeunes Femmes in about 1963, I considered my voluntary service to be professional work, meaning that the national meetings and related work had priority for me" (Mrs. A). "Activities which proceed from involvement with a movement are different from a mere search for something which can occupy one's spare time—a search which can lead, for example to office or secretarial jobs executed free of charge" (Mrs. L). A search for responsibility? A willingness not to confine oneself to routine execution of predefined tasks but to be involved in the definition of a collective (and militant) plan of action?

As a result, as Mrs. L emphasizes, this period of quasi-professional voluntary work served as a transition for many women to resume studying, which then allowed them to obtain positions available in the business market, or to find a professional opening requiring the education acquired in the movement. It is the second case that seems to us to occur most frequently, confirmed by a good many statements, particularly those of Mrs. D and Mrs. A. "The training I got through voluntary service is at least equivalent and probably quicker than what I could have received in a professional occupation. . . . I don't think that a firm would have given me responsibilities so quickly" (Mrs. D). "I thought that being a treasurer would not have opened the door for something else. But then, in 1973, I was offered a part-time job. . . . All that I had learned in on-the-job training about bookkeeping was what I needed. And I have been working at this job ever since" (Mrs. A).

The training received in Jeunes Femmes can be reflected in work when the situation allows. "I had to organize a team . . . in a collegial, nonhierarchical fashion. The philosophy of Jeunes Femmes and everything I learned there as a volunteer helped me a lot. I try to have a critical mind and to communicate it to my colleagues" (Mrs. G).

Implications for Women's Work Roles

As an approach, self-help may have been dictated by the family situation and responsibilities of these women as well as by the Protestant ethic. But it was a form of self-help very similar to work because of its serious commitment and the length of service. The combination of the bad financial situation of the movement and the availability of the women made the self-help approach both feasible and appropriate. It should perhaps be noted that the women were able to give time to the organization partly because they had few other expectations for themselves. In this regard, a short article in the *Jeunes Femmes Review,* criticizing the film *Cleo from 5 to 7* for its emphasis on luxuries, pleasures, and clothes, is significant.

These women, most of whom had many children, could never have worked full-time during the period when Jeunes Femmes flourished. This was also a period of social creativity, when self-help was a necessity for women. Perhaps in the 1980s women with children who have the same training would work. Furthermore, the work formerly done through self-help is now professionalized. Now there would be antagonism and competition. Twenty or thirty years ago, there was not.

As an example of the potential for antagonism, some women pointed out that self-help does not accord any status. Professional work is better in this regard. "My evolution as a woman has taught me under what conditions I could obtain respect: professionalism" (Mrs. J). According to Mrs. G, some of the young women were not able to obtain status through participation in Jeunes Femmes. In general, although husbands and children respected what they were doing, friends and others around them did not.

Attitudes toward money and salaries were diverse and ambiguous. A salary was seen as justified for professional activity. "I'm glad to work and be paid for it. This work is an opportunity for me. My husband was jobless for 2½ years. It really helped that I had a salary" (Mrs. A). Another long-term member, who had been paid for involvement for part of the time, said, "I can't hide the satisfaction of being paid; it is normal to feel that way" (Mrs. J). On the other hand, Mrs. J also said that she had previously given time and effort without any idea of or worry about being paid. Another woman (Mrs. G) said, "Money is unhappily the criterion of success in our society . . . but a salary would be absurd for all the time I have spent in Jeunes Femmes. I was paid nicely by all the opportunities I had to think better and develop my personality." Mrs. D said, "I am persuaded that every generation invents a new way of giving free service, absolutely necessary in a world where money is the principal criterion."

The members of this movement were motivated by the need for social integration, relationships, stimulation, the desire to build a common project through common norms. It may be that all women look for a place to form, confront, and discuss ideas. The woman at home has only the family for social reference, sometimes friends and neighbors. She lacks the culture of work where norms are elaborated (Sainsaulieu, 1977). An alternative can be found in informal groups. Self-help thus provides a symbolic salary in social integration. Women at home get bored.

Ann Oakley (1974), in her book on the sociology of housework, shows that, in her study, three-fourths of the housewives were bored. They found their work to be fragmented, monotonous, and lonely. Compared to assembly-line work, there was a low level of interaction with others. The opportunity to engage in social relationships with other workers is one of the most prized aspects of any job.

Nevertheless, self-help brought wealth in human terms that no paid work could offer. Partly because the power hierarchy was not determined by salary scale, power could be more widely shared. Second, the Jeunes Femmes groups created new relationships for their members based on self-help principles. Third, there were no explicit penalties for participation or nonparticipation. Women could participate more flexibly and juggle the demands of their families better than if they had paid jobs. The "salary" for participation in self-help was also survival, remaining in the know, escaping the ghetto of the family and the trap of housework. It was not a sacrifice but an emergency exit. The words "rewarding" and "pleasure" were used often: "the pleasure and power of friendship"; "The meeting was often a feast." (Mrs. M).

Dependence on one's husband's salary was generally well accepted by these women, at least when there were no real money problems. They were generally from middle-class backgrounds. They were quite willing to be involved in self-help as long as it gave them the free time that paid work would not. "Certainly self-help is devouring, but I can choose the limits of my obligations. For example, I can stop during school vacations in order to have time for the young and the old in my family" (Mrs. D). Patterns of participation in self-help may actually correspond to what would be ideal working patterns for many women.

Motivation for Involvement

Behind the general good feelings toward the organization, there were some conflicts. One example that we noticed was that there the two different attitudes about the purpose of the movement. One was militant and utopian. The aim was to change mentalities, to do something entirely new. This attitude was not only feminist but also political. The intent was to "trick" institutions, which were viewed suspiciously, by using the relatively innocuous guise of self-help to bring about social changes. The self-help form of organization permits types of action that a paid and chartered organization would not be able to undertake. The chief target was the Calvinist church. The Jeunes Femmes had used the familiar, easy-to-understand appearance of the traditional women's self-help group to hide new fights and courageous battles: family planning, political fights, battles for women's rights and oppressed people (for example, during the Algerian War).

The other prevailing motivation was the more typical day-to-day, Calvinist self-help. A good example is the "professional" volunteerism of the clergymen's wives. Women's organizations, focused on self-improvement, are traditional in Calvinist churches, rooted in puritanism. But the two attitudes were not totally opposed. Self-help in Jeunes Femmes was mostly of the militant sort.

We have noted that Jeunes Femmes was a peer activity. "We have the common experience of historical events" (Mrs. H). "I share the reactions of a generation" (Mrs. C). In fact, one can distinguish three generations:

(1) The generation of women who had difficulties during World War II but also new freedoms and afterward. They were uncomfortable at home. They chose self-help as a means to add status to their positions as housewives.

(2) The generation of women who had husbands, brothers, or other relatives in the Algerian War. They fought for political rights, equality, and cultural development.

(3) The post-1968 generation of women who became distrustful of power and social institutions. Many divorces resulted from that crisis. French students at that time were saying that under the paving stones there is the beach. Under the hearth, women discovered not the beach but their utility and their inutility.

Participation in Jeunes Femmes often led to other types of commitment, especially in religious movements, parents' organizations, neighborhood associations, and the like. Generally, members of Jeunes Femmes did not get involved in political commitments. The organization had political objectives but they were a part of larger goals. The commitments were certainly militant, far removed from charitable activities.

Their involvement was a way of making new relationships, for example with Algerian women. But it also was a way of creating new relationships at home, of giving the women better understanding of world problems and more equality with their husbands. "It gives satisfaction and thirst for life" (Mrs. G).

Their own testimony, as well as the name of the organization—Young Women—which did not change for thirty-five years, are evidence that the goals of the movement were certainly women's goals: a commitment to feminism, to self-help among women, and "to have a man's life" (!). But antagonism between the sexes? No. One former member says, "So many women!" and another one, "For women, by women." Many women remarked on having been the only woman on one board or another. In fact Jeunes Femmes was a social movement, with the criterion: "Women similar and different, who met to change mentalities and social structures" (Mrs. F). Given the times, to include men would have been to increase discrimination. Men would have taken power.

Summing Up

But, in the end, what can be concluded? The organization helped in women's social and professional integration: "Many of our former leaders are now leaders in various associations or in adult education" (Mrs. L). It helped women who were at home to survive. Self-help, which allows flexible commitments of time, is congruent with housework. It is a cultural continuation. This is not contradictory with the status and pleasure that women found in self-help. What was seen as a burden or injustice was the unrelenting responsibility women still had for their household duties: "I was obliged to slip it among family priorities and housework" (Mrs. D). Some members felt guilty about leaving the dishes for the husband or performing acrobatics to get the housework done. In this regard, perhaps one of the results of the organization has been better recognition of women, more equality with their husbands, better acceptance of going outside the home. Things have changed. Women now gain these rights through professional status, but self-help also had an influence: "It was a melting pot of young women, where little by little they went out of their homes to find new commitments" (Mrs. L).

Many associations come into the world and eventually disband. Jeunes Femmes was created at a time when there were no professional alternatives. Social work was just beginning. The organization was born in a particular context. Women participated in self-help at their own risk but also at the risk of their household.

The meetings and the structure of the organization reflected the problems and needs of the members. The women were in search of identity, solidarity, and women's help for women. Jeunes Femmes is a good example of self-help with social action objectives because it led to community work and adult education, both of which are now in the forefront of social action and social change in many countries. The development of the organization occurred in three stages: post-World War II, Algerian War, and post-1968. Each stage was associated with specific fights and particular tasks. Likewise, the lives of the members were affected differently at each stage. Many won new freedoms and raised new issues during the years when men were the unquestioned leaders in the home. Many had important roles in struggles such as social planning or the defense of Algerian women. Many experienced doubts about the social structure in 1968 and discovered the real face of power and institutions. This third generation sometimes won divorces and chose to take paid work. In this last generation we found attitudes more typical of the women's movement.

The movement ended in 1981; as is the case for most associations, the fire eventually went out. But one can also emphasize that this demise is the historical consequence of increasing opportunities in the profession of social work. We have seen motivations for participating in self-help originating from professional, trade unionist, religious, political, and family concerns. But to study self-help without scrutinizing the psychological background would have been insufficient.

We have also tried to discover the main rewards of this association. Self-help affords better-quality relationships. Behind its unassuming exterior, Jeunes Femmes provided social identity and warm solidarity.

Finally, the normative background of this instance of self-help should be stressed. In the group one could find values and norms, guides to attitudes, and strong models democratically built. Participation involved the members in a strong, militant commitment, characterized by equality despite inequalities in education and status.

Because Jeunes Femmes was essentially a women's self-help movement, its members were able to withstand any form of external leadership that would inevitably have led to domination by men (in the Protestant hierarchy, for example). The women's movement is a social phenomenon characteristic of the twentieth century and thoroughly imbued with the principles of self-help.

CONCLUSION

Self-help and informal helping, which seem new, are actually a rediscovery. What seems new is actually a retrenchment. After a period of massive increase in social services, economic constraints must pull expenditure up short if it is not to grow exponentially. Self-help provides one alternative. But it can be justified not only on economic grounds but also for qualitative reasons. Professional action has dysfunctions that self-help seems to avoid. On the other hand, however, professional activity can provide technical competence while self-help can be amateurish. The two approaches have different functions. They are complementary in their standards of efficiency and competence. Properly used in tandem they could have positive social effects in reducing inequalities, increasing the autonomy of individuals and groups, and diminishing social standardization and stigmatization.

The modern state, in its concern about the limitations of social welfare policies, has rediscovered self-help. However, the choices for society are difficult in a debate where values are constantly interposed in economic calculations—and often in political ones. The demands of professionals at all levels of social work, threatened in recent times by unemployment, have swung the balance of opinion toward the creation of employment, in the hope that costs might be minimized through better management and efficiency rather than by cutting back personnel. France is a relative latecomer to a recognition of the benefits of self-help, and further developments will have to occur within this context of cutbacks in governmental expenditures and increasing professional protectivism. The strong legal framework of restrictions on associations, the suspiciousness of trade unions, a historical background of religious charities and industrial paternalism, a high degree of state control of social policy regarding children and the aged, a lack of mutual aid traditions such as in the United States and Canada, and the low status of social work are other factors that impede the development of complementary relationships between formal services and informal care. Renewed vitality in associations and new governmental policy favoring self-management could change the situation and encourage better utilization of informal solidarities.

We have presented two case examples: the elderly and the Jeunes Femmes. They demonstrate that peer groups and social classes engage in self-help not as a way of competing with professionals but as an extension or complementary activity with a different value system. Older, retired people find a new place in society through self-help activities and associations. Women in Jeunes Femmes used their movement as a springboard into better social and professional status.

REFERENCES

Blum-Girardeau, C. *Les tableau de la solidarité.* Paris: Documentation Française, 1981.

Davies, B. Social work and social control. Presented at a conference in Aix, December 1979.

Ferrand-Bechmann, D. *L'anti-ville, les residences secondaires.* Nanterre: Université de Nanterre, 1975.

Ferrand-Bechman, D. *Be a good neighbor, les marguerites à Meylan, étude d'un systeme de voisinage.* Observation du Changement Social, Centre National de la Recherche Scientifique, Quai Voltaire, Paris, 1980.

Ferrand-Bechman, D. Le bénévolat face à l'etat providence. *Report to the Ministère de l'Urbanism et du Logement, Paris, 1982.*

Godin, J. B. *La solution sociale.* Quimperle: La Digitale, 1979.

Kniebiehler, Y. *Nous, les assistantes sociales.* Paris: Aubier, 1981.

Laroque, P. *Commission d'étude des problems de la vieillesse.* Paris: Documentation Française, 1962.

Meyer, P. Où va le travail social? *Paris Revue Esprit No: Special, 1972.*

Oakley, A. *Sociology of homework.* London: Robertson, 1974.

Questiaux, N. *Rapport d'orientation sur le travail social circulaire du Ministère de la solidarité.* Paris, mai, 1982.

Sainsaulieu, R. *L'identité au travail.* Paris: Fondation Nationale des Sciences Politiques, 1977.

Sand, G. *La ville noire* (2nd ed.). Paris: Michel Levy Frères, 1861.

Schwartz, B. *Rapport sur l'insertion sociale et professionelle des jeunes.* Paris: Documentation Française, 1981.

Sewandono, I. *What people owe to each other.* Rotterdam: Université Erasmus, 1980.

Weber, M. *Economie et société.* Paris: Plon, 1971.

10

ENGLISH SELF-HELP

Varied Patterns and Practices

ANN RICHARDSON
England

In England, as in many other countries, there has been a substantial growth in the number of "self-help" or "mutual aid" groups over the past decade or so. Defined loosely as groups of people who have joined together with the aim of alleviating or solving some common problem, these organizations are concerned with a wide range of medical, social, and behavioral conditions. Not only have many new organizations been created, but also existing organizations have extended the spread of their local groups. It has been a period of very rapid development in this particular corner of the voluntary sector.

Surprisingly, however, little has been known about these groups beyond the simple fact of their proliferation. What do they do and why do members join? What affects a local group's success, so that some fail and others thrive? How do they fit into the wider pattern of care for those in need of help? Research carried out at the Policy Studies Institute in London, on behalf of the Department of Health and Social Security, was addressed expressly to those (and other) questions. Although focused on a few individual organizations, this research was concerned to develop a broad picture of self-help groups in general by analyzing the causes of particular patterns and problems. It is from this research that the following discussion is derived.

This chapter presents a brief introduction to self-help groups in England, followed by a discussion of their relations with some providers of care in the statutory (public) sector. If there is one clear message to emerge, it is the very striking diversity of self-help groups in practice. Some are small, unaffiliated to any larger body, and surprisingly ephemeral. Others are sizable and enduring organizations with large numbers of members at the local level and a well developed national structure (Robinson & Henry, 1977; Robinson, 1979; Robinson & Robinson, 1979). Some are wholly inward-looking, with no interest in generating contact with professional people in their area. Others are so purposively active in creating joint endeavors with the public sector that the relationships between statutory and voluntary resources are not readily disentangled. In consequence, it is difficult to make many generalizations about self-help groups as a whole or to describe a "typical" group. There is simply too much variation among them.

A brief comment on the study should be added here. It focused on four organizations comprising people with social and caring problems, rather than those of a strictly medical or behavioral nature: widows, one-parent families, parents of mentally handicapped children and adults, and women caring for elderly or infirm relatives (known as "carers"). The organizations ranged widely in their size from roughly 4,000 members to about 50,000 and from 45 branches ("chapters" in American terminology) to over 450. They also ranged in age, one having been formed in the late 1940s, one in the 1960s, and two in the early 1970s. Finally, they varied in their organizational resources; while all had a headquarters office, for instance, their total staff ranged from 2 to 53. The study entailed research on the local groups of these organizations through a postal survey of their secretaries and more detailed case studies in a few locations. In addition, information on individual members was gained through a second postal survey and supplementary interviews. The results are not described in detail here, but are drawn upon where relevant to illustrate particular points (Richardson & Goodman, forthcoming). All of the data discussed below stem from this study.

THE NATURE AND FUNCTIONS
OF SELF-HELP GROUPS

One of the principal problems that confronts anyone attempting to describe self-help groups is establishing a workable definition. This is not simply a matter of academic niceties; it affects not only the territory considered relevant but also the conclusions arising from its investigation. If they are defined solely as small, spontaneously formed, highly participative groups of wholly like-minded people, as suggested in much of the existing literature on this subject (Katz & Bender, 1976; Gartner & Reissman, 1977), then the area is a small one and analysis relatively easy. In Britain, however, such a definition would exclude a large proportion of those groups who both see themselves as providing self-help and are seen by others in this light. In consequence, they are more loosely defined here as groups of people who feel they have a common problem (generally concerning a medical, social, or behavioral condition) and wish to do something about it. This makes the terrain more extensive and generalizations more difficult.

No one has yet tried to chart the rise of self-help groups in England over the past ten or twenty years, and this research made no systematic attempt to do so. There is simply no readily accessible information either on the number of groups at various times or on the number of members belonging to them. Indeed, in part because of the definitional problems indicated above, there is no commonly agreed-upon list of the relevant "population" of such groups. Nonetheless, an examination of the formation dates of a large number of groups demonstrates, at least casually, that their genesis has been largely recent. Only a handful of organizations predate the 1960s, and many, perhaps the majority, were formed in the early 1970s. Furthermore, from discussions with the organizers of some groups, it is apparent that the number of branches associated with each organization grew considerably during the last decade or so. In sum, self-help groups are essentially (although by no means wholly) a recent phenomenon.

Before attention can be given to the relations of these groups with other providers of care, it is important to clarify more exactly what they are and what they do. First, who are the members of self-help groups? Contrary to the common assumption that they are composed only of people with a particular problem, many groups involve members who do not themselves have the relevant condition at all. Such people are usually, but not necessarily, a minority of the total membership. In the organizations studied, those in the relevant category ranged from 97 percent in the case of widows to 30 percent in the case of carers for dependents. Some of the remainder (the majority, in the latter case) were members who had chosen to retain their affiliation to the group, although they no longer had the problem for which they joined. Others were people who had no personal experience of the problem, but were either general sympathizers or people with a professional interest in it. Many organizations welcome the involvement of such members for the time and resources they can contribute. Others discourage their participation on the grounds that they cannot identify so readily with the experiences of other members. Organizations also differ considerably in their ability to retain or attract such members.

Members also differ in a number of other ways. Few groups appear to be as homogeneous as tends to be expected from the outside. Among the groups studied, members were found to come from many different walks of life, varying not only between groups but also within them. They often ranged considerably in age. They also varied, more significantly, in the length of time they had experienced the relevant conditions, thereby creating different demands on their group. The needs of the newly bereaved, for instance, are not the same as those of women who have been widowed for many years; the needs of new parents of mentally handicapped babies are not identical to those of aging parents of mentally handicapped adults. Individual self-help groups attract quite disparate people where they have a wide umbrella; this can prove the source of both cooperation and fellowship and some uneasy tensions among members.

Second, how do self-help groups work? In contrast to the provision of informal care, discussed in other chapters, self-help groups are essentially small (although in some cases not so small) organizations. This means that they typically entail all of the official personnel roles and other paraphenalia of ordinary organizations. They have chairpersons, secretaries, and committees, who are generally responsible for taking certain decisions. They have consitutions, minutes, and account books, all helping to impose order on what might otherwise simply be informal relations among friends. They are not necessarily highly formalized organizations; committees may meet infrequently and minutes may be kept to a minimum. Nonetheless, they *are* organizations and not solely informal arrangements for occasional mutual aid.

Moreover, despite the rhetoric of total equality among the membership of self-help groups, most groups—and certainly all of those studied—have a few key members who do most of the work. They not only take on the responsibility of running the group but also provide much of the help members gain from it. They are the ones who undertake fund raising, organize outings, take on the task of informing themselves (and subsequently others) about sources of help in the area, and tend to run major projects financed by their group. In this pattern, self-help groups resemble traditional voluntary organizations much more than is commonly supposed. These key members are generally the officers, but often not all of them and not necessarily limited to them. They are frequently not typical members, having both belonged to their group and experienced the relevant problem far longer than the average member. In many cases, they are people who have little need of help at all, whether or not they continue to have the relevant condition, having stayed to give back to others the help they received when they first joined. This serial reciprocity (in contrast to reciprocity between the same people at the same time) can prove a significant resource for many mutual aid organizations.

When one looks beyond the local level, the organizational resources of self-help groups can prove very sizable indeed. Some groups are, of course, purely local bodies, independent of any larger institutions or sources of expertise. Many of the best known, however, and all of those studied, are affiliated in some way to a national structure and in some cases have regional help as well. The national organizations vary enormously, from one or two paid staff who do whatever they can to tens or even hundreds, with highly differentiated functions. Clearly, the amount of help that can be given to local groups varies with the nature of such resources. Most organizations, however, try to keep their local groups informed about policy developments, provide advice on publicity and other group maintenance problems, and offer help to individual members with unusual queries.

Third, what do these groups actually do? Are they simply a chance for tea and a chat? The principal activity of many groups, certainly, is a regular meeting, enabling members to discuss mutual problems, exchange information, and plan future developments. The frequency of such meetings ranged widely among the organizations studied, from weekly or fortnightly among many single parents and some widows groups to bimonthly or less often for many groups for carers and parents of mentally handicapped children. As a supplement to such meetings, and in some cases as a substitute for them, most groups also provide a number of explicitly social occasions, such as outings and get-togethers in members' homes. Again, provision ranged from weekly events to annual occasions only. But many groups also seek to help their members in other ways, providing not only regular information about sources of help but also a number of direct services. Thus, groups issued regular newsletters, invited informative speakers to meetings, and often assigned one or more members to act as an information resource on welfare and legal problems. Such provision was again highly variable, however, both in its frequency and in the sorts of information covered. Many groups also set up systems for delivering specific forms of help to their members, ranging from informal visits to the housebound or casual babysitting to large-scale projects, such as formal playgroups for children or hostels for the mentally handicapped. Some had welfare funds to help members in financial distress. Again, the extent and effectiveness of all such provision ranged widely from one group to another.

All of the activities described above are means of helping members directly—enabling them to cope more easily with the problem in question. But many self-help groups also aim their attention beyond their immediate membership to help the general population with the relevant condition. They act, in other words, as pressure groups to get more benefits and services and generate public sympathy for their particular problems. In some cases, groups were found to do little more than write a letter to their local newspaper; in others, they undertook large-scale campaigns to change national or local policy. In some cases, such work was seen as the major purpose of the group; in others, it provided an occasional change in the month's routine. It was often not undertaken in any spirit of aggression or even defined by the groups themselves as "political." Nonetheless, it should be appreciated that mutual aid groups often undertake much more than just mutual aid.

In summary, self-help groups, at least in Britain, can be seen as both more active and less uniform than is commonly supposed. They undertake to help members in a wide variety of ways and sometimes embark on highly ambitious projects. Not all members are equally involved, however, and certain key people tend to bear the responsibility of both taking decisions for the group and acting as official spokespersons for it. Furthermore, groups are often able to call on paid staff from central or regional offices to help them both with internal organizational problems and with their dealings with other agencies in their area. All of these characteristics have some bearing on the relations of self-help groups with other providers of care, to which it is now possible to turn.

SELF-HELP GROUPS AND STATUTORY CARE PROVISION

A study of the "relations" of self-help groups and statutory care providers can refer to two very distinct issues. On the one hand, it can be interpreted to mean the relation of service *provision* between different organizations. Who provides what sorts of help? To what extent are activities duplicated in several different contexts? Who does what job better? On the other hand, it can be interpreted to mean the relations between service *providers* in different sectors. Do they have any contact? If so, what is its nature and purpose? How do they respond to one another? These two sets of questions must be approached in very different ways; they are concerned with very different problems. Both are much too broad to be given more than cursory attention here. Nonetheless, an attempt is made to lay some groundwork for each issue in turn.

To what extent do self-help groups provide similar services to those available from public agencies? On a very general level, taking groups as a whole, the kinds of help they try to provide members are not so different from those stemming from the statutory sector. As described above, they aim to assist members in a wide number of ways, from emotional support and social diversion to practical advice and particular services. Some even undertake ambitious projects, such as day centers and residential homes. All such help is also available under certain circumstances from a considerable diversity of caring professionals employed by the many administrative arms of the welfare state. But to say this is not to get very far. Individual groups rarely provide all such help, and some do little at all. The availability of statutory help is similarly variable, much of it provided by local authorities (locally elected bodies) with some discretion over what they do. Discussing these issues in such a general way, in other words, is not very illuminating.

One means of being more specific is to consider how particular services are viewed by those on the receiving end. In many eyes, there is an intrinsic difference in the help provided by self-help groups and that available from paid professionals, expressly because of its source. The emotional support of a group of people in the same situation is not the same as such support from a social worker; a play scheme run by a voluntary group is not the same as one run by a public agency. Whatever the ostensible overlap in functions, they would argue, what people *receive* is very different. But the data from this study suggest that such generalizations must be treated with some caution. Some forms of help are thought best derived from self-help groups; others are sought from professional providers; others still are sought from whatever source that provides them.

First, to what extent do members join self-help groups because they lack help from any other source? How often does the group represent the *only* place to go? Among the members of the organizations studied, few appeared to join their group in any sense of desperation; the great majority (roughly two-thirds or more) had some help from other sources at the time they joined. Indeed, the proportions are much higher if attention is limited only to those who joined when their problems might be expected to be most acute: when first widowed or divorced or their handicapped child was born. Altogether, of those who had *no* other help at the time they joined, roughly half felt they needed some. They viewed their group as something of a lifeline. As one parent of a mentally handicapped child said: "I was banging my head against a brick wall and nobody cared." For this minority it was a question not of choice but of clutching at any help available. The remainder (of those who had no help at the time they joined) felt they were not in any special need, often because they had been living with the condition for some time. Some, indeed, had joined only because they wanted to be of help to others.

In most cases, then, the self-help group was seen as a useful supplement to other forms of help members were receiving. Much of this assistance stemmed from the informal sector: family, friends, and neighbors. Nonetheless, many members indicated that they had help from professional sources: doctors, social workers, and miscellaneous others such as health visitors, depending on their particular situation. They were not generally critical of such help and were often anxious to praise the efforts others had made on their behalf; they simply felt there was a limit to what could be expected from (and imposed upon) those with other work to do. The self-help group, by providing a ready source of people in the same situation, was seen as a valuable addition to the help available to them.

Second, what do members expect to gain from a group? Is it somehow different from what they get from other sources? The exact reasons for joining, not surprisingly, varied between different sorts of groups. The two organizations for people who had lost a marriage partner (widows and lone parents) tended to attract members for the company and emotional support they could provide. In their own words "you need people around you to realize it's not happened just to you." They were more likely to feel that their group had, because of its composition, a unique ability to help. As one divorced parent indicated, "Seeing people in the same situation as myself and coping gave me an incentive to soldier on"; and a widow stated that "other widows are the only ones who can understand." In other words, such support could not come from professionals, however well-meaning, and however hard they tried.

Members of the other two organizations, in contrast, were much more concerned to gain various forms of practical help and advice. Parents of mentally handicapped children, particularly, tended to explore every path: "We went everywhere; you find out everything you can." They saw their group as one obvious source of assistance because members would have had to face similar problems and would, as one carer said, "know all the snags that have cropped up." They were also, however, more likely to see the group as a means of finding out about other sources of help, including that from statutory agencies. As one parent of a mentally handicapped child suggested, "If you want to find out something, they will give you a steer." It should not be thought that they did not also view the group as a valuable source of emotional support, however. Talking to other parents, for instance, was clearly important: "A person who hasn't had a child like it has no idea what it's really like for 24 hours a day; they can make cooing sounds and be full of sympathy, but they're not actually in your shoes." Similarly, simply meeting other people in the same situation engendered a sense of identity; in the words of one carer, the group "made me feel less isolated, not a freak."

Where groups provided more substantial services, such as clubs for the handicapped or playgroups, members clearly benefited from this help, but there is little evidence that they viewed them as in some way different because of their source. As noted above, these were generally run by a few individuals (and, in some cases, paid staff), rather like any other voluntary organization. The study was not able to evaluate these projects, especially in comparison to those provided by statutory agencies, but they appeared to run smoothly and efficiently. In the eyes of members, they were a welcome resource—but so were their counterparts provided by the state. As they were typically set up where statutory provision was absent, there was rarely any competition for the consumer. Whoever provided them, such services were used and appreciated.

In all cases, self-help groups did have one clear draw over help from professional sources—the opportunity to give help back to others in the same situation. A substantial proportion of members joined in part because they wanted to work to help others, and many indicated that this had been one of the principal benefits of involvement. As suggested above, this help often came from those who no longer had the relevant problem or had come to terms with it. As one former carer said, "If I go to meetings, it is because I might be able to talk to people and assist them"; a single parent of some duration similarly remarked, "They need me, which is as it should be; it is the old members that are the only ones who can carry it for the new ones." There is no question that this is an important aspect of self-help groups, at least to some.

On the other hand, there were certain kinds of help that many members did not expect to gain from their group, despite efforts in some cases to take them on. These included both help requiring some professional expertise and various forms of practical assistance with their particular problems. With respect to the former, members tended to seek the relia-bility of expert knowledge; as one widow said, "It's not enough to be a widow—you need someone trained to help." With respect to the latter, the reasons were more complex. Some were reluctant to accept direct help from others, despite their common problems, out of a feeling of pride; as one officer of a carers group reported, "Pride and independence would lead them to disaffiliate rather than accept charity." Others were reluctant to take on any commitment to reciprocate—at least very often—and therefore did not want to impose. As one lone parent stated, "You can't help each other a lot as you're all bloody well struggling." The parent of a mentally handicapped child summed up her attitude to her group as "a self-help thing" but added, "Once you've got one of these children, you can't self-help; you're so literally tied." The ability to give help back to others, in other words, was not always great and tended to limit the amount of mutual aid (as opposed to mutual emotional support) mustered by groups.

In summary, what is being argued here is that, for the most part, self-help groups and statutory agencies tend to be sought for different sorts of help by people with problems. The two sorts of "services" are largely complementary. Practitioners of the helping professions can offer a great deal of advice and information, but they are not seen to have the depth of understanding that comes from someone who has been through the same problems. Furthermore, they do not provide the sense of a haven of like-minded or like-situated people. Nor, of course, does receiving help from the state offer the same sense of involvement as helping others. It was in these sorts of ways that members felt self-help groups made the most significant contribution to their welfare.

All of these benefits, however, were typically derived in the context of a considerable amount of help from a variety of professionals, and few members suggested that their self-help groups were anything more than a very desirable "extra" on top of such assistance. It is difficult to generalize about such help, because individuals' needs vary so much over time and there are periods during which little, in fact, can be done. Where members needed medical or legal advice, not to mention financial assistance, these were not generally seen as the province of their group to supply. As noted above, some groups did organize large-scale projects, such as playgroups and hostels, but for most members such assistance was gained, if at all, from other sources. Many felt that the statutory services could be improved, and some indeed had joined expressly in order to press collectively for change, but they were generally highly appreciative of public efforts made on their behalf.

There were certain kinds of help, however, which seemed to fall too frequently between the two stools of statutory and voluntary provision. These were often the unexciting but nonetheless valuable supportive services that could help people cope more easily with their lives: baby-sitting, running errands, providing transport, or simply visiting the housebound. Such activities are often thought to be the ideal territory of self-help groups, but as indicated above there is in fact a limit to what members can do for one another. Many members, particularly officers, put in long hours and invested considerable energies into organizing such mutual assistance, but in the final analysis their collective abilities were heavily constrained. The very fact that self-help group members have problems (which is, after all, why they join) means that they have problems in doing very much to help others. The blind can lead the blind only so far.

SELF-HELP GROUPS AND
STATUTORY CARE PROVIDERS

If most self-help groups and most statutory agencies *do* different things, the question then arises of how they relate to one another on an everyday basis. To what extent do they have any contact, and what do they think of one another? As indicated at the beginning of this chapter, there is enormous variation between different groups. Some have virtually no contact with any public agencies in their area, some have occasional discussions, and others work closely with local professionals concerned with their particular problems. Organizations, like ordinary individuals, do not have regular contacts with one another purely randomly; they get together for some reason. Groups tend to initiate discussions with outside organizations for one of three purposes: to help their individual members, to help the group itself, and to help the wider population of people with the relevant problem. The extent and nature of such contact are discussed in turn below.

It has been shown above that most self-help groups are concerned to help their members in a wide variety of ways, and securing the help of statutory agencies is clearly one of these. This is often simply a matter of giving individual members a helping hand with specific queries: checking what benefits they are entitled to or investigating how to go about applying for a place in a residential home. Some self-help group officers tried to keep one or more useful contacts among workers in statutory agencies expressly for this purpose, enabling them to make an inquiry by a quick telephone call. In addition, officers often made some effort to provide their members general information about sources of help in their area. They not only collected leaflets and other publicity put out by public agencies but also invited representatives of key local departments to talk at meetings about their services. The majority of groups studied had some contacts for these purposes.

The second reason for some contact between self-help groups and statutory agencies is to help the groups themselves. Local professionals often helped groups indirectly by publicizing their existence and referring potential members to them. Some personal contact was typically found to be useful in bringing the group to a worker's attention. Much more crucial, however, certain local government departments (particularly the Social Services Department) often helped groups directly—giving financial grants, offering premises in which to meet, and generally helping them to function more efficiently. Such help was found to be surprisingly common. Financial grants ranged from only a few (9 percent) of the widows' groups to a substantial proportion (40 percent) of the groups for mentally handicapped children. Many of the sums involved (1979-1980 data) were small: £50 or £100 (roughly $85-$170) to help them distribute a newsletter or pay for a meeting room. Nonetheless, some were sizable indeed; one-quarter of those to groups for mentally handicapped children were for £1,000 (roughly $1,700) or more. These were generally for some specific purpose—to pay for transport expenses or running clubs for the handicapped—but some were untied. In addition, many groups had the rent-free use of premises from their local authority, ranging from a few carer groups to one-third of those for mentally handicapped children.

All local groups that had any such help from their local authority clearly had to have some contact with its representatives. The extent and nature of their relations, however, varied enormously. In some cases, contact was kept to a minimum. The self-help group officers simply filled in a form to renew arrangements made some years previously and seemed happy to carry on with little further discussions. At the other end of the spectrum, some groups worked very closely with local statutory personnel to develop what could virtually be seen as joint projects. This was most in evidence in the case of the groups for mentally handicapped children. One, for instance, was in the process of setting up a Special Care Unit (a day center for the very severely handicapped) in its area at the time of the study. While active in fund raising for this project, it had attracted a large government grant toward its capital and running costs. The group planned to run the unit itself but hoped to hand it over at some future date to the local authority to finance and run. A separate management committee had been established for the unit, involving both the officers of the self-help group and key professional administrators in the area. The details of these arrangements need not be elaborated here; the essential point is the obvious closeness of the relations necessary in order to develop them. As the group chairman himself stated, "Everyone knows what everyone else is doing; this works to mutual benefit."

Groups can also be assisted indirectly by local-authority staff employed expressly to liaise with and advise local voluntary organizations, including self-help groups. Many authorities have such community workers, whose functions are both to help develop new groups and to assist existing groups to mobilize their resources more effectively. They can also help groups by publicizing their existence to potential members and to professionals who might refer people to them. A few of the groups studied had received some attention from such workers, although not typically on more than a very occasional basis.

The third reason for contacts between self-help groups and local statutory agencies is to help the wider population of people with the relevant problem. Put in another way, this refers to all the pressure-group or political activities of self-help groups. As noted above, self-help groups are not solely concerned with the problems of their own immediate members; they also try to influence government policy, at both central and local levels, on their behalf. While some of this activity can be undertaken at a distance, by letters to the local papers, for example, it is commonly carried through as well by personal discussions with key figures with some influence. Many self-help group officers carefully initiate and maintain relations with such people, from local-authority (elected) councilors and officials to their Members of Parliament. They invite them to group meetings from time to time or ask to see them about specific issues. In some cases, such people are brought onto the group committee in order to ensure regular contact and opportunities for discussion.

Again, groups were found to vary enormously in the frequency and nature of such contact. Some, very simply, had none at all. They chose to take little interest in policy issues and did not pursue any political or professional figures in order to influence their thinking. Others took such an interest only occasionally, when prompted by their head offices or by a particular local issue or problem. But for some groups such discussions were seen as an integral part of what they were about. They kept a careful watch on local and national policy developments and aimed to make themselves an effective voice on their members' behalf. A few of those studied took part in regular consultation sessions with relevant local officials for this purpose.

One obvious, but also critical, feature of the relations between self-help groups and local statutory personnel is that they are cumulative. Although contacts may be initiated solely for one purpose, they can be—and often are—maintained for others. Groups that have frequent relations because they are in receipt of some financial assistance, for instance, may be more able to get help with members' enquiries or get their voice heard on policy matters. Conversely, groups that have no reasons for any ongoing contact can find that they are less able to make their views known when they wish to do so. Some groups, in recognition of this fact, made an explicit effort to keep in touch with local professionals. One chairwoman of a carers group, for instance, said she regularly invited those holding particular posts to speak at meetings, so that "having seen us, they know who we are when we need things." Other groups, as noted above, actually involved key statutory workers directly on their group committees.

The value of regular contact can also become evident when there is much turnover, either in the external professional posts or in the officers of the self-help groups themselves. One chairwoman of a widows group expressed considerable disappointment that she had just got on familiar terms with a key social services official only to find that he was moving to a new area. New chairpersons, similarly, had to take time to build up good relationships with local statutory personnel. A history of previous relations between the two organizations could prove helpful, but individuals none-theless had to develop their own mutual trust and acceptability. There were some groups with no contacts in the statutory sector in part because of this problem.

The extent and purpose of contacts have been shown to vary, but what of their nature? To a very large degree, the relations of most of the groups with their local statutory agencies were very good. The self-help group officers felt that the professionals were helpful to them, appreciative of their needs, and responsive to individual requests. Similarly, local officials spoke well of the groups and their dealings with them. Few group officers felt that local professionals were obstructive or unhelpful; few statutory workers felt that the group officers took advantage of their access. There was a great deal of goodwill on both sides.

Interviews with officials at a number of different levels, from heads of departments to junior personnel, elicited a surprising degree of unanimity about the value of self-help groups. They wanted to "work in harness, rather than against them" and were full of praise for individual officers: "strong, able and committed people." Some were apologetic for their own inability to act as quickly and efficiently as outside groups would like, feeling, in one official's words, "shackled by officialdom and bureauc-racy." They generally gave the impression of trying to help groups func-tion as effectively as possible, even where this could mean some criticism of their own departmental work.

But good relations were not always seen as a blessing. Some officers were criticized by their members for being too close to those in positions of authority, too anxious not to "rock the boat." It was suggested that their desire to appear cooperative meant that they could not operate effectively as a pressure group. This was often particularly an issue when money was at stake, as officers would not want to prejudice a local grant; as one said, "We must always be looking over our shoulders; we've got to be careful not to put our heads on the block." Interestingly, it was a criticism that was also made by local-authority officials themselves. Some felt that the self-help groups in their area were too undemanding, too unwilling to stick their necks out on controversial issues. There were times, in other words, when good relations were felt to get in the way of effective action.

Where relations were particularly close—for instance, where local-authority personnel were co-opted onto group committees—it could prove difficult to distinguish whose opinions were whose. One local administrator, for instance, said that he often tried to get his group's support for services his department "wanted to see expanded." Another said he tried to educate members to appreciate the constraints on local authorities, so that they could be a more effective pressure group. The very frequency of contact, in other words, meant that they generally worked together, each learning from the other side.

It should not be thought, however, that relations were always of a positive nature. Some officers felt they receive little help from local agencies and, in a few cases, actual hindrance. A secretary of a group for lone parents said that one local office not only refused to display a notice but also seemed "to intimate that, as far as they are concerned, the group is a figment of my imagination." Problems could also develop where a community worker became actively involved in a group. In one case, a well-intentioned worker was co-opted onto a group committee to, in his eyes, "show them how to run the group." He had many good ideas but introduced such substantial changes that many of the original members promptly left. Relations deteriorated to such an extent that he eventually resigned, turning his attention to other groups in the area. Such difficulties could prove discouraging for both sides, making groups suspicious about outsiders and community workers uncertain about their own roles.

One might well ask what factors affect the relations between self-help groups and local statutory agencies. To some extent it is probably a matter of luck—active and outgoing group officers, on the one hand, and receptive and interested professionals, on the other. But this is not the whole of the story. It has been shown that frequent contacts are generally beneficial, enabling the two sides to approach each other more as friends or colleagues than as intrusive outsiders. This means, perhaps counterintuitively, that those groups making most demands on local professionals may have better relations than those who modestly try not to impose. It also means that those groups that develop some sizable projects, or take an active interest in local policy issues, are more likely to be known and generate some sympathy than those that keep to themselves.

But self-help groups are not *all* identical bodies, and there are undoubtedly striking differences in the ways they approach local professionals and are seen by them. Some represent unquestionably worthy causes, while others may be seen as peripheral or concerned with problems whose moral status is in some way uncertain. The demands they make may similarly be seen as more or less legitimate. Some groups involve officers who are more accustomed to dealing with authority and may prove more acceptable to administrators solely on the basis of their social class, sex, or general personal style. The key officers of one of the groups studied, for instance, were retired local government staff themselves; they clearly had an advantage in making any approach to their council. Some groups, furthermore, are more able to mobilize other resources, not only financial but also other forms of support, such as the endorsement of leading local figures, giving them more status in the public eye. Furthermore, it must be added that local authorities themselves do not speak with a single voice; some are much more concerned to respond to local groups than others, and the same holds for individual staff and elected members *within* individual authorities. There is a wide range of factors, in other words, that will affect the legitimacy and effectiveness of self-help groups in the outside world.

One resource that can prove helpful, made available by some organizations to their local groups, is professional assistance from within. As noted in the introductory discussion, many self-help groups have more organizational resources at their disposal than the time and energies of their own members. Those groups with some assistance from professional workers within their own organizations were often at an advantage. These workers, whether operating from a national headquarters, a regional office, or more informally from their own homes, were often able to smooth the path of local groups to other local agencies. They could chat informally with local statutory workers on a more equal basis than could ordinary members, but at the same time relate to the groups themselves as insiders. In so doing, they had to be extremely cautious not to be seen as outsiders from both sides, especially as self-help group officers could become hostile to any interference in their own sphere of activity. Nonetheless, where the individuals involved acted with some sensitivity, they could prove very helpful indeed.

CONCLUDING COMMENTS

Surprisingly little academic attention has been given to the growth of self-help groups in Britain. The research on which this chapter is based represents one of the few major studies in this field. While the territory covered by this study was fairly large, there was clearly a limit to the number of issues that could be explored in any depth. Furthermore, only a few groups could be given proper attention. It would thus be inappropriate to endow any conclusions with too much significance. They represent, rather, a first step to understanding what self-help groups are all about.

This chapter has sought to demonstrate the very considerable diversity to be found among self-help groups in practice. They come in many shapes and sizes, undertake to provide many different activities and services, and have quite varying relationships with the outside world. Some are able to develop sizable projects, entailing their own premises and paid staff; others do little more than meet on an occasional basis, having limited funds and presumably equally limited energy. Some are well-known in their areas, keeping in regular touch with local agencies to help their members or to campaign on their behalf; others are so withdrawn as to be little known to anyone. However, one of the more constant factors found in this research was a high degree of amicability between groups and those working for other organizations in their area; their relations were generally of a very friendly nature.

What implications for those working for statutory agencies follow from these findings? First, it is clear that they can play an important role in the development of self-help groups. Those in touch with potential members, such as social workers and health visitors, can make a contribution by simply referring people to a relevant group. Those with access to local resources, not only funds but also premises and transport, can help groups to learn about and make use of them. It is important that professional workers get to know the key groups in their area. They should find out not only what groups exist and what they do but also the names of the principal officers. This is not as easy as it sounds, since there is often considerable change and turnover—in the individuals running groups, in what they do, and in the very existence of groups themselves.

Second, as a corollary to learning about individual groups, professionals must begin to recognize the lack of a single pattern among them. They must not assume that one group is quite like another or adopt a single stance toward groups as a whole. Like the individuals of whom they are composed, groups have differing strengths, differing limitations, and, indeed, differing life spans. An appreciation of these differences and a willingness to work within the constraints they necessarily impose can lead to both more realistic policies and more effective practices with respect to this component of the voluntary sector.

Finally, self-help groups should be seen as a significant resource for those living and working in local areas. They are not typically in competition with public agencies either in what they do or in how they are seen by those involved with them. By helping members to cope better with their particular problems, they probably act to reduce demands on certain statutory services—not to increase them. On the other hand, by informing members about other sources of help, they perform an important consumer rights function, probably increasing taking-up of benefits and services among those entitled to them. Mobilizing the goodwill and energies of those familiar with particular conditions and problems, they represent a bargain for the community at large. Furthermore, where they are active as local pressure groups, they may be seen as useful allies by those concerned to improve individual public services, including those working for them. Their interests are not necessarily at variance with one another, but quite the reverse; they have many concerns in common.

In the final analysis, the very diversity to be found among self-help groups and what they do makes generalization difficult. Those who believe in limited public expenditure and the importance of individual responsibility will welcome those groups who provide for themselves and do not demand increased services from the public sector. Conversely, those who believe that people with problems have a right to more statutory services will give particular welcome to those groups who emphasize their political role. Not only do both kinds of groups exist, but individual groups swiftly take on new attitudes and activities as they feel circumstances warrant. It is difficult, in other words, to adopt a blanket stance because of the variability among different groups and within the same ones over time. Those working for statutory agencies, along with any others interested in these groups, must adapt themselves to this complexity. It represents the essence of self-help in practice.

REFERENCES

Gartner, A., & Riessman, F. *Self-help in the human services.* San Francisco: Jossey-Bass, 1977.

Katz, A. H., & Bender, E. I. *The strength in us: Self-help groups in the modern world.* New York: Franklin Watts, 1976.

Richardson, A., & Goodman, M. *Self-help and social care.* London: Policy Studies Institute, forthcoming.

Robinson, D. *Talking out of alcoholism: The self-help process of Alcoholics Anonymous.* London: Croom Helm, 1979.

Robinson, D., & Henry, S. *Self-help and health: Mutual aid for modern problems.* London: Martin Robinson, 1977.

Robinson, D., & Robinson, Y. *From self-help to health.* London: Concord Books, 1979.

III

PROSPECTS FOR POLICY

11

CITIZEN PARTICIPATION IN HEALTH CARE

FRANCINE LAVOIE
Quebec

Quebec, one of Canada's ten provinces, has a population of 6,230,000 of which 80 percent is French-speaking and 15 percent English-speaking. During the past three decades this province has experienced profound and varied social changes. First of all, this period has been marked by rapid urbanization. While in 1950, two-thirds of the population lived in cities, by 1971 this proportion had jumped to 80 percent, with half the population living in the region of Montreal alone (Orban, 1976). A second important social transformation has been the rapid decline of the Catholic church's influence. In 1960 the Catholic church was a key social insitution: Health, education, and welfare services (which it often owned) were under its control. It was relegated to its spiritual role when the state took over these services ten years later (Renaud, 1978). At the same time that this urbanization and this rapid decline of ecclesiastic power were occurring, a technocratic elite was developing, favoring expansion of the state's role and centralization of the human services (Lesemann, 1978). Finally, a strong renewal of Quebecois nationalism has been experienced in the last three decades, leading to the election in 1976 of a government advocating sovereignty from Canada.

These social changes, which other countries have also undergone, are characterized in Quebec by the rapidity with which they have taken place.

AUTHOR'S NOTE: *I wish to express my gratitude to Dr. François Doré for his critical comments.*

The expression "quiet revolution" is generally used to designate the changes which took place in the 1960s, though the expression "quiet reform" would be more fitting. Political decisions concerning the maintenance and promotion of good health in the population have obviously been influenced by these characteristics.

INSTITUTIONAL REFORMS

A look at a few prominent events in the history of the human services in Quebec will give a better idea of the institutional and political context in which the values of self-responsibility for health and autonomy with respect to the intervention of specialists developed.

During the 1950s, the province of Quebec was governed by a political party whose health care policies were distinctly outmoded and reactionary; this led to predominance of the federal government in this field (Lesemann, 1981). Hospital insurance was introduced by the federal government in 1961. In 1966, this same government promulgated the Health Insurance Act, establishing a universal and obligatory program which was not to be adopted by Quebec until 1969. During the same period, the government of Quebec was attempting to take back control of the administration of human services policies. It set up a commission of enquiry on health and social welfare, the Commission Castonguay-Nepveu of 1967-1973, whose mandate was to examine the services in this field. The conclusions of this commission gave rise to major reforms which were all the more efficient because the commission's principal leaders were named to key positions in the government administration. The roles of present institutions were to a great degree defined during this period.

Like other reforms of the government of Quebec, this calling into question of the human services had three particular features (Renaud, 1981). First, the reforms were heralded by elaborate ideological pronouncements that were highly publicized and that took shape around social democratic objectives (equal distribution of wealth, citizen participation, and so on), creating high expectations in the population. Second, the massive administrative reorganization that followed was carried out without any trial runs. Third, there was a large gulf between the ideological pronouncements and the concrete realizations, which ended up being similar to those that had appeared in other Canadian provinces but in very different social climates.

As regards citizen participation, the reforms of the 1960s and 1970s created institutions in which in principle they had a say in matters. The essential ones were the "hospital centers," in fact a new name for the hospitals; the "social service centers," which united once separate social welfare services under one administration; and the "local community service centers" (LCSC), which are front-line institutions with a community vocation. The LCSCs are oriented toward prevention as much in the medical as the social domains and their work is handled by multidisciplinary teams.

Generally speaking, the creation of the hospital centers and the social service centers had the effect of accentuating professionalization in the areas of needs analysis, problem definition, and service delivery. Their role consists essentially in ensuring the health and productivity of workers and in managing marginal groups (delinquents, the elderly, and so on) through the delivery of services or government benefits. The LCSCs, according to the reforms, were to promote citizen participation and diminish the recourse to "curative" institutions; they suggested the possibility of radical change and became because of this bearers of hope. However, the ideological declarations concerning the LCSCs, founded on citizen participation, decentralization and more efficient delivery of services to marginal groups, proved to be far removed from the actual practice (Divay & Godbout, 1978; Lesemann, 1981) in spite of some interesting attempts such as community involvement in the pre-implementation period and participation in program development and personnel selection (CLSC-Santé, 1979).

In sum, the reforms in the human service institutions gave rise in general to an increase in the centralization of decision making, to growth of the curative rather than the preventive sector, to the neglect of workers' and users' participation, to bureaucratic rationalization working against rank-and-file workers and in certain cases to the taking of control again by medical doctors (Renaud, 1978, 1981). The creation of a new place of practice and new institution, the LCSC, as well as the administrative reorganization of the traditional institutions were not sufficient to realize the community objectives of these reforms and even reinforced professional prerogatives.

PROFESSIONAL PRACTICE

During the 1970s, a new movement again took up the goals of community ideology but applied them above all to the modification of professional practice. Developed by unsatisfied professionals, this new movement took the form of intervention through networks and was implemented in

various human service institutions. Two principles inspire the protagonists
of this movement: reappropriation of demand for care by network members, that is, the collectivization of the demand of the patient; and
self-determination of the network members in the process of taking
responsibility for their problems based on confidence in their capacity to
resolve them (Alary, 1980). These principles approach the definition of
participation as formulated by Green, Werlin, Schauffer, and Avery
(1977).

We choose to describe documented interventions; one will not find a
complete picture of this movement in the province of Quebec. The
principal groups are Network Intervention (*Intervention en réseau*) of the
Douglas Hospital Center and the Research Group on Network Practice
(*Groupe de recherche sur les pratiques de réseaux*), which is affiliated with
the School of Social Work at the Université de Montréal. Since the two
groups draw on a strategy of action research for inspiration, they propose
decentralization of access to knowledge and decision making in interventions (Mayer & Desmarais, 1980; Rousseau, 1980). Despite the similarity
of their respective objectives and strategies, the two groups have different
histories, probably related to the differences in their institutional ties.

Network Intervention has been affiliated since 1977 with the Community Psychiatry Center of the Douglas Psychiatric Hospital Center. Subsidized by external funds, a multidisciplinary team of researchers and
intervenors dissatisfied with the traditional mode of intervention, experi-
mented with the Speck and Rueveni (1977) model for one year to develop
their own mode of intervention through primary network in noncrisis
situations (Desmarais, 1980). Blanchet, Cossette, Dauphinais, Desmarais,
Kasma, Lavigueur, Mayer, and Roy (1982) tested its applications in a
traditional intervention setting during 15 months, by taking charge of
twenty-five patients of a city district referred to the hospital center. The
specific objectives of their intervention were as follows: to increase the
number of participants in the primary network; to improve the quality of
the relations between the patient and his or her network, for example, to
generate a certain reciprocity; and to encourage openness toward the
network on the part of the patient. Their general objective was to formu-
late an alternative to psychiatric care and to be a source of institutional
renewal.

The team succeeded in using a network approach, sometimes combined
with individual psychotherapy, with fourteen of the twenty-five patients.
They conclude that resistance came often from the professional, who
judged the patient unprepared; in other cases, the patient refused—had no

network or a negative one. Their outcome measures, referring to symptoms, to satisfaction, or to the size of the network, are not truly informative. The results attained seem similar to traditional interventions and the team does not discuss the effect of their five years' endeavor at the institution. In conclusion, it would seem that for taking charge of a city district or for a high number of crisis patients, the application of this model is not very appropriate. Significant innovative tendencies do not appear to have been introduced into the institution. In addition, the institution has been critical of the group's insular nature, the experimental and extravagant character of its activities, and its being out of touch with the day-to-day experience of other workers. The experiment was terminated in 1982.

A team of university professors forms the core of the Research Group on Network Practice, which, like the preceding group, enjoys government subsidies. Their model is disseminated partly through the training sessions they offer to practitioners and partly by graduate students trained in the group. One of the characteristics of their experiment has been the variety of institutions in which attempts to implement their model have been made. The underlying philosophy involves the promotion of a double shift of the initial demand for aid: first, from the individual to the collectivity, and second, from dependence on the institutional services to autonomy and the concomitant utilization by the collectivity of its own resources (Brodeur & Rousseau, 1980). The action research process permits the participation of any practitioners interested in having such experimentation going on in their workplace and even of the administrators of these institutions. The clientele most often singled out for this type of intervention consists of multiple-problem families and psychiatric patients, depending on the choice of the practitioners.

Despite the theoretical value of this approach, adoption of the model presents certain difficulties. Beausoleil (1980) reported the problems that were brought up in case studies of network interventions carried out in two institutions. First, the workers at these institutions said that they were already applying this model, when in fact this does not seem to have been the case. Second, the administrators criticized the lack of evaluation of these trials; for them, the model's effectiveness had not yet been demonstrated, particularly when considering the use of novel human resources, the reduction of institutionalization, and the cost. As no planned evaluation was used, the reports of qualitative changes like reduction of the intensity of crisis, reduction of demands for material aid, and increase of demands for advice and discussions do not influence the administrators. Lately, this group has split into two research teams, one further documenting the network interventions, the other working on the organizational factors that influenced the development of eight alternative modes of practice in human service institutions. Final reports are not yet available.

THE FUTURE OF NETWORK INTERVENTION
IN HUMAN SERVICE INSTITUTIONS

Though it is too early to evaluate the impact of these attempts to change professional practice in the human services, it is on the other hand possible to mention a few factors that may influence the adoption or the rejection of network intervention in such settings.

First, we will ask which workers in the caregiving system would be the most likely to adopt this type of innovation and what their reasons for adopting such a model would be. Social workers, psychologists, and paramedical workers would be the most likely ones to be won over to a model of intervention through networks because they have the least power of any in these institutions and have only to gain by an intervention that involves the dismantling of the hierarchical organization of care delivery (Bozzini, 1981). In addition, this model might constitute an effective means of slowing down the growing trend toward Taylorization (or compartmentalization) of their work that has appeared in recent years.

Second, intervention through networks might also have a certain attraction for institutions that are little inclined to radical self-questioning. The social determinants with which this model is concerned (the family and the neighborhood) are recognized by tradition, and their analysis gives rise to less profound ideological debate than would other determinants, such as the organization of work or poverty. Many administrators perceive network intervention as a variant of family therapy, so why not try a revamped version proclaiming a toned-down community ideology?

Third, it can be noted that in all cases, intervention through networks is aimed at populations that overuse professional services and suffer from chronic or multiple problems. These populations show little response to the traditional treatments given by institutions and therefore the risk of failure is high no matter what method of intervention is tried. The testing of the model of intervention through networks with such populations is demanding and may lead to a negative evaluation.

Although the two experiments described above are promising and could make up for the failure of the governmental reforms of recent years to involve the citizens, they entail a considerable risk, given the conditions that prompt the adoption of intervention through networks and the clientele toward which it is currently directed. This new model could, in the hands of technocrats, become a tool used to limit the access of the most disadvantaged groups in Quebecois society to professional services, which would then be reserved for the affluent. Furthermore, intervention through networks does not necessarily live up to its promises of participation, collectivization, and autonomy.

CONSUMERS OF SERVICES

Have the reforms in Quebec human service institutions prompted attempts at change other than those affecting the practitioners? More precisely, have there been attempts at change on the part of the consumers of these services?

It is interesting to note that in an evaluation of 62 clients of *Coupe-Circuit* (an alternative psychiatric clinic in Quebec city), Langlois (1982) concludes that of the four types of lay helpers implicated (permanent members of the clinic's collective; family and friends; neighbors and members of citizens' groups; ex-clients), the ex-clients and the members of community groups were the most efficient. This shows the importance of the mutual aid movement and the potential of groups.

On the other hand, among consumer groups, the self-help ones have had the strongest voice in claims for participation at all levels in the caregiving system and the taking of self-responsibility for health. Though the presence of these groups has made itself felt more markedly since 1976, their development has been and remains slow. Given the potential for change that the self-help groups represent (Romeder, 1980), interesting questions can be asked concerning their present situation and the reasons their growth is held back.

Lavoie (in press) identifies six types of self-help groups currently active in Quebec. They handle the following types of cases: drug addiction; long-term psychosocial problems (*Déprimés anonymes, Parents anonymes, Association de personnes obèses du Québec*); crisis situations; chronic physical illnesses; close relatives of people with problems; and social identity problems. A Canadian study (Romeder, 1980) showed that in Quebec and in Canada the most numerous groups are those concerning themselves with the problems of addiction and obesity. Contrary to what is happening in the United States (President's Commission on Mental Health, 1978), the advantages and innovative potential of the self-help groups have not been emphasized by either the federal or provincial governments or even by citizens' committees. They are often ignored: professionals in insitutions are not very open to this form of consumer group. What is the source of this indifference?

The federal and provincial governments could have followed in the footsteps of the U.S. government and have argued that self-help groups can be used to reduce the costs of the human services without reducing their quality. However, the current economic crisis in Quebec and Canada has sufficed to justify the considerable cutbacks recently applied to these services. Resorting to self-help groups' ideology to introduce a reduction of costs has thus become of no use, and the governments have escaped the inherent risks which dealing with such potential claim makers could entail. Nor are the governments ready to make use of the self-help groups to break the monopoly held by professional groups on the definition and treatment of health and social problems. This role is already played by various public service unions, which have been working for many years in Quebec on the dismantling of the hierarchical organization of service delivery (Bozzini, 1981; Cartier, 1979). The government administrations are willing to make room for the self-help groups only in cases of chronic problems or marginal clientele, areas in which the medical hegemony is least and for which the traditional solutions are extremely costly. This analysis leads us to believe that the federal and provincial governments will continue to treat the self-help groups just like they do voluntary organizations. In other words, governmental support will probably be limited to tax exemptions, circulation of information, and training of leaders. The only direct financial contribution will take the form of grants for a few pilot projects conforming to priorities defined by the government itself.

The attitudes of Quebecois professionals toward self-help groups vary considerably: They go from total rejection to help in setting them up. Medical professionals provide support to self-help groups concerned with physical problems such as handicaps by collaborating in the raising of funds for the latest research. This type of support obviously remains oriented toward cure rather than care (Navarro, 1975). Certain other professionals find nothing original about the self-help group experience because they themselves are working with "their" group of clients on taking self-responsibility and developing autonomy. Others perceive the self-help groups, like the volunteers, as a threat to their jobs. This reaction has become more and more common since the government of Quebec imposed heavy budget restrictions on human service institutions, often leading to cutbacks in personnel. That very few professionals are interested in alternatives in mental health care may be due to the ideology that the latter may convey and the potential for institutional reform that they represent (*Syndicat des Professionels des Affaires Sociales de Québec,* 1981).

Adult educators are one particular type of professional working with the self-help groups. Financed largely by the public education system, they offer courses conveying values that contradict the experience of these groups: The use of a professor, even when the latter is defined as a resource person, hardly encourages the calling into question of experts; furthermore, these courses are characterized by their focus on self-actualization, resulting in partial, individualist analysis of problem causation, and their duration is limited. This formula is particularly attractive for self-help groups with a poorly developed ideological base. It is easily accessible and responds to the strong inclination of Quebeckers for things that are presented in the form of a course. The alienation thus hidden within this sophisticated package contributes to the choking of the potential for change that the self-help groups offer.

Interestingly enough, there exist reports of the points of view of four Quebec self-help groups concerning their experiences with professionals (Cantin & Daoust, 1981; Beaudry, 1981; Langlois, 1981; AUTO-PSY, 1981). Generally speaking they report that the development of their group begins with a critique of traditional professional practice. The four groups maintain ties with professionals as individuals, but this choice is determined by the quality of the relationships thus established; three groups exclude the institutions' representatives by ignoring their existence or by confronting their philosophy.

In sum, professionals do not generally constitute dynamic elements in the formation and development of self-help groups. This conclusion must be qualified by the observation that the working conditions of professionals rarely permit them to enter into contact with the self-help groups; thus, their typical reactions, apart from a few fortunate exceptions, are mistrust, a wait-and-see attitude, and fear of the threat of deprofessionalization (Bozzini, 1981).

Given the inertia of government administrations and the resistance on the part of professionals, other interest groups are one of the most effective sources of self-help group development. Among these interest groups, the recently formed alternative resource organizations (AUTO-PSY, 1981; Beaudry, 1981) deserve mention.

An Illustration

The history of the Service d'entraide des veuves will serve to illustrate the roles of the diverse social actors involved in self-help groups. The Service d'entraide des veuves, run by nonprofessionals who are themselves widows, is meant for recently widowed women. Its goals are to help them overcome this crisis, to inform them of their rights, and to facilitate their reintegration into society.

It was set up five years ago by a pressure group uniting groups and individuals interested in the status of women: the Fédération des femmes du Québec. Aware of women's problems and considering widows as among the worst off, the Fédération wanted to aid in the setting up of such a self-help group in the mainly francophone city of Quebec so as to create a model for the other regions of the province. This association received a grant from the federal government for the setting up of the project. It intended to withdraw itself several years later out of respect for the desire for autonomy of the Service d'entraide des veuves. The two groups still maintain some ties however, by which the latter benefits through, among other things, more advanced training for its personnel and participation in an advocacy group that unites many women's organizations with common concerns (pensions, for example). The presence of the Fédération des femmes du Québec has proven to be essential to the development of this self-help group. In the conservative field of helping widows, the Fédération helped further an innovative approach. In addition, by dealing with the main demands regarding the laws and institutions, it has made it possible for the Service d'entraide des veuves to concentrate on the immediate needs of its members.

Government participation has varied over the years. A federal government subsidy facilitated the group's emergence and bolstered its innovative image. The provincial government, whose aid is less but constant, has treated the Service d'entraide like a traditional voluntary group. It did, however, encourage circulation of the group's principles by financing a provincial symposium. The existence of a large budget right from the beginning has rendered the group suspect in the eyes of other organizations, has forced it to adopt a bureaucratic management model far removed from its leaders' interests, has probably made the recruiting of volunteers more difficult, and was the source of a major crisis when the three-year federal subsidy came to an end. Established in a prosperous period, the group might not make it through the present budgetary crisis.

Professional involvement in the Service d'entraide des veuves experience has been minimal. Even though this self-help group is not in competition with the professionals, since few of them are interested in this clientele, this is not a sufficient condition for the creation of a collaborative relationship between the two. In fact, the professionals either look upon the group as a leisure club or—and this occurs more and more frequently—refer people with multiple chronic problems to it. In addition, professionals treat the group this way without first informing themselves about its objectives and methods. It goes without saying that few of them offer their support excepting occasionally as lecturers; never do they call their role as experts into question.

Another social actor with a predominant role is worth mentioning: the public charitable organizations. The Service d'entraide des veuves has appealed to them on a regular basis in an attempt to diversify its financial sources, but to no avail. These organizations influence the self-help group all the same through the criteria they set down. They attempt to impose an essentially technocratic working method on voluntary groups by, first, grouping them according to clientele served, ignoring differences in ideology or modes of intervention, and second, requiring that the clientele include a certain number of referrals from professionals. One of these organizations has criticized the Service d'entraide des veuves for its lack of interest in the real needs of widows. Quite obviously, such a self-help group is constantly in contact with the problems of these people. This group benefited from two professionally conducted studies on the needs of widows, one of which was used in preparing the setting up of the group. How is it that a public charitable organization refuses to recognize the expertise of a widow self-help group concerning the needs of widows?

Following this overview of the involvement of advocacy groups, governments, professionals, and public charitable organizations in the history of the Service d'entraide des veuves, one can see the importance of such groups forming alliances with other pressure groups.

Generally speaking, the formation of alliances among different self-help groups or between self-help groups and pressure groups makes for better dissemination of innovative approaches and for wider-ranging discussion of the causes of problems experienced by the members. Moreover, these exchanges provide a forum for the development of strategies for dealing with the concerned social agents (Beaudry, 1981). It must also be stressed that such coalitions can influence the practice of professionals and even of researchers because they can bring attention to some new explaining factors (Gregg, Preston, Geist, & Caplan, 1979).

CONCLUSIONS

Neither institutional change alone nor attempts to modify professional practice through the network approach seem to lead effectively to the participation of citizens in health care and maintenance of quality of life. It remains to be seen if the mutual aid movement, even with the formation of coalitions, will have a greater impact than these two initiatives.

Considering this situation, what can we do as professionals? I suggest two ways of getting involved. First, we should reflect on which institutional structures can lead to innovation with regard to the professional's role and to the contribution of lay helping resources. There will always be institutions; we should not be naive and we should learn to better them.

Second, we should work to implement some projects pertaining to helping networks. Even more, we should disseminate what we learn (the results, the problems of implementation, and so forth), and we should evaluate those projects in ways respectful of their values (small size, centered on process more than on results, and so on). The professional should be more than a consultant, he or she should be involved in action research following two approaches: research on definite problems identified by the people involved in the networks (through participation, training, and the like) and development of explanatory models (on the causes and the evolution of the problems, on the helping factors, elaborated from the people's experiences; Lavoie, 1982). Action research is a way to avoid the professionalization of lay helpers and, combined with evaluation, a way to sensitize the administrators.

Finally, we should all work to promote valuable citizen participation in health care.

REFERENCES

Alary, J. Les antécédents de "l'approche feseau" en service social. *Service social,* 1980, *29,* 267-275.

AUTO-PSY. Pas assez fou pour mettre le feu. *Santé mentale au Québec,* 1981, *6,* 161-167.

Beaudry, M. Les maisons de femmes battues au Québec: Du groupe autonome à la prise en charge par l'Etat. *Revue internationale d'action communautaire,* 1981, *6-46,* 151-160.

Beausoleil, J. Une double expérience d'implantation de la pratique de réseaux en milieu institutionnel. *Service social,* 1980, *29,* 342-358.

Blanchet, L., Cossette, D., Dauphinais, R., Desmarais, D., Kasma, J., Lavigueur, H., Mayer, R., & Roy, L. *Réseau primaire et santé mentale: Une expérience de recherche-action.* Unité de recherche psycho-sociale. Centre de psychiatrie communautaire, Centre hospitalier Douglas, Avril 1982.

Bozzini, L. L'expertise et la hiérarchie sanitaire en question. In L. Bozzini, M. Rénaud, D. Gaucher, & J. Llambias-Woeff (Eds.), *Médecine et société, les années 80.* Laval: Editions cooperatives Albert Saint-Martin, 1981.

Brodeur, C., & Rousseau, R. Essai de formalisation du projet d'intervention de réseaux. *Service social,* 1980, *29,* 313-321.

Cantin, L., & Daoust, G. Les déprimés anonymes. *Santé mentale au Québec,* 1981, *6,* 180-182.

Cartier, G. Le mouvement syndical et la réforme du système de santé. *Revue internationale d'action communautaire,* 1979, *41,* 37-42.

CLSC (Centre Locaux des Services communitaires) Santé. Special volume on power: "Pouvoir . . . dans nos institutions." 1979, *3,* 1-20.

Desmarais, D. Un modèle bio-psycho-social d'intervention de réseau. *Service social,* 1980, *29,* 366-379.

Divay, G., & Godbout, J. *La décentralisation en pratique.* Rapport de recherche 5, Institut national de recherche scientifique (INRS)–Urbanisation, Montréal, 1978.

Green, L. W., Werlin, S. H., Schauffer, H. H., & Avery, C. H. Research and demonstration issues in self-care: Measuring the decline of medicocentrism. *Health Education Monograph,* 1977, *5,* 161-189.

Gregg, G., Preston, T., Geist, A., & Caplan, N. The caravan rolls on: Forty years of social problem research. *Knowledge: Creation, Diffusion, Utilization,* 1979, *1,* 31-61.

Langlois, R. Coupe-Circuit: Une alternative à la psychiatrie. *Santé mentale au Québec,* 1981, *6,* 119-125.

Langlois, R. *Coupe-Circuit: Une alternative communautaire à la psychiatrie.* Master's thesis, Université Laval, Québec, 1982.

Lavoie, F. Action-research: A new model of interaction between the professional and self-help groups. In A. Gartner & F. Riessman (Eds.), *Mental health and the self-help revolution.* New York: Human Sciences Press, 1982.

Lavoie, F. Santé auto-gérée et entraide. In Y. Villedieu (Ed.), *Les psychothérapies* (tentative title). Québec: Québec-Science Editions, in press.

Lesemann, F. De la communauté locale à la communauté multinationale: L'état des monopoles et des politiques communautaires dans la gestion de la santé et des services sociaux. *International Review of Community Development,* 1978, *39/40,* 49-98.

Lesemann, F. *Du pain et des services: La réforme de la santé et des services sociaux au Québec.* Laval: Editions coopératives Albert Saint-Martin, 1981.

Mayer, R., & Desmarais, D. Réflexion sur la recherche-action: L'expérience de l'équipe d'intervention de réseau de l'Hôpital Douglas à Montréal. *Service social,* 1980, *29,* 380-403.

Navarro, V. The industrialization of fetichism: A critique of Ivan Illich. *International Journal of Health Services,* 1975, *5,* 351-371 (Translated into French in L. Bozzini, M. Renaud, D. Gaucher, & J. Llambias Woeff (Eds.), *Médecine et société, les années 80.* Laval: Editions coopératives Albert Saint-Martin, 1981.)

Orban, E. (Ed.). *La modernisation politique du Québec.* Québec: Editions du Doreal, 1976.

President's Commission on Mental Health. *Task panel report: Community support systems.* Washington, DC: U.S. Department of Commerce, 1978.

Renaud, M. Quebec new middle class in search of local hegemony-causes and political consequences. *International Review of Community Development,* 1978, *39/40,* 1-36.

Renaud, M. Les réformes québécoises de la santé ou les aventures d'un Etat narcissique. In L. Bozzini, M. Renaud, D. Gaucher, & J. Llambias-Woeff (Eds.), *Médecine et société, les années 80.* Laval: Editions coopératives Albert Saint-Martin, 1981.

Romeder, J. M. *Self-help in Canada.* Paper presented at the annual meeting of the American Orthopsychiatric Association, Toronto, 1980.

Rousseau, R. Recherche-action et intervention de réseaux. *Service social,* 1980, *29,* 322-331.

Speck, R. V., & Rueveni, V. Treating the family in time of crisis. In J. Masserman (Ed.), *Current psychiatric therapies.* New York: Grune & Stratton, 1977.

Syndicat des Professionnels des Affaires Sociales du Québec [SPASQ]. La psychiatrie et le monopole médical: Les professionnels en tutelle, la population en otage. *Santé mentale au Québec,* 1981, *6,* 89-98.

12

SHUTTLE DIPLOMACY IN THE PERSONAL SOCIAL SERVICES
Interweaving Statutory and Informal Care in a Changing Britain

GILES DARVILL
England

The stranger is an important member of the community. As Simmel says (1950, pp. 402-408), he is the person "who comes today and stays tomorrow, the potential wanderer: although he has not moved on, he has not quite overcome the freedom of coming and going. . . . His position in the group is determined, essentially, by the fact that he has not belonged to it from the beginning, that he imports qualities into it, which do not and cannot stem from the group itself. . . . To be a stranger is naturally a very positive relation; it is a specific form of interaction." As an illustration of the stranger, Simmel describes the trader required by the community that is not self-sufficient. Communities also take in strangers to be impartial judges. The stranger receives all kinds of confidences withheld from the more closely related person. However, the role of stranger contains many dangerous possibilities. "In uprisings of all sorts, the party attacked has claimed, from the beginning of things, that provocation has come from outside, through emissaries and instigators."

When the stranger finally settles in his or her place of activity, the role of stranger, with its advantages and dangers, may, as Jew and Gentile have found, linger.

Communities also take in strangers for arbitrating in the ever more complex business of managing human relations. In addition to the priest there is now the family doctor, social worker, district nurse, or agency volunteer.

Relations between the stranger and the community were once defined by agreed-upon rules; often the stranger lived at a slight distance. Now, however, we are more actively than ever inviting professionals or other paid workers in the personal social services to spend all their working hours with us, even to identify with us. But who is this stranger? Is he an equal partner with the community? Can we send her off over our boundaries if she cheats or puts first the interest of a more powerful master? Perhaps he works for the state, and he can send us to mental hospital, deny our parents entry to a residential home, take our children away from us. Perhaps she is an "accredited volunteer," with a signed card of authority containing her photograph. We cannot easily send such strangers away. Let us see how all this has come about.

EMERGENCE OF SEPARATE DEVELOPMENT

Statutory Services

The British welfare state has not been tried and found wanting. It has been found to be expensive and never fully tried. After World War II a socialist government set in motion a program of legislation on education, health, housing, and social security, aiming at a universally available baseline of services run by central or local government. Members of the public who could afford them could opt for privately run alternatives. The program for the final link in the chain of welfare provision, the personal social services, emerged much later. The personal social services include domiciliary and residential services to the elderly, mentally and physically handicapped, mentally ill, and family and child-care services. Collectively, the social services departments that administer the personal social services have responsibility for the vast bulk of statutory social work in Britain. The impact of much of the eventual social services legislation was softened because it was permissive (you could do it if you liked) or did not lay down minimum quantitative or qualitative standards, did not provide adequate money to get things going, or to train staff, and did not even make clear whether services should employ paid staff or could involve volunteers. Large gaps remain, most notably for the elderly who still want a comprehensive government policy with accompanying legislation.

Whereas in the fields of health, education, housing, or social security statutory inadequacies had to be tolerated by the poor and could be filled for the better-off by private provision, the gaps in personal social services really only affected the poor or stigmatized, and so there was no impetus for a parallel private system to emerge (a major exception being the private nursing homes for the elderly). Volunteers stepped in to fill some of the gaps; otherwise the burden of care remained with relatives and others willing to take it on, or personal breakdown led to the person coming under the wing of other services, such as the health service or prison.

The main statutory agency in the personal social services is the social services department (SSD; there are 116 in England and Wales) or the social work department (12 in Scotland). (Northern Ireland has a system that is not comparable with the rest of the United Kingdom.) These are run by elected local authorities (where one political party has overall control), but central government provides the legislative framework and has a major influence on the overall levels of spending. Most of the money and staff time are spent running residential homes for children and the elderly, and there is little additional provision for the recovering mentally ill and the mentally or physically handicapped. Departments make thinly spread provision for day centers and various home-based services (lunches, cleaning, and the like) for some of those in special need, mainly the elderly. Additionally, SSDs employ social workers, whose main task is to carry out the departments' mandatory responsibilities for providing a social work service with respect to children at risk. Social workers occupy about 12 percent of the posts in departments, but their conventional wisdom permeates the agencies.

A small but significant proportion of the paid professional and semi-professional staff employed in the personal social services work in what are termed voluntary organizations, which in some cases are 100 percent funded by local authorities. Often they carry out services on behalf of the statutory services. It is important not to confuse these voluntary organizations with the alternative system of private schools and health services. Like the statutory services, they exist, in the main, for the poor or deviant, and their services are not bought. Voluntary organizations are the equivalent of private, nonprofit agencies in the United States. It is also important, especially for the purposes of this chapter, not to confuse voluntary organizations with volunteers. Many voluntary organizations, of course, involve volunteers, but, until very recently at least, some have been entirely staffed by paid workers and may dislike, even loathe, volunteers. At the same time, many volunteers are attached to statutory services.

While the statutory welfare state has struggled to develop, volunteers and informal carers have continued to provide the main contribution to personal care, as they did before the welfare state emerged. Furthermore, they continue to occupy a world quite separate from the statutory. The statutory cuts across the nonstatutory to carry out specific and limited operations largely out of the context of what else was happening. Their staff are usually housed in remote offices in large population centers. There has been no attempt nationally, or until very recently in any locality, to plan a comprehensive interweaving of such statutory services as exist in the networks of volunteers and informal carers.

Volunteers

Although there have always been informal carers (families, friends, and neighbors), the emergence in large numbers of "volunteers"—strangers who retain the freedom of coming and going in the informal world—is a recent phenomenon. Volunteers are quite unable to provide a sustained service for large numbers of people in need; for example, they are unable to provide services for large numbers of frail, confused elderly people. The kind of volunteer groups that might be termed neighborhood care groups or community care schemes may occasionally be able to provide an extensive service for two or three elderly, but more commonly they offer a very small service for a large number. Only in the former case can the volunteers be said to be preventing the immediate need for residential provision.

Informal Care

The so-called informal system of care has, like volunteers, existed mainly in a world apart from statutory activity. Who are these informal carers? Both common sense and academic scrutiny suggest that the informal system of care consists of a number of not always compatible elements (see, for example, Froland, Pancoast, Chapman, & Kimboko, 1981: Ch. 2; Robinson & Abrams, 1977). Family, friends, and neighbors— its three constituent elements—are often experienced as contrasting. Philip Abrams (1980, pp. 12-23) has to date carried out the most academic work, and sparked off the most controversy, on the nature of the informal system, especially on the subject of neighboring:

> Notwithstanding the supposed "death of the family," kinship remains the strongest basis of attachment and the most reliable context for informal social care that we have. . . . The bulk of the helping reported as "neighborhood care" in the sense of neighbor-

liness turns out on scrutiny to be kin care of this sort. . . . Beyond
that, our strongest bases of informal social care are those of the
non-located moral communities associated with churches, races,
friendship groups and certain occupational groups—not neighborhoods. Neighbors and local communities come in a very poor third. I
suspect that this was true even in the nineteenth century and it is
certainly true today (emphasis added).

It is perhaps interesting to note that many of the "webs of affiliation"
that form the basis of Abrams's nonlocated moral communities are derived
from the sacred rather than the secular; they are theaters of action with
preexisting rituals. Given their communities' religious or ethnic foci, participants derive their values from beyond the neighborhood and have their
eyes and ears open to events beyond the neighborhood which they seek to
change. In practice, within the neighborhood itself there may be considerable religious and ethnic conflicts—a point not apparently adequately
assimilated by Abrams when he sought to define the modern neighborhood as based on a sense of identity acquired from political action
designed to "wrench control of the local milieux from outside authority
and vest it in strictly local hands" (Abrams, 1980). Abrams did not at any
point address the issue of how neighborhood groups in deeply divided
neighborhoods approach their conflicts.

Such a sketch of the juxtaposition of statutory, volunteer, and informal
care has run the risk of being both too long and too short. What one sees is
"separate development," notably between statutory services and the rest.
As a result, volunteers and informal carers provide care up to the limits of
their capacity, which may be very considerable in the case of many caring
relatives or the exceptional friend, neighbor, or stranger volunteer. The
state does little to reinforce or relieve this care. When nonstatutory care
breaks down, the state has to step in with drastic remedies, lifting the
person in difficulty psychologically and perhaps physically out of his or
her familiar world. Examples could be given from the situation of families
at risk of breakdown, the mentally ill, or the young criminal, but I shall
concentrate hereafter on the elderly, as they constitute the largest group
of "consumers" of the personal social services and the forthcoming growth
in the percentage of the population who are frail or mentally infirm is
probably the major factor behind official interest in informal care.

The following example illustrates the potential impact of "separate
development" at the family level. An elderly mentally infirm person would
typically live alone or with a frail spouse, receiving regular help from other
family members and occasional help from old friends or neighbors, some

of whom might visit under the wing of the local neighborhood care scheme. A "home help" (approximately a household cleaner) might visit twice a week, and a hot lunch might be delivered three days a week (rarely on a weekend). As things become more serious, pressure would be put on a relative other than the spouse to take on full-time care. A daughter might give up a paid job and, astonishingly, once the old person moves in with her and her family, all domiciliary services could be withdrawn. After a year, the unsupported relative would be unable to tolerate the intensity of 365 days a year caring for her infirm parent and would refuse to provide care any longer, probably in a mood of acute guilt and distress. The elderly person would move with great suddenness from the informal world to the statutory, entering full-time residential care either in a local-authority home or a psychogeriatric ward, depending on the severity of his mental impairment.

REASONS FOR SEPARATE DEVELOPMENT

Can the wide canyon between statutory and informal care in the 1960s and 1970s be explained merely by reference to bureaucratic and professional inflexibility and isolationism—the inability of paid services to develop the versatility necessary to relieve and reinforce informal and volunteer care? This seems too easy. Attitudes in British society underlie this state of affairs. There seem to have been two clusters of attitudes. Some people adopted one rather than another; many seemed to hold contradictory attitudes from both. Those holding one cluster claimed to welcome paying taxes and local rates in order to be relieved of responsibility for awkward people and to be freed of extended family ties. They vaunted professionalism and expertise in every matter under the sun. They welcomed the availability of low-paid jobs in the social services to help sustain full employment. If they were receivers of care, they preferred help from outside their familiar, perhaps stigmatizing, environment. (Ronald Blythe, 1979, thinks we underestimate the sense of relief with which many an old person leaves his daughter's house to enter a residential home). Above, or beneath, these attitudes was an "establishment" perhaps still sufficiently apprehensive of the seething proletariat to underpin the increased public expenditure involved.

The contrary cluster of attitudes held its own, with the result that statutory services never became comprehensive, and volunteer and informal help remained essential. There was a desire among a significant number *not* to spend too much on public services, especially for the poor, and they disliked large local government bureaucracy, and, to them, empty-headed elected officials and bossy, ill-educated semiprofessionals like social workers. Their suspicion of unions also contributed to the slow pace of growth of the personal social services. Volunteering grew mainly in default of statutory services, but there were forces that might have created more volunteering anyhow—the aftermath of the late 1960s uprush of "doing your own thing" in groups. Perhaps these impulses really had practical results only in conjunction with ethnic, religious, or political institutions—for example, the growth of the alternative movement within the churches (Clark, 1977) and the growing power of the Liberal Party in local, if not in national, government. There was an increasing interest in privacy, too, and a desire to exclude the state if not one's neighbor from family affairs.

It seems with hindsight that, because the divisions between the two clusters of attitudes did not fall neatly within party political lines or religious denominations and were often unresolved within the individual himself, there was a conspiracy to minimize the incongruities by establishing two quite separate worlds: a statutory world embodying one set of attitudes and a nonstatutory world embodying the other. I would not want to hang too much on this argument, as public planning on a large scale is rarely very rational. However, there is no doubt that for whatever reasons those whose needs placed them on the boundaries of residential care continued to suffer from the discontinuity between informal and statutory welfare provision.

INTERWEAVING: THE FIRST STEPS

The mid-1970s saw the first tentative steps by SSDs toward interweaving statutory services with volunteers and informal carers. Anticipating that finance would be saved in residential provision if the home help and home meals services began to be provided more comprehensively for groups on the margin of requiring full-time residential care, SSDs spent comparable sums on increasing domiciliary provision. (A recent official report charts this and indicates that much progress in this respect remains to be made (Department of Health and Social Security, 1980). A number of SSDs employed special staff to recruit volunteers who were "strangers" to visit people in their homes (Darvill, 1981) and others to create local networks of familiar faces acting as street wardens to keep an eye on the elderly and encourage other local people to get involved. Some SSDs provided generous expenses (semipayment) to volunteers, including neighbors, who would undertake regular helping tasks—for example, with the elderly (Darvill, 1975). Rigid fostering rules were modified to allow perhaps rather disreputable neighbors to be paid to provide temporary care when, for example, a mother was hospitalized. The first volunteer or neighborly sitting-in services (daytime or overnight) were established.

Additionally, it was no longer always assumed that once a relative assumed care, services could be withdrawn; on the contrary, they might be stepped up. Day centers for the elderly were more inclined to include rather than exclude the mentally confused elderly, who would disrupt games of bingo with their reminiscences or tears. Community health teams also modified some of their practices—for example, providing professional training and advice to neighborhood care schemes—and, exceptionally, SSDs and health authorities joined forces to set up a new kind of paid worker, combining the roles of home help and nursing auxiliary in order to offer flexible help to informal carers, especially in rural areas. These steps, however, were taken mainly by departmental staff other than social workers, who continued to work at a distance from communities of shared concern or shared locality. (Holme & Maizels, 1978, Barclay, 1982).

Approaches to Interweaving Become More Common and Systematic

In the early 1980s there was a sudden increase in interest among staff of SSDs in the departments' capacity to reinforce and relieve informal care and create networks of informal care where they did not exist. The pioneers of these approaches had been experimenting for several years and traced their roots to way in the past, but the widespread interest and imitation, especially by social workers, was new. Whereas hitherto a handful of staff were interwoven with nonstatutory care, now whole teams of disparate staff were reorganized and their jobs redefined to meet the new objectives. The objectives and terminology have never been officially spelled out, but a commonly shared aim is to provide an *interweaving* of statutory and nonstatutory services so that informal care can be maintained and residential care postponed for the maximum possible period of time. (The term "interweaving" was introduced by Bayley, 1973.) As a person's disability or other needs intensify, his or her carers require a greater quantity or more complex or specialized quality of support. He and his carers will therefore receive support from a *continuum* of increasingly sophisticated volunteer and statutory services—for example, through domiciliary care two to seven days a week, or relief day care on an increasing number of days and in increasingly sophisticated milieux (such as a special volunteer-run club, perhaps set up by a social worker, a local-authority day center, or a day hospital, with periods of short-stay residential relief care). Relatives will be closely supported by social workers during changes in the infirm person's condition or perhaps will be invited to join a relatives' group set up by statutory staff.

The philosophy of the continuum of care was held in common by social services teams, which adopted quite dissimilar structures. As the Barclay Report (1982, pp. 206-209) outlined when discussing social work, there have been two main approaches, based on shared concerns and shared locality. The former approach has been based on specific client groups—for example, the elderly mentally infirm on the boundary of residential care—and has aimed to establish a continuum of care within quite a large population. The approaches based on shared locality have usually endeavored to "go patch," the shorthand term used by social services staff. With patch systems social services facilities and staff of varying levels and specializations are reorganized into small staff units, each specializing in a very local patch of from 5,000 to a maximum of 25,000 people, and dealing with all "client groups."

Interweaving Based on a Shared Concern

The system in parts of Buckinghamshire, a county to the northwest of London, is based on the needs of the elderly mentally infirm. The objective is to prevent wherever possible any long-term hospitalization of elderly mentally infirm people or admission to a local-authority home or private nursing home. The scheme is of double interest since it demonstrates cooperation between the social services department and the health authority's Department of Mental Health of the Elderly (DMHE), itself almost a unique set-up, employing, among others, approximately a dozen community psychiatric nurses for the elderly. Both informal carers and "stranger" volunteers are also crucial in establishing the continuum of care.

Informal carers are encouraged to assume and maintain care by regular provision of necessary domiciliary services; home helps and community nurses are not withdrawn if a relative assumes care, and waiting times for aids and adaptations (such as walking aids and ramps for wheelchairs) are kept to a minimum. Additionally, there is an increasingly comprehensive network of facilities for relief day care and for short-term residential care.

Relief day care is provided in the first instance where available by semi-formal clubs, organized in the elderly person's immediate neighborhood and mobilizing both "stranger" volunteers and local people whom he or she is likely to know. These clubs have normally been set up and financed by either the SSD or the DMHE. There are also local-authority day centers where more intensive and extensive care can be offered, and SSD residential homes for the elderly also open their doors for day care. Short-term residential care can be provided either in an SSD home or, if necessary, in a psychiatric ward. While elderly people are being cared for by relief services, informal carers may attend support groups that are now developing for relatives and other carers. No single aspect of the above arrangement is in itself very unusual. What is unusual in Buckinghamshire is the comprehensive continuum of services and the purposefulness with which the DMHE and the SSD combined to establish it, both by reorganizing statutory facilities and by setting up and supporting local nonstatutory clubs.

Interweaving Based on Shared Locality

Going patch has been a much more popular approach to the continuum of care than the above; indeed, the "moonies" of patch systems (for the movement has a sectarian frenzy about it) would scarcely recognize the radicalism of the Buckinghamshire approach as in any way akin to theirs. Within the patch movement there are some conversions of greater intensity than others. A halfhearted approach to "going patch" can mean social workers dismantling large teams in an area of, say, 100,000 people and working in small groups in an area of approximately 20,000. The cynics say that the social worker, by hanging about for an hour or so longer than normal in pubs and launderettes, will achieve little more than getting to know some of the local "earth mothers" who can be persuaded to take on the care of the department's more unrewarding foster children and to inform the department before the press does about any elderly found dead in their back gardens. This may be unfair, but departments whose staffs have been unwilling to make real changes have nonetheless claimed to have gone patch.

More serious attempts involve a thoroughgoing attempt to reinforce and relieve existing informal care and to create it where it does not exist. A recent important text has gathered up examples of eight patch-based teams

(Hadley & McGrath, 1980, p. 96). The essential features of this model are cited as:

(a) locally based teams, focusing on small areas or patches,
(b) the capacity to obtain detailed information about the patch,
(c) accessibility and acceptability to the patch population,
(d) close liaison with other local agencies and groups,
(e) the integration of all field and domiciliary workers within patch teams,
(f) participative forms of management in patch and area teams, and
(g) the exercise of a substantial degree of autonomy by patch and area teams.

To which should be added: adequate provision of day and short-stay residential care places under the management of the patch team.

Staff commonly specialize in very small localities, normally about 10,000, where they get to know social need at a very early point, make close links with local voluntary organizations, set up new volunteer programs, and support informal carers with whom they may have almost daily contact. No department can really claim to have set up a continuum of interwoven care unless it has involved not only social workers but also the domiciliary services (home helps, home deliverers of lunches) so they too are working as the "eyes and ears" of the department in the villages, suburbs, and neighborhoods and are supporting informal carers, and unless it has provided extra places for day care and relief residential care, using money saved by reduced numbers of children and elderly people in permanent residential care. (At least, that saving is the fervent hope). Links with other departments, notably health and to a lesser extent housing, are also likely to be important. Very few patch systems have achieved this degree of comprehensiveness to date. The Normanton scheme described by Hadley and McGrath (1980) is especially interesting; it has integrated domiciliary care staff, newly created posts of patch workers (approximately, social work aides), and street wardens, in patches of 5,000 population. It has also played an important part in setting up a political forum in the town.

The Dinnington project is also important, though its authors claim it is not strictly a patch system: "It is a project concerned with integrating all health and welfare services, statutory, voluntary and informal, at neighborhood level. Working on a patch basis is one, but only one, of a number of fundamental features" (Bayley & Parker, 1980, p. 71). A small office campus in Dinnington is shared by housing workers and social services staff, with a senior-level interdepartmental steering group overseeing it. The writers add: "It should be emphasized that the team of three workers (the two social workers and the housing assistant) are only the core team. Potentially the 'team' (insofar as one can use the word) consists of all the health and welfare workers in Dinnington (and other members of the community as well) and part of the task of the core team is to help this team to focus and coordinate its work" (p. 79).

One feature that both the "shared concern" and "shared locality" models demonstrate is a change in the use of time of professional and other paid staff. Rather than carrying out or managing services themselves, community nurses, home help organizers, social workers, and others are encouraging people to start things up, helping people discover their latent skills and relevant experiences, passing on parts of their training, disbursing funds, and so on. Where ancillary staff are involved, higher-level staff also have a greater role than before in helping them develop the scope of their work. Staff are discovering quite a new interpretation of what it means to be a "professional."

Each of the two methods of interweaving has its strengths and weaknesses. The model based on shared concern has the advantages of any specialized service—experience of the details of a particular set of needs. The model based on shared locality has the advantage of knowing the key local leaders, the recent history of alliances, and disputes between organizations. Proponents of each model claim that if only the statutory side is appropriately organized it will find a community of common interests that can, if the will is there, be organized to fight for those interests. Furthermore, each sometimes accuses its rival model of fragmenting community effort.

Innovations such as those described above have almost all been introduced by local authorities. Central government departments have played only a small part in establishing interweaving, mainly by small changes in the national social security system and by timely provision of research grants to enable the monitoring of these experiments. Central government support of volunteering and informal care have been mainly rather general—exhortations and finance for a variety of ad hoc developments, without any overall understanding of the need to develop the continuum of care more systematically. On the negative side, the widespread cuts in public spending have made it harder for SSDs to undertake the extra spending needed to finance innovation.

"Stranger" volunteer organizations have also had a role to play in interweaving with informal carers. In Buckinghamshire, MIND (the local branch of the National Association for Mental Health) and the local Red Cross played important roles in mediating between the statutory and informal systems of care. Organizations like good neighbor schemes can occupy (not merely stand astride) crucial middleground, holding in creative tension the best elements of formal and informal caring.

Forces for Interweaving

What tipped the balance in favor of greater interweaving of care? Pragmatic considerations joined with idealistic and ideological ones, the relationship between them not being entirely clear so close to the event. Simultaneously, other considerations continued to work against partnership.

Perhaps the most important force for community partnership has been the creative energy of the key professionals involved, who were determined to lead their teams out of the dead forms imposed on all of them. Writers on the social services habitually underplay the importance of leadership: Most of the early patch systems, for example, were established, often in the jaw of opposition, by team leaders who were driven by a profound if unobtrusive inner strength, not unlike the power the Spanish poet Garcia Lorca described as the *duende,* which cannot be defined because it is "a power and not a behaviour, a struggle and not a concept. . . . The appearance of the *duende* always presupposes a radical change of all forms based on old structures" (Garcia Lorca, 1982, p. 43).

Another powerful force in favor of community partnership has been the continuing willingness of informal carers to assume responsibility for care. We are always in danger of taking this for granted, but without informal carers being responsive both to relatives' need and to the supportive intrusions of stranger-professionals, no interweaving of care would be possible. The information available about the actual and potential availability of people willing to undertake informal care is not extensive and is sometimes open to contradictory interpretation (for a summary, see Tinker, 1981, Ch. 9; Moroney, 1976). The evidence suggests that a high proportion of elderly are cared for by members of their families; in fact, the proportion increases as elderly people become more infirm, and approximately 50 percent of the very severely handicapped are cared for by families.

However, some analysts feel that social trends will diminish the availability of informal carers. The larger number of women in work has to be considered but some argue that part-time work need not hinder people's ability to undertake informal care—it might even stimulate people. The higher divorce rate also leads people to predict that there will be fewer informal carers. In one marriage in three, one of the partners is remarrying. Will people be prepared to undertake care of stepparents in addition to stepchildren? Some trends are indecipherable—for example, the fact that so many people marry and have children compared to fifty years ago. This means fewer elderly have unmarried daughters to undertake care, but more do have children of some marital status who can be considered as potential carers.

Informal carers have not taken an entirely passive role in promoting the emergence of interwoven care. Pressure groups composed of relatives of the mentally handicapped and of schizophrenics have been active in campaigning for relief care. Relatives of the dependent elderly have been slower to organize for themselves, which is surprising, given their much larger numbers, but in the last two years an Association of Carers has been established, with local branches (sometimes developing out of relatives' support groups). Pressure with respect to the elderly has normally been carried out by pressure groups, not by groups of carers. Campaigning informal carers have been handicapped by the lack of hard evidence about the pressure they are under or the extent to which this pressure leads to breakdowns of caring arrangements and could be prevented by interwoven statutory care (but see Sainsbury & de Alarcon, 1974). This information is arguably more important than speculative data about demographic trends. A study of the support of informal carers is currently being concluded at the National Institute for Social Work, London. Meanwhile, however, a powerful influence stimulating the interest in partnership has undoubtedly been the accumulation of evidence that has been presented to administrators concerning individual examples of care disintegrating under pressure.

A further incentive to partnership is the heavy weight of evidence about the accumulation of need and demand, especially among the elderly (Tinker, 1981, pp. 9-17). The elderly population is not growing as a percentage of the whole population, but dramatic changes are taking place in the structure of the elderly population itself, and over the next ten years there will be approximately 30 percent more elderly over 75 years old. This is due in the main not to an extension of the expectation of life at any age after childhood, but to the huge reduction early in the century in infant mortality rates. Social services administrators have understandably become alarmed at the steady increase which will occur in the numbers of frail, perhaps mentally impaired, elderly. When one also considers the uncertainty outlined above concerning the willingness of relatives to care, it is clear that action has to be taken. Above all, it is widely felt that everything possible must be done to aim paid resources at crucial targets, such as caring relatives, even though, as discussed later, there is little evidence yet that informal care supported by statutory services is either cheaper or more agreeable to the recipient or his or her family than institutional care.

The increased pressure of need has come at a time of cutbacks in statutory spending, and this too has acted as a pragmatic force toward partnership—working on the assumption that interwoven care is cheaper than is insitutional. Those in favor of interweaving for ideological or idealistic reasons cannot help offering a measure of gratitude to the financial situation; for all its devastating effects, it is at least forcing people out of their inertia to do the right things, if for the wrong reason of (assumed) saving.

A further factor in favor of interweaving is the existence in Britain of a single agency, the Social Services Department, for a wide range of statutory and professional social services activities. Habitually practitioners grumble about the size, scope, and impersonality of SSDs, but Froland, Parker, and Bayley (1980) argue, "It is important to point out that the existence of a single agency which deals with the full range of client groups . . . offers a potentially helpful foundation for developing worker flexibility. The range of work undertaken and knowledge gained can lead to a relationship with the community and its many resources, both informal and voluntary, which a multiplicity of smaller specialist agencies could not be expected to equal."

Alongside these more pragmatic forces for partnerships, various ideological or idealistic influences can be identified. Some professionals have seen interweaving of care as a way of combining the best of each of the two sets of attitudes, which in the 1970s seemed irreconcilable. The welfare state could be preserved, protecting clients and their families from overexposure to deprivation and pain, and professional skills could be used to the full. At the same time the public could be mobilized to prevent difficulties arising—especially with respect to young people—or to meet needs within a framework of mutual help or informal care. Professionals could work with, rather than for, the community, strengthening it in the process. Social work and community work could be combined.

The political support for models such as patch systems has been considerable and from all tints of political opinion, albeit for different reasons. Political support has undoubtedly been pragmatic in part—it is assumed money is saved—but community-oriented systems of care have also been seen as a way of promoting political values. This variety of political support has come at a time when consensus politics has given way to more sharply defined ideological differences between parties. Many hitherto neglected aspects of social life are being scrutinized for their political content.

The Left has seen interweaving as a way of achieving standards and continuity in the welfare state by bringing statutory decision making, including decisions over levels of resources committed to welfare, under greater community control. It is seen as a check on the growth of autonomously exercised professional power, which undermines the confidence of ordinary people to be masters of their own fate; community-based service delivery can, it is felt, be a catalyst for stimulating and underpinning local political activities. For example, a community association can recruit members for its political work by mobilizing the commitment of people who in the first instance are more likely to become involved in meeting welfare needs than joining political organizations. Political awareness, it is argued, will follow, and suitably motivated and trained professionals will be close at hand to pass on political skills. This view, of course, tends to suppose that local ethnic, religious, and other differences can be readily reconciled.

The Right has supported interweaving of care as a way of handing back responsibility to people who need encouragement to stand on their own feet. It is seen as a gradual way of redirecting the socialist-inspired welfare state away from dependence on the state to interdependence and, for the far Right, ultimately to independence in which people would rely on a network of commercially managed welfare facilities.

The political center has supported interweaving of care because it embodies a number of elements of which it is fond: participation by the people, professionals as educators of the public, and so on. But as with the other parties, no clear view has emerged of tangible matters, like the extent to which the state retains the responsibility to ensure continuity and minimum standards of care, whether provided commercially or by the state itself.

That all parties can see something for them in interweaving of care is a strength and a weakness—a strength because it demonstrates that the models themselves are politically neutral structures that are adaptable within limits to varying political approaches (although clearly an extreme approach from Left or Right would be likely to destroy the essential give-and-take of interweaving), and a weakness because innovatory service delivery can be killed by neglect in certain localities while a political struggle for its custody rages over its head.

Interweaving of care has also been welcomed and fostered by idealists not heavily influenced by professional values or political ideologies. They struggle to develop forms that can provide formal structures within which informal relations can grow, and often start by condemning impersonal, uncaring, and above all overbusy institutions, including the so-called caring ones, such as schools, doctors' surgeries, and hospitals. Often Christians, they single out the institutionalized church for special criticism, because it is insufficiently concerned with "being" and because its "doing" is of the wrong sort. Community-oriented systems of care are seen as a way of encouraging "being within doing." These idealists are not by any means all "sandal-wearing dropouts." Indeed, among directors of social services and researchers who have done most for interweaving are Christians, including disguised clergy, who are sometimes inclined to wonder whether social workers and other paid staff are able to generate interweaving unless they embody the special commitment of the best parish clergy. There is often a bond between these more distanced analysts and managers and the duende-bound practioners at the "front."

Forces Against Interweaving

There are pragmatic obstacles to increased interweaving and idealistic or ideological objections. Perhaps the greatest obstacle to interweaving is the sheer lack of knowledge about informal care, not only about the large-scale issues, such as demographic trends, but also intimate issues related to day-to-day events. Until we have a more sophisticated understanding of the different kinds of informal care, varying types of stress, and need for support, it is hard to underpin it effectively. Parker (1981) has identified four dimensions for analyzing the nature of informal care. In order to discriminate among different kinds of problems and support needed, one must analyze informal care, he argues, in terms of its duration, intensity, complexity, and prognosis. In the "Report of a Study on Community Care" (Department of Health and Social Security, 1981) were recently identified a number of attempts to measure effectiveness, including cost-effectiveness of interweaving. The report concluded that no fully adequate method of measuring effectiveness has yet been devised. If cost-effectiveness of service delivery is assumed, it is usually because the costs to the carer have not been fully understood or computed. The not dissimilar experience of supporting foster parents suggests that many expensive lessons remain to be learned on the subject of statutory support of informal carers.

Moving from the personal to the neighborhood context, Abrams, Abrams, Humphrey, & Snaith (1981) investigated community care schemes and asked many pertinent questions still to be answered about the schemes' capacity to carry new work as part of interweaving arrangements and about the correct level and style of formal intervention and underpinning. Answering such questions is intrinsically tricky: McGrath and Hadley (1981) have discovered the methodological problems involved in evaluating patch systems, for example. There is a range of obstacles to interweaving that derive from the behavior of most large organizations (see, for example, Froland et al., 1980, Ch. 4). Inertia is partly due to vested interests among both managers and unions, but also to the lack of special skills needed to introduce innovation. People who can combine the necessary vision with management skills of any sort, let alone those skills required to mobilize staff within new forms, are hard to find. Not only are large bureaucracies inert; volunteer groups and neighborhood projects can also succumb.

Another important obstacle, regularly discussed in the debate about patch systems, is the nature of local government accountability. Social service workers are part of local authorities, answerable not to professional bodies but through local-authority managers to the local political committee, and they have less freedom than even probation officers to make their own professional decisions. This tight hierarchical accountability is a serious impediment to the risk taking—with money as well as with people—involved in establishing interweaving. Accountants demand financial returns that stretch beyond what is reasonable for the recording capacities of front-line staff and informal carers; managers, at the behest of committees, demand referral back of decisions which, if not made rapidly while informal carers are motivated, may never be implemented.

Another obstacle to interweaving continues even when one can find innovating managers and establish a flexible accountability system. Frontline staff lack the basic skills involved in supporting interweaving. I am talking not only about the generous attitudes required or the ability to live with ambiguity. Front-line staff need to be trained in specific skills and knowledge—for example, in how to tell when the stress of informal caring is building up. Elderly people with neurotic tendencies or personality disorders can be as wearing as the demented or antisocial, but one study showed how the existence of the former and their effect on dependents' families is less often identified than the latter, even by visiting psychiatrists (Sainsbury and de Alarcon, 1974).

In the national context, the tax and social security systems present serious obstacles to interweaving. Although there have been advances in financial support by agreement of informal carers, there are important steps still to be taken, especially with respect to married women who give up work to look after invalid relatives. (Unlike men and single women, they are not entitled to Invalid Care Allowance.) Additionally, their pensions suffer: In other countries, for example, Czechoslovakia, work undertaken in looking after dependent relatives qualifies the carer for credits toward his or her own pension equivalent to those that would have been earned by staying in paid employment.

Idealistic or ideological obstacles stand in the way of interweaving. These can be either personal or political. The dependent and their informal carers themselves may hold values that make external support difficult. Dependent people may feel profoundly uncomfortable about receiving care from neighbors, volunteers, or state professionals. How to be a receiver is a skill that has to be learned like any other. "Little is heard about the moral contribution made by those who receive without whom no giving would be possible" (Parker, 1981, p. 32). Relatives may feel acutely unhappy with outside help. "No one else could cope with my mother" is a familiar phrase when volunteers offer to relieve relatives. The dynamic forces that lie beneath this suspicion and the sometimes excessive privatization of family problems are little understood. Perhaps sharing care activates latent fears and feelings of inadequacy.

On a more ideological level, some deny that statutory or other formal structures can ever support informal care without destroying the latter, either by overloading it with responsibility or by intruding on its values and procedures. Abrams at one time held this view, although he later softened it, in the light of his own and others' research on a number of projects where it proved possible to "have things both ways":

> The intrusion of artificial helping networks, whether voluntary or statutory, into a neighborhood does not have to occur at the expense of natural helping networks. Indeed there is some evidence that the former can positively stimulate and sustain the latter. In other words the ambiguous goals of neighborhood care policies and projects now seem to me to point towards tension rather than contradiction. (Abrams, 1979)

It seems especially likely that there will be tension where the so-called clients are in some way deviating from generally acceptable behavior—for instance, young people whom the courts have made subjects of supervision ("intermediate treatment") orders, or who are members of the still flourishing alternative society in Britain, in particular those with ethnic or radical religious ties.

Interweaving has its political and professional enemies also. It has already been argued that the models are politically neutral, and where one party has infused them with its values and the appropriate practical outcomes, another identifies these values with the model. Nor is this opposition necessarily merely empty ideological rhetoric. Once one political group has turned the model in its direction—aiming at extensive community control or slow hiving off of services ("social monetarism")—then interweaving is a legitimate political battleground. Professionals, too, may see interweaving models as a threat to their vested interests. Other, perhaps more detached, analysts are fearful of interweaving. If implemented extensively, will it provide the different forms of the public world, including neighborhood groups, with channels for spreading their tentacles into the privacy of family life further than is acceptable? Will we be forced to be active, forbidden to be lazy? Will grandma and her granddaughter ever be allowed to be free of each other? The growth of semipayment is also suspected, not only understandably by unions, but by those who wonder whether it will encourage people to put a price on every form of caring. (Against this it is argued that semipayment removes obstacles to altruism; see, for example, Qureshi, Davies, & Challis, 1979).

THE FUTURE

There are various practical measures essential to establishing interweaving. These include unambiguous central government policy in favor of experimenting with interweaving of care and power sharing with the informal system; extra finance for local authorities to underpin experiment; changes in the tax, pensions, and social security systems to encourage informal care; legitimization of the risks involved, for example, via insurance; training and career incentives for staff to support informal carers; criteria and machinery for evaluating the effectiveness of interweaving from the points of view of the cared for, the carers, and different political, professional, and financial perspectives (especially monitoring the stress on informal carers to ensure agencies are not offloading their responsibilities); and provision of incentives other than financial to informal carers, including training, social opportunities, and a chance to share problems with other carers.

We have seen that pending these changes the decaying forms of statutory welfare have been transformed by outstanding professionals and, to a lesser extent, by local politicians. These "strangers" have bridged the gaps between statutory and informal care, and we murmur "the duende" and applaud. But the duende by its nature can, if frustrated or misdirected, quickly turn from the creative to the destructive. Both the informal carer and the innovator need reasonable control over the power released by the changes.

As well as the practical measures listed above, therefore, new structures must be created that can ensure equilibrium will be maintained between the "strangers" and their adopted communities of interest or residence. There is an equally urgent need for structures that will enable people to try to deal with conflicts among themselves within their communities, conflicts which, in the absence of negotiating forums, can be handled only by withdrawal or violence. In some Scandinavian countries—for example, Norway—there are health and social welfare committees of local people for mediating between clients and their families, and the professionals. The British models along these lines—for example, where parents and other members of local communities are elected to governing bodies of schools, and where patient and volunteer groups are members of community health councils—have to date made no impact on professional and political power and betray an overoptimistic view of people's readiness to form community-based alliances across ethnic, religious, or other differences. In the personal social services, not even these limited models of consultation have been introduced, but it is generally healthy that the ideological aspects of social welfare are more apparent and have been brought into wider ideological debates, even if, as a result, those involved in the personal social services must share the uncertainty over the future that is experienced in other areas of national life.

REFERENCES

Abrams, P. Unpublished paper, 1979.

Abrams, P. Social change, social networks and neighborhood care. *Social Work Service Magazine,* February 1980.

Abrams, P., Abrams, S., Humphrey, R., & Snaith, R. *Action for care: A review of good neighbor schemes in England.* Berkhamsted, England: The Volunteer Centre, 1981.

Barclay Committee Working Party Report. *Social workers, their roles and tasks* (Chairman, Barclay, P.). London: Bedford Square Press, 1982.

Bayley, M. *Mental handicap and community care.* London: Routledge & Kegan Paul, 1973.

Bayley, M., & Parker, P. An experiment in health and welfare cooperation. In R. Hadley & M. McGrath (Eds.), *Going local: Neighbourhood social services.* London: Bedford Square Press, 1980.

Blythe, R. *The view in winter.* London: Allen Land, 1979.

Clark, D. *Basic communities.* London: Society for the Promotion of Christian Knowledge, 1977.

Darvill, B. *Paid visiting and street warden schemes: Their contribution to community involvement*. Berkhamsted, England: The Volunteer Centre, 1975.

Darvill, G. *Prepared to share*. Berkhamstead, England: The Volunteer Centre, 1981.

Department of Health and Social Security. *Report of a study on community care*. London: Author, 1981.

Froland, C., Pancoast, D., Chapman, N., & Kimboko, P. *Helping networks and human services*. Beverly Hills, CA: Sage, 1981.

Froland, C., Parker, P., & Baylery, M. *Relating formal and informal sources of care: Reflections on initiatives in England and America*. Paper presented at the First World Congress of the International Voluntary Action and Voluntary Associations Research Organization and l'Organisation Internationale pour la Recherche sur les Associations et l'Action Volontaire.

Garcia Lorca, F. *Deep song and other prose*. London: Marion Boyars, 1982.

Hadley, R., & McGrath, M. *Going local: Neighbourhood social services*. London: Bedford Square Press, 1980.

Holme, A., & Maizels, J. *Social workers and volunteers*. London: Allen & Unwin, 1978.

McGrath, M., & Hadley, R. Evaluating patch-based social service teams: A pilot study. In E M. Goldberg & N. Connelly (Eds.), *Evaluative research in social care*. London: Heinemann, 1981.

Moroney, R. *The family and the state*. London: Longman, 1976.

Parker, R. Tending and social policy. In E. Goldberg & S. Hatch (Eds.), *A look at the personal social services*. London: Policy Studies Institute, 1981.

Qureshi, H., Davies, B., & Challis D. Motivations and rewards of volunteers and informal caregivers. *Journal of Voluntary Action Research*, 1979, *8*(1/2).

Robinson, R., & Abrams, P. *What we know about the neighbours*. Durham, England: Rowntree Research Unit, University of Durham, 1977.

Sainsbury, P., & de Alarcon, J. The cost of community care and the burden on the family of treating the mentally ill at home. In D. Lees & S. Shaw (Eds.), *Impairment, disability and handicap*. London: Heinemann, 1974.

Simmel, G. The Stranger. In K. Wolff (Ed.), *The sociology of Georg Simmel*. New York: Macmillan, 1950.

Tinker, A. *The elderly in modern society*. London: Longman, 1981.

13

BRIDGING THE DIVIDE

A Maori Initiative in Linking Formal and Informal Care

STEPHEN UTTLEY
New Zealand

New Zealand is a geographically isolated country consisting of two main islands with a land area of almost 270,000 square kilometers. The population consists of just over three million people, giving a population density of just less than 12 persons per square kilometer, which is low by international standards. As in other countries, there has been a movement of population from rural to urban areas; almost 70 percent of the population now live in urban areas. There has also been a movement of population from south to north island and a growing concentration of population in the upper part of north island.

An important feature of life in New Zealand is the pervasive role of central government. One of the few political issues to polarize political opinion in the early period of colonization was the argument between centralists, who favored strong central government, and provincialists, who wished to see power remain with the six provincial councils. The contribution of central government to the creation of a transport and communication infrastructure helped to resolve the argument, and provincial councils were abolished in 1876. Low population density, the need for investment capital for economic development, and the protection of citizens through welfare systems have been factors contributing to the creation of a tradition of extensive central government intervention.

DEVELOPMENT OF THE FORMAL
SERVICE SECTOR IN NEW ZEALAND

The Liberal government of 1893 to 1914 is usually seen as having laid the foundations for the welfare system in New Zealand, although some initiatives in health and education had their origins in the 1870s and 1880s. The enfranchisement of women, changes in land development policy, the introduction of an extensive system of labor legislation, and the payment of old-age pensions in 1898 were some of the major innovations introduced during the Liberal government. New Zealand in this period stimulated immense interest from America and Europe. Lord Asquith described it as "a laboratory in which political and social experiments are every day made for the information and instruction of the older countries of the world" (Sinclair, 1969, p. 187). The effect of the Liberal program was to extend considerably the role of central government and, with it, the size of the public service bureaucracy. The increasing complexity of the task facing the state apparatus led to a Commission of Inquiry into the public service in 1912. The report of the Commission criticized the degree of departmental autonomy and the lack of standardized procedures and called for greater efficiency, careful job classification, regular inspections, and clear procedures for handling appointments, promotions, and transfers. The New Zealand public service has never lost sight of these objectives, with their implied emphasis on strict control from the center of the organization.

If the Liberal government of the 1890s laid the foundations of the welfare state in New Zealand, then the Labour government of 1935 to 1949 created the framework for contemporary state provision of social services. Among the measures introduced were the provision of public housing, the development of a social security system with an extensive range of statutory, income-tested benefits, the provision of free hospital and pharmaceutical services, and access to general practitioner services at a relatively small cost to the consumer. By the early 1940s it could be said that "the state now provided welfare services appropriate to a modern, urban society" (Dalziel, 1981, p. 277). The government was also active in trying to minimize the impact of external factors on the domestic economy and in particular in ensuring full employment. The growth of state intervention involved in these measures by necessity meant a further rapid expansion in the size of public service.

It has been suggested that the inability of the church and charitable organizations to meet the welfare requirements of the country was instrumental in stimulating state involvement from the latter part of the nineteenth century onward (Oliver, 1977, pp. 6-10). The growing urbanization of the population toward the end of the nineteenth century did lead to collective action among citizens and the development of voluntary organizations, although in rural communities the emphasis remained on informal systems of support linked to family, friends, and neighbors (Olssen, 1981, p. 257). The creation of an extensive system of state-provided social services by the late 1930s has not deterred the subsequent growth of voluntary organizations (Oliver, 1977, p. 25; Jack & Robb, 1977, pp. 37-40). Growth has manifested itself in the emergence of a relatively small number of national or federated bodies, which are centrally organized and provide the bulk of services to a particular group, such as the mentally handicapped, with substantial financial support from central government. Growth has also been apparent in the plethora of small organizations and groups located at neighborhood, suburb, or territorial local-authority level, whose existence may be transient and whose focus is essentially on mutual aid.

THE EXPENDITURE CRISIS

Divergence in the rate of growth of the economy and public expenditure was not a question of public concern until the mid-1970s. However, this masks the very dramatic growth in government welfare spending since the end of the 1960s. From 1950 to 1969 the growth of welfare spending exceeded the growth of the economy by about 0.5 percent each year, but from 1970 to 1978 this jumped to a differential growth rate of 5.3 percent each year. In these circumstances it is not surprising to find many of the policy discussion documents in the social and economic policy area published in the second half of the 1970s concerned about the spiraling cost of state-financed social services and speculating about the future of the welfare state. An examination of documents produced by the New Zealand Planning Council (1978, 1979, 1981), the New Zealand Task Force on Social and Economic Planning (1976), and the New Zealand Council of Social Service (1976, 1978) reveals two rather different perspectives, although both may be found coming from the one advisory body and indeed within the same document.

In the first perspective, the effectiveness of many state-provided social services in meeting consumers' needs is questioned, and the inadequacies of current services and methods of delivery are highlighted: "All in all, it could be argued that there is no direct relationship between the amount of state spending and the activities of public *institutions* on the one hand,

and the real welfare of *people* on the other" (New Zealand Planning Council, 1979, p. 23). On this basis it is argued that public expenditure on social services may be contained and/or curtailed with little deleterious effect on consumers, and that a close examination of services for more efficient of resources may allow both cost containment and improvement of services. There is talk of moving from a "welfare state" to a "welfare society" in which private enterprise, voluntary organizations, churches, communities, and the family assume many of the responsibilities currently undertaken by the state (New Zealand Planning Council, 1981, p. 21). The meaning of the notion of a "welfare society," the capacity of institutions other than the state to meet welfare needs, and the mechanisms by which the state can assist such a transfer of responsibility remain obscure. One is left with the feeling that the transfer of responsibility actually means allowing the costs of reducing state services to rest on the individuals, groups, and institutions affected.

The second perspective takes us back to the centralist-provincialist argument, because there is a strong commitment to devolving responsibility from central government to local or regional bodies. Part of the rationale for this stance is the rejection of the notion of standardization of service and procedures, which has been a dominant ideal in the New Zealand public service since the 1912 report. The emphasis on a multicultural society and on the welfare requirements of particular geographical communities provides the spur for focusing on diversity in service, decentralization of provision as far as possible, and participation by people in the planning and delivery of services—the so-called bottom up approach. As in the first perspective, there is an assumption that local communities, neighbors, friends, and family will take more responsibility for caring services, but unfortunately little attention is paid to the capacity of these institutions to achieve this objective. The proposals for change become focused on the coordination of services within the formal service sector and, in particular, on the relationship between voluntary organizations and central government.

At present, action appears very much confined to the first perspective, with attempts to curtail growth in social service expenditure to the rate of inflation. In 1982 it appears that a 3 percent cut in real expenditure is likely in all aspects of public expenditure. So far, cost constraints have affected mainly manpower in the social services, through reduction in either nonprofessional support services or the future size of professional occupations by restricting access to training (for example, in medicine, teaching, and dental nursing). The influence of what one writer refers to as the social technocratic approach (Easton, 1981) appears to be focusing policy decisions narrowly on cost and efficiency rather than on the more radical options offered in the discussion documents mentioned above.

SELF-HELP AND INFORMAL CARE SYSTEMS

As in many other countries, self-help activity has grown considerably in New Zealand during the last ten to twenty years, although this growth has been only partially documented. The compilation over recent years of directories of social services available in particular territorial communities, or to particular groups within those communities, gives some indication of the type and range of groups involved. A recently published directory of services for disabled people in Wellington (Wellington Co-ordinating Council for the Disabled, 1982) suggests that self-help groups are either focused on specific physical conditions such as blindness, asthma, multiple sclerosis, and so on, or offer more general help by providing opportunities for social interaction and personal development. Informal care available through kinship and friendship networks remains an important and preferred source of help for the elderly, sick, and handicapped. There is no reason to believe that the availability of such care has diminished in New Zealand during the last thirty years (Uttley, 1981).

To suggest that informal care systems still exist and that family and friends are the first source of help is not to claim that the system has not changed in response to urbanization and changes within the family and friendship networks themselves. Complex changes have taken place (Townsend, 1976), but these networks in modified form are still available to many members of the community and are the preferred source of help. There are reasons to believe that there are specific factors supporting the existence of social networks in New Zealand. First, New Zealand has a small and relatively homogeneous population, which is also highly urbanized. Second, in Maori cultural tradition, personal identity is located by identifying one's position within the extended family and tribal systems. These two factors perhaps help to produce the situation in which "when New Zealanders meet previously unknown fellow countrymen they often prefer first to establish connections: 'Do you know so and so?' " (Levett & Bradley, 1973, p. 61). Establishing one's position relative to a social network is important in New Zealand society and may produce larger and more interlocking networks than exist in many other countries. There is little reason to accept the argument that growth in the formal sector has

damaged the informal and self-help sectors. It does, however, seem likely
that some degree of specialization has taken place, with the formal care
system concentrating on manipulating control over access to real resources
through action in relation to income, housing, health, and so on, while the
self-help and informal care sectors focus on what has been termed the
"quality of life" (Allardt, 1976). The quality of life refers to action to
enhance relationships in family, friendships, and community networks and
action to enhance and retain status and prestige in a personal, social, and
political sense.

BRIDGING THE DIVIDE:
FORMAL AND INFORMAL CARE

In New Zealand there seems to be a growing self-help system and an
informal care sector that has adapted to social change. The formal care
sector has a long tradition of direct provision by central government, with
close attention being paid to standardization of service and procedures, a
tradition which has been transferred to a number of large voluntary
organizations serving particular client groups. In these circumstances
attempts to achieve planned linkage between the two sectors are fraught
with difficulties. One such attempt will be described involving a government department that is about to bridge the sectors not by using the
informal care system to achieve the goals of the formal system but by
encouraging the informal system to set the goals and the strategies for
achieving them while the department plays the role of adviser and resource
broker.

MAORIS IN NEW ZEALAND SOCIETY

Just under 9 percent of the population identified themselves as Maori
or part Maori in the 1976 census. The Maori population is a youthful one;
about half are under 15 years of age. During the last fifty years Maoris
have moved from being a rural-based population to an urban-based population. Official statistics are often compiled in such a way as to render
comparisons by ethnic background difficult, however a preliminary analysis of a 10 percent sample from the 1981 census indicates Maoris have a
considerably higher rate of unemployment than the non-Maori population.
A recent review of available health statistics shows that mortality rates for
most diseases and for all age groups are appreciably higher for Maoris
compared to non-Maoris (Pomare, 1980). One can cite similar evidence in
relation to housing, education, income, and so on which suggests that,

although the Maoris are the indigenous people of New Zealand, their social position is closer to that of a minority immigrant group.

DEPARTMENT OF MAORI AFFAIRS

Central government involvement in the concerns of the indigenous people of New Zealand goes back to the early days of colonial rule, when a Native Secretary was appointed in 1846 and a Native Affairs Department formed in 1869. The statutory framework within which the present department operates was largely laid down in the 1945 Maori Social and Economic Advancement Act and the 1962 Maori Welfare Act. An important feature of the legislation is the dichotomy between a developmental focus based on the aspirations of the Maori people and the concerns of the Pakeha (European) population about "problem" behavior among Maoris. Section 18 of the 1962 Maori Welfare Act contains clauses concerned with promotion of the general well-being of the Maori people and the preservation of Maori language and culture. The same section contains clauses about the prevention of excessive drinking and personal problems and the fostering of respect for the law among the Maori people. The difficulties inherent in the dual focus are apparent in the internal documents of the Department of Maori Affairs during the 1950 and 1960s. There was concern about the effects of continuing urbanization on traditional support systems and the retention of Maori custom and culture, and about the material hardships experienced by Maoris in the urban environment: poor housing, lack of child-care support, low levels of income, and so on. The Department was under pressure from the Pakeha community to respond to these problems in terms of those individuals and families in difficulties; for example, the Department's support of budgetary advice services was in part a response to pressure from the business community to facilitate recovery of outstanding debts. In these circumstances it is not surprising that the Department in its welfare operations became focused on individual pathology. The influence of the public service environment on the perception of the workings of the Department was significant. Emphasis, for staff, was placed on knowledge of the legislative framework within which the Department operated, on knowledge of departmental procedures, and on linkage with other parts of the central government system. Overall staff were described as conveying to other parts of the bureaucracy, and to clients, the objectives of the Department.

The impetus for change came partly from staff of the Department, who raised various concerns with the Minister at their annual conference in

1976. A two-man committee of inquiry was formed, drawn from the State Services Commission, the government body with overall responsibility for the public service, with terms of reference reflecting the concerns expressed about the internal management of the Department and the broader question of the adequacy of the community services offered by the Department to the social needs of the Maori people. It is worth noting the committee's method of working, as this set the pattern for subsequent developments. The committee not only consulted staff in the various district offices but also held extensive public meetings, usually on maraes (the traditional location for discussion in the Maori world). On the basis of these consultations the committee felt able to resolve clearly the dichotomy identified above, because among the communities, "the Maori people are in full pursuit of a modern westernised way of life *moulded to suit their own character*," and on this basis they recommended "a major shift of emphasis from the present indulgence in social casework to youth and community development activities" (Haber-Thomas & Puketapu, 1977).

The report of the committee and the appointment of one of its members, Kara Puketapu, as the head of the Department has led to dramatic changes during the last four years. The acceptance by the committee of the goal of achievement as defined in the Pakeha world, but through a distinctly Maori approach, laid the foundation for a new ideology in the Department: *tu tangata,* to recognize the stance of people. Puketapu recognized the way clients of social service organizations are incorporated into such organizations at the bottom of hierarchical structure. The tu tangata ideology involves inverting this system of organization so that the client group becomes the center of the organization. Not only must the stance of the people be recognized, but the possibility of achieving the aspirations identified will rest on identifying the contribution that each individual has to make. The views of the people were identified using the methods employed by the committee, with staff, particularly senior staff—including the head of the Department and on many occasions the Minister too—holding public meetings on maraes and in community centers. The difficulties of establishing an effective dialogue, when past communication had been firmly grounded in directive communication downward, so common in the public bureaucracy, can be well imagined. Perhaps the tradition among the Maori people of frank discussion on the marae has assisted the change in communication. These meetings became not only the forum for identifying objectives and devising programs to meet them, but also a place in which departmental staff were held accountable directly to the people. It is easy to describe this process in terms of decentralization, consultation, and accountability, but

Puketapu (1982) sees the process as having greater significance in a Maori context. It is an attempt to identify and mobilize each person's *wairua* (the spirit, the whole being). The social, economic, and political environment can constrict the wairua, but the process of dialogue is regarded as helping each individual get in touch with his or her wairua, thereby releasing the creative energies of the whole person. The broad objectives identified were to improve educational attainment, to provide opportunities for self-fulfilment within the community, to raise the socioeconomic status of the Maori people, and *kokiri* (to advance). Based on these objectives, development programs have emerged focused on Maori culture, the encouragement of economic entrepreneurship, including the acquisition of business and work skills, and social programs, with the main emphasis on education and youth development. What is conspicuously absent from any description of the programs is any reference to the term "welfare." The policy is to make this term extinct in relation to the Department's activities.

There have been numerous organizational changes since 1977, and increasingly the goal has been "to make the Department move from its 'in office' character to a position within the client community itself" (Puketapu, 1982). In 1980, community advisory groups were set up in every departmental district. These groups had not only advisory functions but also control over the allocation of financial resources and some direct control over the implementation of particular programs. In 1981, a number of kokiri units in the Wellington area were started in which departmental staff were taken out of district offices and placed in particular geographical areas. Each unit has a senior department officer, about four paid staff, and community volunteers. The staff are predominantly Maori, although there is representation of Pacific Islanders. The leader of one of the units is a trained social worker, but this is certainly not regarded as a necessary qualification. Part of the rejection of the "welfare" tag attached to the Department in the past is the rejection of an individual-problem orientation conveyed in social work education. Staff are expected to commit themselves to the developmental philosophy of tu tangata. Volunteers are increasingly recruited around specific projects. The Porirua kokiri unit, for example, is seeking to establish a day-care center located on a marae, in which part of the objective is the promotion of Maori language. About thirty volunteers have been recruited; they are local people who are either fluent Maori speakers or are parents who want to see such a facility available for their children. The volunteers' task is both to develop and promote the idea within the community and then to assist in providing the service. As the knowledge of Maori language tends to be concentrated among the elderly, the setting up of this type of day care may help to recreate the links between young and old around language and custom, which were so important in a rural marae-oriented community. The priorities and tasks of the kokiri unit staff are determined by local community management groups. It is usual for these management groups to consist of all people attending monthly meetings, which are open to all, although a formal chairperson is normally elected. Attendance varies from month to month, but the Porirua unit, for example, averages between thirty and forty people for its meetings. The inaugural meeting of the Hutt Valley kokiri unit attracted over seventy people, and after having identified a large range of concerns, these were ranked according to their importance and the time required to achieve them. The meeting set down a series of tasks for unit staff around issues such as truancy, after school programmes, and employment needs. Staff are expected to work on tasks and report to the next management meeting, where progress can be assessed and tasks modified. The kokiri units represent the logical extension of the tu tangata philosophy by making resources available directly to the people at a local level to help them achieve the objectives they themselves determine. This kind of radical change cannot be achieved quickly and without difficulties. In the annual review of the tu tangata program in 1981 by people from all parts of the country, the need to make available resources, in the sense of knowledge and techniques, to community management groups was stressed as an urgent priority.

How have these changes been possible, given the highly centralized and formalized approach to state provision in New Zealand? The answer to this question is complex. Elements in the answer might include the fact that initiative for change came from within rather than from external criticism of services leading to an inquiry and thus encouraging a closing of ranks around the existing system. It is unlikely that the staff, in seeking change, foresaw the types of change that were to come. Their concerns were with both the objectives of their service and the internal functioning of the Department. For some, the latter was probably to the fore, in particular the dominance of the financial control staff in senior positions in the organization, who were predominantly Pakeha. The political acceptance of change can be seen as a genuine commitment to experimentation with a "bottom up" approach. On the other hand, it could be seen as a token gesture in the sense that Maori Affairs is a small department, and therefore changes are unlikely to flow on into other areas of central government activity. The last one hundred years have seen a shift in the public discussion of relationships between the Pakeha and Maori from ideas of assimilation to integration, and more recently to the notion of a multi-cultural society. One may question how real such a commitment is, but within sections of the Pakeha community, a strong interest in and respect for Maori culture perhaps made the political acceptance of a more distinctly Maori approach easier to achieve.

Any consideration of why and how change has occurred cannot ignore the influence of Puketapu. Before being appointed as head of the Department, he had established a reputation in the public sector as an incisive manager and an acute analyst of organizations. Rather than seeing a highly centralized government system as an obstacle, he sees it as a potential strength in that in a small society like New Zealand a centralized system should make flexibility and rapid response to change much easier (McAllister, 1979). The notion of wairua underpins a commitment to the potentialities of creative action by people to develop their situation. In recognizing that in our working and social environments control over decisions affecting the individual are often removed from their control, Puketapu identifies the destructive effect of this process on the individual's confidence to solve problems. It is this type of analysis that is central to the ideas of democratization of work, particularly among Scandinavian writers (Gustavsen, 1977). Just as the Scandinavians see the restoration of creative problem-solving abilities coming about through the step-by-step transfer of control over work to workers, so Puketapu places great emphasis on action and the gradual transfer of responsibility for action.

Staff in the Department, in particular community officers and senior management staff, have faced a continually changing situation since 1977. The community officers prior to this were the agents of the Department in the community and had two main functions: first, to convey Department policy and requirements to the people; second, to offer a predominantly casework-oriented service for which some of them had acquired professional training. During the initial stages of change, the necessity for the central administration to establish a dialogue with the people effectively left staff in limbo, with little idea of what was going on. Gradually their role has been clarified and developed. They have been required to abandon their interest in social casework, to stimulate and promote creative resources in their communities, and increasingly to act alongside and under control of local communities. Senior managers perhaps with a lifetime of service in the public sector, have been required to accept mutual criticism from within the Department and to be openly accountable to the people they serve in numerous public arenas. A phrase often heard during the first few years of change has been "shape up or ship out," which reflects the tough stance taken toward staff to ensure as rapid a change in ideology and method of working as possible. It is interesting to contrast this pattern with the more conventional approaches to major change in social service organizations. This often involves an extensive public inquiry and report, which is subsequently debated, modified, and legislated. Change is usually introduced some time later to allow for planning and often allows for considerable time for adaptation in methods and staff working. Workers in this situation face a prolonged period of uncertainty followed by a differential rate of transition to new methods of working, and at some stage the blueprint from which the change is constructed is held to be achieved. (An example would be the Seebohm reorganization of personal social services in Great Britain.) In the changes described in Maori Affairs, the gap between report and action was short; staff were and are clear that they must change their method of working. The realization of the tu tangata ideology involves a commitment to continual change—there is no blueprint or end point as such.

LINKAGE: ASSIMILATION OR ACCOMMODATION?

The changes that are taking place within the Maori Affairs Department are only part of a broader pattern of change, as the different parts of the welfare system respond to the pressure of resource constraints associated with the overall economic environment. New Zealand has a long tradition of central government involvement in social services, both through financial support to voluntary organizations and through direct provision. The overall emphasis in public service on standardization of provisions and procedures has been of great importance in the formulation and implementation of social policy. The objective that social service consumers should receive the same service administered in the same manner wherever they live may not always be achieved, but it remains the dominant goal.

Within an ethos of central control and standardization, attempts to link the formal service sector with the informal care sector can entail mere assimilation of the informal sector by the formal sector. One example of this has been the growing recruitment and deployment of volunteers by both voluntary organizations and government departments. The Department of Social Welfare, which is responsible for social security and social work services for families and children, has instituted a program making extensive use of volunteers. The scheme originated in a provincial town as a response to local needs and conditions. The adoption of the scheme on a national basis has occurred with a considerable degree of standardization and the incorporation of volunteers within the public service hierarchy, with volunteers being given individual caseloads, a volunteer team leader, and a casework supervisor drawn from the paid staff.

It has to be acknowledged that ideas about helping networks and linking formal and informal care systems can become part of a strategy, adopted within the formal care system, to minimize the effects of resource constraints. The expansion of social services has been a significant component in the overall growth of the service sectors in industrialized countries and a movement toward what Bell (1976) has termed the postindustrial society. It is possible to distinguish between different parts of the service sector, and some writers (such as Foote and Hatt, 1973) have argued that social services are distinct because they involve changing, rather than merely maintaining, the service consumer; that is, social services are people-changing enterprises. The service consumer is faced with a complex webb of roles in the position of recipient of a social service. Gersuny and Rosengren (1973, p. 139) describe the position as follows:

> The service society has transformed the consumer into buyer, worker, client and resource all in one. The buyer role implies a voluntaristic relationship. The worker role calls for a negotiated contractual inequality. The client role implies subordination to the possessors of an esoteric body of knowledge to which he is not privy. Finally, the characteristic of being a human resource for the agencies selling services implies yet further potential for the exploitation and alienation of the consumer.

An important feature of the growth of welfare systems has been the extension in provision of services from a small part of the population regarded as the poor or deprived, to the provision of services in such a manner as to make nearly all citizens consumers of social services. In a country such as New Zealand, where social services are provided predominantly by central government, consumers become clients of the state organization. The social services are people-changing enterprises, but to achieve this change they have to employ relatively large amounts of labor; they are labor-intensive activities. The cost of labor is therefore important in determining the cost of social services. It is against this background that the possibility of making greater use of the consumer as a human resource for the social service organization becomes attractive. As Gersuny and Rosengren (1973) imply, the incorporation of the consumer as either a low-paid indigenous worker, a volunteer, or, as in some instances, an enforced worker through community service sentences in the courts, allows social service organizations the possibility of reducing the effects of resource constraints. These lower-cost resources do replace, at least in part, more expensive labor. The incorporation of the consumer as a resource does not necessarily present a challenge to the dominance of centralized control in the formal service structure. The consumer is located firmly at the base of the organizational hierarchy and is subject to the same system of control as other staff. To the extent that the use of consumers in this way involves more effective linkage with the voluntary and informal care systems, it could be regarded as an extension of central control to the periphery rather than part of a process of devolution of control. What we may be witnessing is the transformation of the formal social services to a self-service system, as people are required to service themselves under the close scrutiny of "the management" and according to the service organization's manual.

Are the developments in the Maori Affairs Department that have been described merely part of this process of exploiting the consumer? The program is open to many criticisms, ranging from the rejection of the goal of a westernized way of life through to concern about the lack of evidence about the effects of the program in practice. It does, however, offer a real questioning of what Roger Hadley (1981) has termed a "pre-Copernican" view of the caring system in which the informal self-help and private market sectors are seen as satellites of the state. It seems to be a genuine attempt to place the client or consumer at the center of the caring system. There is a sense in which the consumer is regarded as serving himself or herself, but this in return for an attempted inversion of the organizational pyramid in which the consumer acquires a marked degree of control over the objectives and actions of the formal care system. The changes in the division of labor between consumer and paid worker in this scheme are fundamentally different from those in the volunteer scheme run by the Department of Social Welfare. The cultural tradition in the Maori world of open decision making in a group discussion setting does hold out the possibility that these developments may be a radical step toward a truly community-centered approach to social service provision.

Can the experiments within Maori Affairs be successfully transferred to other parts of the welfare system in New Zealand? The tradition of active involvement by citizens in service provision is still apparent in the dramatic growth of volunteer programs and self-help groups, and this commitment to action could be a crucial resource in attempts to link formal and informal care systems. The obstacles to change, however, are formidable. I have argued elsewhere (Uttley, 1980, pp. 202-203) that welfare institutions are examples of what Schon terms dynamic conservative institutions which try to remain the same in the face of pressure to change. This view is confirmed by examining current responses of New Zealand social services to a deteriorating economic situation. Faced with an increasingly difficult resource position, the decisions that are made represent a retrenchment of services around core activities. In this environment the use of the idea of natural helping networks can easily be adopted as part of a strategy to conserve service institutions by using natural helpers in the same way as agency staff, thus maintaining the same form of service but at lower real cost. Another major obstacle is the rigid hierarchical system of organizing services. Attempts to achieve a closer link between formal and informal care services involve a definite community orientation and can be achieved only, as Maori Affairs has done, by moving services from their "in office" format. This makes staff less easily managed within a hierarchical structure and standardization of service harder to achieve. Any attempts to make the necessary changes have to be seen against the historical development of the public service and the mounting pressure for more stringent, centralized systems of financial control of public services to monitor resource use.

Is it possible to overcome these obstacles and utilize the creative strengths for action that do exist? An affirmative answer rests on two propositions. First, when trying to link formal and informal care systems, it is neither theoretically appropriate nor realistic, in our current economic and social environment, to plan changes at the macro policy level. The idea of self-exciting, small-scale experimental programs has been a characteristic of the Maori Affairs approach and is likely to be the most successful strategy to adopt in the pakeha world, too. The second proposition concerns the necessity to see the discussion of natural helping systems as part of a much broader set of ideas about participation and control over decision making. The Maori Affairs Department has made an unambiguous commitment to the economic advancement of the Maori alongside cultural and social objectives, and the programs focused on educational attainment, work skills programs, work cooperatives, and land development are a reflection of this commitment. The literature about natural helping networks is closely identified with development strategies, which emphasize the decentralization of control over resource allocation decisions. The Maori Affairs programs emphasize the need for returning control in all aspects of social life, not just in the provision of social services. In the pakeha world, the cultural traditions of collective discussion and decision making are not as strong as within Maori culture. The link, which was previously noted, between the development strategy in Maori Affairs and the literature on worker democracy is of central importance if such a strategy is to succeed within the pakeha world, because it is only by maximizing the opportunities for participation and control that the potentialities for change can be realized.

REFERENCES

Allardt, E. Dimensions of welfare in a comparative Scandinavian study. *Acta Sociologica,* 1976, *19,* 227-239.

Dalziel, R. The politics of settlement. In W. H. Oliver & B. R. Williams (Eds.), *The Oxford history of New Zealand.* Wellington: Oxford University Press, 1981.

Easton, B. R. *Pragmatism and progress: Social security in the seventies.* Christchurch: University of Canterbury, 1981.

Foote, N. N., & Hatt, P. K. Social mobility and economic advancement. *American Economic Review,* 1973, *43,* 364-378.

Gersuny, C., & Rosengren, W. R. *The service society.* Cambridge, MA: Schenkman, 1973.

Gustavsen, B. Liberation of work and the role of social research. In R. McLennan (Ed.), *Proceedings of a seminar. Research on organizations: Problems, methods and data.* Wellington: Victoria University of Wellington, Industrial Relations Centre and Department of Business Administration, 1977.

Haber-Thomas, P., & Puketapu, K. *The community service.* Report to the Minister of Maori Affairs, 1977.

Hadley, R. Social services departments and the community. In E. M. Goldberg & S. Hatch (Eds.), *A new look at the personal social services.* London: Policy Studies Institute, 1981.

Jack, P. A., & Robb, J. H. Social welfare policies: Development and patterns since 1945. In A. Trlin (Ed.), *Social welfare and New Zealand society.* Wellington: Methuen, 1977.

Levett, A., & Bradley, R. Networks, social status and attitudes to change in urban Wellington. In S. D. Webb & J. Collette (Eds.), *New Zealand society.* Sydney: John Wiley, 1973.

McAllister, D. Puketapu's leap. *Public Sector,* 1979, *2,* 3-4.

New Zealand Council of Social Service. *Roles of central government, local authority and voluntary agency in social welfare.* Wellington: Government Printer, 1976.

New Zealand Council of Social Service. *Sharing social responsibility.* Wellington: Government Printer, 1978.

New Zealand Planning Council. *Planning perspectives 1978-1983.* Wellington: Government Printer, 1978.

New Zealand Planning Council. *The welfare state? Social policy in the 1980s.* Wellington: Government Printer, 1979.

New Zealand Planning Council. *Directions.* Wellington: Government Printer, 1981.

New Zealand Task Force on Social and Economic Planning. *New Zealand at the turning point.* Wellington: Government Printer, 1976.

Oliver, W. H. The origins and growth of the welfare state. In A. Trlin (Ed.), *Social welfare and New Zealand society.* Wellington: Methuen, 1977.

Olssen, E. Towards a new society. In W. H. Oliver & B. R. Williams (Eds.), *The Oxford history of New Zealand.* Wellington: Oxford University Press, 1981.

Pomare, E. W. *Maori standards of health: A study of the 20-year period 1955-1975.* Auckland: Medical Research Council of New Zealand, 1980.

Puketapu, K. *Reform from within.* Unpublished manuscript, January 1982.

Schon, S. *Beyond the stable state: Public and private learning in a changing society.* Harmondsworth: Penguin, 1973.

Sinclair, K. *A history of New Zealand.* Harmondsworth: Penguin, 1969.

Townsend, P. *Sociology and social policy.* Harmondsworth: Penguin, 1976.

Uttley, S. The welfare exchange reconsidered. *Journal of Social Policy,* 1980, *9,* 187-205.

Uttley, S. Social work and the destruction of family and community services. In D. McDonald (Ed.), *Social work and the family.* Christchurch: University of Canterbury, 1981.

Wellington Co-ordinating Council for the Disabled. *Directory of services for the disabled in the Wellington region.* Wellington: Author, 1982.

14

WHEELS IN MOTION

PAUL PARKER, DIANE L. PANCOAST,
and CHARLES FROLAND

> All these associations, societies, brotherhoods, alliances, institutes, and so on, which must now be counted by the ten thousand in Europe alone, and each of which represents an immense amount of voluntary, unambitious, and unpaid or underpaid work—what are they but so many manifestations, under an infinite variety of aspects, of the same ever-living tendency of man towards mutual aid and support? (Kropotkin, p. 282)

So we have invented the wheel again, for which we make no apology. This book has dwelt at some length upon the apparent rediscovery of self-help and informal care, and has attempted to describe these enduring social mechanisms according to the lights of a particular generation. However, the main object has been to consider whether this machinery can be fueled and guided. We make no presumption regarding the necessary locus of such responsibility. After all, even the best metaphors must break; and in this case, the wheel is constructed of people in action, giving and receiving support. Neither governments nor professionals can claim the right of control over such forces, but they, too, have a capacity to give and receive help. In particular, they are in a position to fuel and guide.

The authors of many of the chapters in this book have observed that the reaction of policymakers to self-help and informal care has so far been uncertain and, in some cases, not especially enthusiastic. Branckaerts, for instance, says they "are considered to be minor policy problems, neglectable when necessary." Ferrand-Bechmann perhaps goes even further, discussing a tendency toward conflict, territorialism, and suspicion. Indeed, policymakers have been able to see so many problems that they have chosen to overlook the possibilities. Grant and Wenger, in refuting the argument that statutory welfare systems destroy informal care, argue that the current situation is closer to "innocent neglect." On the other hand, some governments have taken positive steps despite the lack of evidence regarding the true nature and potential of self-help and informal care, and it is likely that they will continue. Professionals, too, are at least paying increasing lip service to the need to work more closely with various elements of the community. Deneke and Richardson, for instance, both found a widespread acceptance of the usefulness of self-help groups among professionals.

CONTEXTUAL INFLUENCES

Self-help and informal care do represent a particularly problematic challenge at both the policy and practice levels; they are not specifically designed to be sympathetic to the values or goals of the formal sector. Indeed some contributors argue that they may have the potential to erode some of the very assumptions about the allocation of power that are implicit in the political structure and also in relationships between professionals and clients. However, at present the evolution of a "social posture" between the formal and self-help sectors is still in the making. Neither side quite knows what to make of the other. Furthermore, some of the contextual factors which are influencing that evolution are already beyond the conscious control of either sector.

Long-standing political, professional, and social principles, such as the notions of subsidiarity, accountability, or complementarity, have by their very existence inhibited the dialogue between the two sectors. For instance, if the principle of complementarity is considered to be immutable, the policymaker will automatically present it as a condition for a policy response to self-help. The self-help sector may see the issue in completely different terms, as an attempt by the formal sector to relegate self-help to a residual role. If policymakers rigidly uphold the principle of subsidiarity, the self-help sector may feel that it is required to try but fail in any area of need before the state will agree to participate. This organizational version of the Peter Principle has a capacity to undermine the morale of even the most resilient groups.

Meanwhile, self-help groups are finding some identity as alternative social forces. Bakker and Karel, in describing the "silent mobilization" they observe in the Netherlands, talk of a change in values, a step toward a counter culture, and a sociopolitical liberation. Ferrand-Bechmann presents self-help in terms of reaction, resistance, and innovation. Deneke observes that self-help groups have been one of the elements of broad social movements, such as the women's movement, in which they have been one of the means of effecting social change rather than being an end in themselves. This has also been true in the United States, where self-help has been identified with such social movements as neighborhood renewal, holistic health, and ecology. In some situations, the endemic sociopolitical structure tends to force new movements into predetermined paths. In Flanders the pillarization of cultural, religious, and political life forces self-help activities to conform to societal cleavages.

Altogether, there is at present no clear picture of a settled relationship between the two sectors. A number of preexisting or external factors militate against a ready mutual confidence. The choices between conflict and cooperation or between a continuum of care and alternative sources of care remain in the balance. This chapter addresses some more specific issues which do lie within the conscious control of the formal sector and ends by reviewing the implications of contributors' suggestions for policy with regard to the future.

WHAT IS THE CARRYING CAPACITY
OF SELF-HELP?

First and foremost, more needs to be known about the prevalence and capacity of self-help and informal care. It is not enough simply to produce figures describing what exists. Policymakers need to know what the potential for growth would be if a sympathetic policy were to be developed, and ask, Would such a policy make any difference, or would the growth have occurred anyway? It may be that informal care is less tractable to external involvement than self-help groups. Furthermore, future demographic trends, for instance, the continued increase in the population of the very old, changes in family structure, and new work patterns, may reduce informal care even further. On the other hand, Ferrand-Bechmann argues that increasing leisure time will lead to more self-help activity.

These chapters can be taken as evidence that self-help activities at present represent a small part of the total service picture, although they are one of the fastest growing. Self-help groups are estimated by several authors to involve 10 to 15 percent of those who would be eligible. While this is a substantial number, especially given the newness of many of the groups and the hit-or-miss nature of their development, it represents only a small proportion of the total number who have such problems and who are probably receiving formal services. The tendency of long-established voluntary organizations to espouse the self-help label for publicity or financial reasons adds to the difficulty of measuring the growth and vitality of the self-help movement. There is little evidence that self-help groups are becoming a substitute for formal services, as much as some of these authors would like to see such a development. Indeed, Richardson argues that "for the most part self-help groups and statutory agencies tend to be sought for different sorts of help"; that is, they are complementary.

The measurement of informal caring activities is much more problematic. It is argued that everyone is, under certain circumstances, an informal carer. But a method of identifying and cataloguing the characteristics of informal carers which will provide a valid and reliable measure remains an elusive goal for researchers. Even so, much of the work that has been done demonstrates clear limitations to the network approach. Cohen and his associates found that the proportion of problems of their chronically mentally ill clients which could be solved through their informal networks was small. The experiments in Quebec, reported by Lavoie, yielded similar findings. Grant and Wenger point out that, even when payment was offered, relatively few helpers could be recruited from the existing networks of their elderly clients.

Generally the conclusion seems to be that those people whose serious problems bring them to the attention of formal services need help because their own social resources are severely depleted. A more preventive community-based approach would probably identify more problems that could be dealt with by blending formal and informal care. However, most of these people are not currently receiving any formal services. Hence, there still seems to be a need for the formal sector to provide intensive, expensive services as well as to support and develop the informal sector. Reviewing the experiences presented here, it seems clear that self-help does not provide a way out of the economic squeeze that is affecting so many Western industrialized countries in the 1980s.

From the perspective of the general public (a perspective shared by professional workers in their roles as citizens), the renewed interest in self-help action may be a manifestation of what Gartner and Riessman (1981) call "the anti-Leviathan ethos," the reaction of people against the large institutions that have so much control over their lives. If the preliminary results can be seen as indicative, however, it does not seem that the public is any more likely to view self-help as a replacement for governmental services than are professionals. Relatives and friends who are helping an old woman stay in her home are more likely to ask for respite services, friendly visiting, or transportation than they are to ask the agency to discontinue a service. Nor are they likely to offer to pay for such services for someone other than a close relative. A self-help group is more likely to be actively lobbying for *more* services for its members than to be advocating their abolition.

HOW CAN SELF-HELP BE RECONCILED WITH GOOD ADMINISTRATION?

Even if it is accepted that there is enough potential in self-help to warrant a response, policymakers are troubled by a number of threats to their traditional models; equity and accountability are frequently cited as major stumbling blocks. Here the problem is to ensure that in permitting greater local participation in and perhaps control over services, the consequent diversity of responses is at least regulated sufficiently to prevent abuses in the distribution of statutory resources, or the usurpation of state responsibilities by unaccountable people. Uttley takes this "devolution of responsibility" issue a stage further, by suggesting that New Zealand could find itself witnessing "the transformation of the formal social services to a self-service system, as people are required to service themselves under the close scrutiny of 'the Management' and according to the service organization's manual." Presumably, such an outcome could occur only if there were no *tu tangata* (recognition of the stance of the people), but merely a soulless dismantling of the centralized bureaucracy.

As well as creating problems for some of the standard tenets of good bureaucratic administration, self-help and informal care rattle the barriers that departmentalize some government structures. Britain seems to have profited from its comparatively unified organizational system of social service departments and the National Health Service in its attempts to develop services that are responsive to self-help. For example, the comparative integration of health and social services for the elderly has made it easier to integrate these services smoothly with the efforts of informal carers. At the other end of the spectrum, the multilayered, disorganized system of services in the United States, with its lack of unifying policies and large gaps in coverage, creates a climate that encourages small-scale innovation (some would even say faddism) and allows self-help groups to proliferate. The most discouraging climates for self-help seem to lie in the middle of the continuum. In France, for example, formal services are highly professionalized and bureaucratized, stifling local innovation. The fragmentation of the Belgian welfare system makes policy initiatives at the national level difficult. In West Germany, the individualizing orientation of the welfare legislation actually discourages self-help, even though the government is theoretically committed to its support. Such a mixed message is likely to generate frustration and an attitude of confrontation on the part of self-help groups. Deneke points out that while relations with professionals are surprisingly good, self-help groups are increasingly aligning themselves with the more radical movements in German society, implicitly challenging the government to respond.

HOW WILL POLITICIANS AND PROFESSIONALS INFLUENCE SELF-HELP?

To add to the policymaker's anxiety, there is an array of issues which, while not directly assaulting the public sector's own position, require answers. Both self-help and informal care are vulnerable to political exploitation. The Right is inclined to use them as a model for reducing government intrusion and promoting individual control; the Left sees them as a source of greater citizen participation and influence over policy. A more apocalyptic vision predicts a serious destabilizing effect. The extreme Right might use them as an argument for drastically cutting direct services that could not be substituted outside the formal sector. The extreme Left might use them (especially the neighborhood-based groups) as a means of circumventing the established political structure, thus effectively disenfranchising people at the local level who do not wish to participate in what can become an alternative political system. These ideas are at present much more the stuff of rhetoric than reality. Self-help and informal care have not yet become important enough to carry that much weight in political debate. It is more likely that they will serve as valuable sources of constituencies for individual politicians than that they will become pawns in the broader political power game.

Another frequent complaint concerns the tendency of professionals to colonize the informal sector. Ivan Illich is one thinker who is very worried about the destruction of what he calls vernacular life by the substitution of shadow work for meaningful, self-generated action. He warns that " 'care' exacted for the sake of love . . . will become manageable by the state" (Illich, 1981, p. 25). Would an active policy inject a destructive dose of professional interference into the delicate equilibrium of the informal sector?

Bakker and Karel alert us to the subtle ways professionals can "pollute" self-help. The shadow cast by their authority, even their choice of language, may subvert the efforts of the groups despite the best intentions. There is also the danger of professional aggrandizement in this as in any other "newly discovered" field of practice. One wonders whether the rapid growth of interest in self-help groups in the United States, the Netherlands, Belgium, and West Germany may not have been fueled in part by young professionals eager to make a name for themselves.

However, these chapters give us reason to think that there may be positive effects as well. If many informal helpers are looking for a new role or status in society, as Ferrand-Bechmann believes, some formalization, whether it be participation in training sessions, a title, a token payment, or organization into a group, will reinforce this motivation. On a more pragmatic level, formalization allows resources to flow from the formal sector to the informal helpers, and such helpers often are in real need of these resources. Grant and Wenger remind us that being paid to care for elderly neighbors offers an employment opportunity to home-based women who have few other means to add to the family income. Ferrand-Bechmann discusses at some length the rich psychological rewards and training for paid employment that many middle-class women received in the Jeunes Femmes movement.

The basic autonomy of most self-help activities, at least in a free society, seems to offer them protection from many threats of takeover. In this sense, their general lack of funding and other forms of support is a strength. As several authors point out, however, many members of self-help groups and a few informal carers are eagerly seeking greater involvement with professionals and policymakers, quick to realize the opportunities for influence on the formal system and for sharing of resources.

HOW WILL SELF-HELP
INFLUENCE PROFESSIONALS?

An advantage of a cross-national perspective is that it throws into question certain assumptions that may have come to be taken as "givens" in one particular context. Interest in self-help groups in the United States has been greatest among community psychologists and social workers, where self-help has generally been described in the context of health or community mental health services. Supporting informal caregivers, on the other hand, has attracted the most interest from programs for the elderly, a development that seems to have been paralleled in England. But these chapters remind us that both self-help and informal caregiving have much wider applicability in terms of both relevant populations and institutional sponsorship. Health care workers and community educators, for example, are two professions that are mentioned as actively involved in supporting self-help in other countries.

Even the redirection of a relatively minor amount of professional attention to self-help and informal caregiving involves significant costs in terms of reorganization and retraining. Listing the various tasks and activities that are seen by the authors as elements of a professional role vis-à-vis self-help would result in a lengthy and demanding job description. Of course, not every skill is demanded in every situation, but if the relationship is truly to be a partnership, the professional must be prepared to find or provide whatever resource the particular situation requires. When it is also realized that most of these skills are outside the direct service, clinical area and involve indirect, facilitative roles, it may be considered remarkable that so may professionals have been able to work effectively with self-help. It does raise questions as to how representative these successful workers may be of their colleagues who have not chosen to get involved. Several of the authors have noted that the professionals who have become involved with self-help have tended to be outside the mainstream: radicals, alternative thinkers, even charismatics—the practitioners of the duende. They have had the freedom to experiment with new ways of working but often lack the power to implement them widely. However, this may not be the whole story. Lavoie suggests that intervention through networks is actually attractive to those institutions that are *disinclined* to radical self-questioning. She argues that because the family and neighborhood represent traditional values, they circumvent a more ideological level of debate and focus interventions on the most inherently conservative social collectivities.

For whatever reasons, the authors seem to be quite optimistic about the ability of professionals to perform these new roles and about the capacity, if not the willingness, of social agencies to make the necessary organizational changes. The implications of their experiences, however, are that fairly large-scale reforms would be required of agencies if they were to adopt these ways of working, especially with informal carers. For instance, confidentiality is a deeply rooted social work principle that has to be radically reinterpreted in the light of social network communication norms if professionals are to work effectively within helping networks. Many of the activities envisioned for the professional working with self-help groups are compatible with the traditional practice of the autonomous professional, particularly in health and mental health. There might even be the possibility in this area of direct fees to the professional from the group for these services. But the approaches to informal caregiving described by Grant and Wenger, Finlayson, Lavoie, and Collins require much more structural change. Many of the benefits of such interventions are preventive, outcomes that are unarguably desirable but very difficult to demonstrate. Therefore, it is especially important that careful, well-documented work, such as that described by these authors, be continued in order to see whether the use of publicly funded workers' efforts in this direction can be justified.

THREE PATHS FOR POLICY

Despite the difficulties, only a few of which have been discussed above, it is the general consensus of the contributors to this book that governments should take this "quiet revolution" or "silent mobilization" seriously. Possible responses can be divided into three main groups: parallel development, structural response, and incremental response.

The policy of parallel development is founded on the assumption that the functions of professionals are fundamentally different from those of the self-help movement; the best prognosis is for a symbiotic relationship rather than a continuum of care conceived within a single structure. In particular, the formal sector can use self-help as a corrective influence on its own practices, by selecting and incorporating appropriate features without attempting to embark on any partnership initiatives. Such a policy would appear to be best suited to a country where the professional role is heavily defended, or where the administrative organization is so fragmented that it has a very low capacity for considered initiatives with forces outside its own domain. France and Belgium respectively have borne out these conditions. However, the "rediscovery" of self-help has been a particularly recent phenomenon in these countries. It may be that parallel development is best seen as an initial phase, in which the formal sector sized up the potential of self-help before taking any purposeful initiatives. Indeed, there are recent signs from the Flemish Ministry of Health that a period of greater political involvement may be beginning.

Our distinction between a structural and an incremental response is actually somewhat arbitrary and subjective, but it hinges on whether a policy undertakes to shape events by changing systems and thus generating consequences, or whether it responds to identified developments that need some support to be able to continue. Examples of a structural response include the reform of welfare benefits, thus giving potential informal carers a realistic choice between going to work and caring for their dependent others in the community, or the development of local non-political citizens' groups to act as intermediaries between professional services and their communities; the establishment of professional advocate/mediators for self-help organizations at the local, regional, and national levels, or the modification of accountability and confidentiality constraints placed on workers, allowing them the opportunity to implement less controlling service delivery plans. Some of the structural responses are essentially revocations of philosophy. For instance, Uttley proposes that any attempt at macro policy development should be abandoned in favor of numerous and varied "self-exciting, small-scale experimental programs." All of these proposals share a proactive commitment; they contain the belief that changes in the formal system will engender a growth or strengthening in the self-help system.

The incremental approach is perhaps the most strongly espoused by the authors of this book. Seed money for self-help groups, money for demonstration projects and research, the setting up of clearinghouses, and training opportunities for professionals are all given as constructive responses to perceived needs, both of the self-help and informal care movement and of those professionals working with them. It is undoubtedly easier at first glance to construct a policy for self-help groups than for informal carers. After all, the existence of an identifiable organization gives the policy-maker something to aim at. Self-help groups can be given money, evaluated, and abandoned; informal helpers are much more elusive. However, it may be that in the long run, the statutory sector will find itself more at ease working with a presence that has no organizational identity, does not seek confrontation or even contact, but is simply there, whether for richer or poorer, depending on the consideration bestowed on informal carers by a sympathetic state. Informal care is ultimately more enduring and in that sense more reliable than self-help groups. As Ferrand-Bechmann says about Jeunes Femmes, "the fire eventually went out."

We have indicated that there are certain respects in which policy toward self-help may differ from policy toward informal care. There is one further dimension to this dichotomy: It may be that if the self-help movement continues to grow, it will develop sufficient strength and unity to generate its own collective policy initiative toward the statutory sector. There are indications in these chapters that self-help groups may be on their way toward developing a free-standing, independent organizational structure, at least in the United States, Belgium, West Germany, and the Netherlands, through national and regional clearinghouses. There are also various sources of support and sponsorship for such independence. Private foundations, businesses, and the media all have certain incentives to assist the growth of the self-help movement, and imaginative use has already been made of such liaisons. It is true that the public sector offers a massive opportunity for self-help groups to develop. But it is also true that they are not without alternatives beyond their own resources. The self-help movement enjoys a genuine opportunity to make choices.

Individual informal carers are less capable of generating extensive, independent structure, but the Good Neighbour system in England and the national organizations of neighborhood associations in the United States provide two examples that are at least partly analogous to the self-help clearinghouses. At the local level, neighborhood groups are gaining considerable influence within city politics, and they have the potential to be as concerned with issues that affect neighborhood helpfulness as they are with zoning and streets. Individual caregivers can also band together around a single issue. For example, family members providing extensive care of their elderly members in New York City and in other areas on the East Coast have lobbied at the state and federal levels for increased medical care for their elderly dependents.

This chapter has pursued a few of the issues relating to the future of practice and policy which have been raised in this book. From the professional perspective, the rediscovery of self-help offers the potential for renewal and revitalization of social services. This comes at a propitious time, since workers in these services are badly demoralized. From the citizen's perspective, which is actually the more important one, the rediscovery of self-help offers one way of meeting new problems engendered by changing lifestyles and social norms. Self-help is also, to a limited extent, a way of coping with governmental retrenchment and with some of the negative consequences of governmental actions and attitudes.

We have argued that the evolution of a social relationship among the statutory, self-help, and informal sectors contains intangible factors that cannot be totally controlled; and furthermore, that the structure of this relationship varies according to cultural, social, and political circumstances. However, future developments are not totally at the mercy of uncontrollable forces. There is a clear distinction between haphazard or pragmatic tolerance, however good-natured it may be, and the pursuit of a policy designed to meet specific conditions. Good nature and innocent neglect will not suffice; goodwill is needed, with all the energy and purpose that *will* implies.

On one point the authors in this book are unanimous. The wheels are already in motion. Formal services are largely in place and meeting the needs they were intended to meet. Informal caregiving remains a vital part of the total service picture. Organized self-help, while not a new phenomenon, is finding new and larger roles to play in contemporary society. Whether these wheels would work more effectively if they were meshed together is still an open question. The specific issues are complex and contradictory, but the themes are simple: *safety:*—Can policy protect the informal sector from exploitation and the formal sector from abdication of its duties? *performance*—Can self-help and informal care be counted on to do what their advocates claim? *economy*—not only in terms of money saved, but in the opportunity cost of a given policy; and *style*—Can a policy be designed that permits the expression of the broader social ethos of the time?

REFERENCES

Gartner, A., & Riessman, F. Self-help mutual aid not a "junior partner." *Human Development News,* December 1981.

Kropotkin, P. *Mutual aid.* Boston: Extending Horizons Books, n.d.

Illich, I. *Shadow work.* Boston: Marion Boyars, 1981.

ABOUT THE AUTHORS

ARLENE G. ADLER is a Clinical Assistant Professor of Psychiatry and Director of Program Evaluation and Research in the Division of Child and Adolescent Psychiatry at the State University of New York Downstate Medical Center. She received her Ph.D. in community psychology from New York University in 1982. Her major research interests include the interplay of social psychological and health indices to the study of stress and adaptation in the elderly, learning disabilities and child development, and the epidemiology of psychiatric illness in children and adolescents.

BERT BAKKER is an andragologist at the University of Amsterdam who worked previously in social work education. He has been involved in research on self-help since 1976. With M. Karel, he has authored several articles and a reader on the subject.

NANCY BARRON received her Ph.D. in social psychology at the University of Missouri in 1970, after which she coordinated state program evaluation and planning of mental health services. She has been a member of several self-help groups and consulted with many others. She is currently the director of the Urban Self-Help Groups and Mental Health Services Project at the Regional Research Institute, Portland State University.

JAN BRANCKAERTS studied philosophy and social and political sciences at the Universitaire Faculteiten Sint-Ignatius Antwerpen and sociology at the Katholieke Universiteit Leuven. He took courses in psychology at the Leuven University Psychological Institute and worked for two years as a psychotherapist. He is currently working as an assistant at the Department of Sociology, Division for Medical Sociology, Katholieke Universiteit Leuven, where he assists in teaching sociology students and is engaged in research on self-help and mental health problems. He has published on the pharmaceutical industry, medicalization theories, social and psychological factors in hereditary diseases, and self-help.

CARL I. COHEN is an Associate Professor of Psychiatry at the State University of New York—Downstate Medical Center and is Chief Medical Officer of the Outpatient Department at Kingsboro Psychiatric Center in Brooklyn, New York. He previously directed the Community Psychiatry Unit at New York University/Bellevue Medical Center. He received his M.D. from SUNY at Buffalo in 1971 and an M.A. in sociology from New York University in 1974. He has written extensively in the areas of social and community psychiatry and gerontology. He is currently engaged in an epidemiological study of aged men on the Bowery.

ALICE COLLINS is a graduate of Smith College and the New York (Columbia) School of Social Work. She has been a social worker in settlement houses, mental health clinics, community organizations, and correctional services. In recent years, she has been involved in research and demonstration of new concepts in professional partnerships with natural networks. She is the coauthor of *Natural Helping Networks* and has written other textbooks and professional articles.

GILES DARVILL has worked as the social services development officer for The Volunteer Centre since it was set up in 1974. His publications include *Bargain or Barricade?* (1975) and *Crossing of Purposes* (1979). He is currently undertaking a study of neighborhood clubs for the mentally impaired elderly and is coediting a book on volunteers and Social Services Departments (London: Tavistock, forthcoming).

CHRISTIANE DENEKE is a researcher in a project on self-help groups in health (*Gesundheitsselbsthilfegruppen*) at the University of Hamburg. The research is funded by the Federal Ministry for Research and Technology.

DAN FERRAND-BECHMANN is maitre-assistante of Sociology at the University of Grenoble, Grenoble, France, where she is studying the role of citizens' solidarity in the general crisis of the welfare state. Her most recent study is entitled *Le Benevolat Face a L'Etat Providence (Voluntarism in the Welfare State)*.

ANGELA FINLAYSON is currently a part-time tutor at The Open University in Scotland and an independent researcher. She has a B.A. Hons. in sociology and a Certificate in Social Science and Administration with Distinction from the London School of Economics. Her professional interests are mainly in the sociomedical field, especially informal support systems. She is the author of numerous articles and one book on coping with various medical conditions.

CHARLES FROLAND, D.P.H., formerly Assistant Professor at the School of Social Work and Research Associate at the Regional Research Institute for Human Services at Portland State University, is currently at Stanford University. In addition to directing a national study of agencies working with self-help, which he reported in *Helping Networks and Human Services,* he has written several journal articles on the role of social networks in mental health and health care. Dr. Froland has designed and administered research and evaluation studies in a wide number of social welfare program areas, including child abuse and neglect, delinquency prevention, vocational rehabilitation, income maintenance, and drug and alcohol services.

GORDON GRANT is a member of a small team of researchers in the Department of Social Theory and Institutions, University College of North Wales, Bangor, United Kingdom. He has been engaged in a series of studies of social care and service delivery in rural areas and thus has direct interests in formally organized systems of care as well as family and neighborhood care. His present work, with Clare Wenger, explores the dynamics of caregiving and care receiving in the social networks of the old elderly and families of mentally handicapped adults.

MATTIEU KAREL has collaborated with B. Bakker on research and writing on self-help since 1976. He recently left the University of Amsterdam to work at Elvas, a clearinghouse for volunteer, self-help, and social action groups.

FRANCINE LAVOIE is Assistant Professor, Ecole de psychologie, Université Laval, Cité Universitaire, Québec, Canada. She was awarded the Ph.D. is psychology from the Université du Québec à Montréal in 1982. One of her major interests is in the study of lay helping networks; she is currently involved in research on widowhood.

JOAN E. MINTZ is Deputy Director of the Division on Aging, Department of Community Affairs, State of New Jersey. She received a M.S.S.W. from

Columbia University in 1976. In 1978-1979, Ms. Mintz was the project administrator for the service program described in her chapter. Her research interests have included the problems of older women and the development of geriatric teaching programs.

DIANE L. PANCOAST, M.S.W., is a social worker and a Research Associate at the Regional Research Institute for Human Services, Portland State University. She served as principal investigator on the Natural Helping Networks and Service Delivery project and was coauthor of the book, *Helping Networks and Human Services* (1981). With Alice H. Collins she wrote *Natural Helping Networks* (1976). She is currently engaged in research on the social support networks of persons with epilepsy and on informal care for the elderly.

PAUL PARKER, M.A., C.Q.S.W., graduated from Oxford University, England, and trained as a social worker at Sheffield University, where he subsequently worked as a Research Fellow and tutor in the Department of Sociological Studies. For two and a half years he served as field director for the Neighborhood Service Project, Dinnington, a major research and demonstration project aimed at implementing a community-based multidisciplinary health and social service delivery model. He first came to Oregon in 1979 on a British government grant to investigate human service programs using a natural helping network approach, and returned to Portland State University in 1981, where he is working on a study of informal care for the elderly at the Regional Research Institute for Human Services and pursuing his Ph.D. in urban studies.

ANN RICHARDSON is a Senior Research Fellow at the Policy Studies Institute in London. In addition to her recent study of self-help groups, she has carried out extensive research on consumer participation in the field of social policy. Among other writings, a book on this subject, entitled *Participation,* is due to be published by Routledge and Kegan Paul in 1983.

STEPHEN UTTLEY is a Senior Lecturer in Social Administration, Victoria University of Wellington, Wellington, New Zealand. Prior to moving to Wellington in 1976, he was a social worker in Manchester, England, and later a tutor in a social work training course at Manchester University. His research interests are in theoretical explanations of welfare state developments and the organization of social services.

CLARE WENGER is a member of a small team of researchers in the Department of Social Theory and Institutions, University College of North Wales, Bangor, United Kingdom. She has been engaged in a series of studies of social care and service delivery in rural areas and thus has direct interests in formally organized systems of care as well as family and neighborhood care. Her present work, with Gordon Grant, explores the dynamics of caregiving and care receiving in the social networks of the old elderly and families of mentally handicapped adults.

RICHARD WOLLERT received his Ph.D. in clinical and community psychology from the University of Indiana in 1977. He is active as a private practitioner, an Associate Professor of Psychology at Portland State University, a self-help group consultant, and a journal editor.